NORMAN TASKER first interviewed Richie Benaud in 1960, when Norman was a teenage sports journalist for the *Daily Telegraph* in Sydney and Richie was the Australian cricket captain. In the years that followed, Norman covered cricket and rugby tours, was sports editor at *The Sun* and *The Bulletin*, and edited major sports magazines. He is the author of a number of bestselling books, including four titles with Alan McGilvray.

IAN HEADS has covered sport for more than half a century, for newspapers and magazines and as author of more than 40 books. In this time, he has collaborated with many champions, including Mark Taylor, Arthur Beetson, Louise Sauvage, Herb Elliott and Jack Gibson. In 2014, Ian and Richie Benaud were among the inaugural inductees into the Sydney Cricket Ground's Media Hall of Honour.

RICHIE

The Man Behind the Legend

EDITED BY NORMAN TASKER AND IAN HEADS
FOREWORD BY JOHN BENAUD

First published in hardback in 2015
by Stoke Hill Press
c/ 122 Wellbank Street, Concord NSW Australia 2137

Pitch Publishing
A2 Yeoman Gate
Yeoman Way
Worthing
Sussex
BN13 3QZ
www.pitchpublishing.co.uk
info@pitchpublishing.co.uk

British edition published in 2016

A CIP catalogue record is available for this book
from the British Library.

National Library of Australia Cataloguing-in-Publication entry:

Richie: the man behind the legend/editors: Norman Tasker, Ian Heads.

ISBN: 978-1785312113 (British edition)

Includes index
Benaud, Richie, 1930–2015.
Cricket players—Australia—Biography.
Television journalists—Australia—Biography.
Radio journalists—Australia—Biography.
Sportswriters—Australia—Biography.
Other Creators/Contributors:
Tasker, Norman, editor.
Heads, Ian, editor.
Dewey Number: 796.358092

Edited & Produced by Geoff Armstrong
Cover Design by Pitch Publishing
Internal Design & Typesetting by Kirby Jones

Printed by TJ International Ltd, Padstow, UK

This delightful book has been thoughtfully compiled by Ian Heads and Norm Tasker. Readers will be entertained by the tales and reminiscences of Richie's many friends and colleagues — there is much fun and laughter, and a few tears as well. The writers have captured their side of Richie's life in a superb way and I am grateful to everyone for their stories.

A special mention from me and the Benaud family to Ian, Norm and publisher Geoff Armstrong for developing the concept — and for the many hours spent bringing the book to reality.

I know Richie would have enjoyed the read.

Thank you to all.

Daphne Benaud
Coogee 2015

CONTENTS

— 1 —
A CERTAIN MYSTIQUE

— 2 —
EARLY DAYS

— 3 —
THE BENAUD ERA

— 4 —
IN THE PRESS BOX

— 5 —
WORLD SERIES CRICKET

— 9 —

A MARVELLOUS INNINGS

— 10 —

POSTSCRIPT

INTRODUCTION

By Norman Tasker and Ian Heads

THE extraordinary reaction to Richie Benaud's death in April 2015 was born of an international respect that is the preserve of a very select group of people. Even the millions who did not know him felt somehow that they did, such was his command of the television medium. He was the ultimate communicator.

To those who did know him personally — as a sportsman, as a television commentator and more importantly as a man — Richie's passing meant so much more. It seemed there was so much to say, so much to thank him for, so much to acknowledge. This book has come about to give expression to those people — the many friends and associates whose lives Richie Benaud touched in such positive ways.

When the idea of such a commemoration was conceived, it was conveyed to Daphne Benaud, who embraced it. So did Richie's sons Greg and Jeff and his brother John, himself an accomplished Test cricketer. The Benaud family has provided valued support and encouragement throughout the gathering of so many personal reflections.

The book grew as a seamless spin-off from a tribute event held on Wednesday, April 15, 2015, at Richie's home golf club, the Australian, at Kensington in Sydney. At an afternoon gathering of family and friends, countless stories were shared — publicly and privately — beginning a process that ultimately expanded across the globe, producing an especially rich harvest for these pages. In total, the tales told illuminate the many highways and byways of an extraordinary life.

In inviting the contributions that fill the following pages, we have tried to encompass the full breadth of Richie's life. Many of the stories are from cricketers who played with or against him in some famous encounters. Some are from people who knew him as a child and grew up with him. There are those who worked with him, in press boxes and commentary boxes around the world. There are tales of summer days in the south of France, of the travails of maintaining his fabled Sunbeam Alpine motor car, and stories of innumerable acts of kindness and comedy.

The gathering of such stories has been tinged with sadness, too. We approached 93-year-old Arthur Morris, Richie's captain when he made his first-class debut for NSW in December 1948. Arthur responded with enthusiasm.

'Richie,' he said, 'what a wonderful boy he was. I did spend a lot of time with those young blokes ... Richie and Jimmy Burke and the others. I'm very happy to talk about them, but can we do it next week? I have to have my hip replaced, but I'll only be in hospital three days.'

We waited three weeks and rang again. Arthur had fallen a couple of times and was feeling poorly. 'Could we leave it another week?' he asked. Sadly, he died before we could hear his stories, one champion on another. Arthur's respect for Richie would surely have been matched by Richie's respect for Arthur, also one of the game's true gentlemen, whose outstanding career placed him in Australian cricket's Team of the Century.

Respect is perhaps the word which best sums up the 90-odd contributions gathered in this book. Respect for the Benaud talent, for the work ethic and the consistency of it, for the gentle nature of his persona, for the way in which he put the game before himself, for the humility he maintained in the face of incredible celebrity and for the many kindnesses he offered on so many fronts.

The tales told here also were told out of an overarching affection. As John Benaud writes in the foreword, there will be many things revealed here that you did not know about Richie Benaud. Of his youth, of his family, of his early working life, of the hard yards necessary to get him to the very pinnacle of his sporting and working careers.

Richie came from a remarkable family. His parents lived through hard times, and instilled in their sons a high character, a sense of fairness and responsibility in the way they lived their lives. Richie's father Lou was a fine cricketer who gave him a love of the game. His brother John was a rich talent, too, both as a NSW captain and as a hard-hitting batsman of Test-match quality. John was also a high-achieving journalist, as sports editor and then editor of the Sydney afternoon paper *The Sun*.

The people who have contributed to this book did so with enthusiasm and a genuine sense that it was an honourable thing to do — to pay homage, in their own particular way, to a man who had been in many cases central to their lives. The stories are rich and heartfelt, poignant and funny, revealing and respectful.

Together they paint a wonderfully expansive and varied picture of Richie Benaud ... the man behind the legend.

Three generations — Richie, John, Lou and Richard — on the eve of Richie's first Ashes tour, 1953.

FOREWORD

By John Benaud

IT'S the late 1970s, Rich soon turning 50. He's en route to a town called Thika, outside Nairobi, Kenya. Sweltering. Agreed to umpire in a cricket match to raise funds for disabled children. The organiser, wife of the high commissioner, thinks because he is the drawcard he should play. And he does — against better judgment, a self-diagnosed rickety back and frozen right shoulder. A generous spirit, cricket and Benaud are synonymous.

It's 1910, our father LR Benaud, Lou, discovering cricket on the grassy banks of the mighty Richmond River, Coraki, his birthplace. Just a little boy with a slash of fair hair having fun with his friends, wielding a rough-cut packing case slat to protect three sticks in the ground from a raggedy soft ball.

It's 1918, a high school friend showing Lou how to bowl a leg-spinner. Dazzles his active mind. He would practise endlessly against a paling fence with chalk stumps, landing area a handkerchief on a length. Fiddled with flight, spun 'em like a top, half-a-dozen different balls, trying for seven. He was captivated by the art of deception, magic tricks for unwary batsmen. In no time at all he was playing with and against men.

It's 1923, Lou making his mark taking all 20 wickets in a match played over two Saturdays on two different grounds. He would recall the men as mostly decent, instinctively good sports. The odd bad experience left him much the wiser: ethics and cricket are like true friends, never at their best when parted.

Lou's father was Richard, a watchmaker and jeweller. A gentleman. Civic-minded too, several times a local mayor. Entrepreneur. Liked to organise match races, rowing and foot sprints for a pot of money, bets on the side. Wily enough to win a few himself.

One evening after dinner, dishes washed and dried, over the cribbage board young Lou told his father that for him cricket was the 'game of games'; that the spirit of cricket had entered his heart; that he had developed what he called his 'great love of cricket'.

It's 1930, Lou naming his first-born Richard, vowing he would play cricket. But Richard Benaud never did roll easily off the tongue. Just a bit too starchy for the Aussie g'day-mate attitudes of the time, between World Wars, the Great Depression, when Johns became Jacks and Williams were Bills. Abbreviation was soon in the air, and 'Dick' was popular.

Our mother Irene, but Rene to everyone, was having none of that. A dairy farmer's daughter, she helped milk 60 to 80 cows morning and night. The product was a rich combination of quiet meditation and unbending determination. Rene took every opportunity to remind the transgressors that 'Richie would do this' or 'Rich would do that'. She issued no edict, just gentle nudges in the right direction. Dick was kaput.

Lou thought parents doting and otherwise should stay in the background. Well intentioned. But when your son aged 16 shows such outstanding cricketing potential that the club's independent selectors name him in first grade alongside you, aged 42 … what to do? Might as well sit back and enjoy the headlines: 'Father And Son Help Beat Premiers: Cricket Shock'.

I was two. The family home was at Sutherland Road, North Parramatta. I was Rich's 'roomie'. Memories. Sharp dresser, *Rinso*-white shirts, cufflinks, striped ties and double-breasted suits, shiny shoes, sometimes brown suede. Handsome. Tanned features. Hair immaculately groomed. Never a hat.

On winter Saturday afternoons Rich would go off to play soccer. Nimble footwork, body swerve. One season scored 50 goals. His home pitch was the Parramatta asylum, patients strolling the sidelines. His junior cricket club was the Rangers, organised by a young man in a wheelchair, Sid Teale. Life's lucky dip did poor Sid no favours, disabled since childhood by spina bifida.

When Rich was KO'd by a bumper, broke a thumb, and once in a Test at the SCG was whacked in the mouth by a square-cut, I gazed at the swathes of white sticking plaster, the bruises and cuts and wondered if my big brother was a cricketer or a prize-fighter.

Lou diligently filled scrapbooks on Rich, good news and bad. Perspective. A ready reminder for the young up-and-comer of cricket's uncertainty. The great leveller.

It's 1953, Rich appearing at Lord's. The most hallowed of cricketing turf, any cricketer's moment in time. Scoreboard: a duck and 5, two-for-plenty, too. There was a newspaper photo of Rich shaking hands with the Queen. Lou gave me the scissors and paste, my scrapbook debut.

It's a few months later, Rich's first Ashes tour behind him. I'm on the front verandah and, out in the middle of Sutherland Road, Lou and Rich. Lou, a combination of backstop and stumps, hanky on a length, Rich bowling. Action is occasionally interrupted by conversations and arm movements, the odd car and, once, the baker's horse and cart. Turned out this was a coaching mission, trying to resurrect Rich's leg-spin bowling career, which had unravelled.

It's 1981, Rich at Coogee reflecting on his Australian Test bowling record, 248 wickets, being overtaken by the great Dennis Lillee. Did he remember that day at Sutherland Road? Yes. Not much ever escaped Rich's memory, but as it turned out that session with Lou was special.

Lou's cricket philosophy was simple enough: always try to play your natural game, but always listen to advice. You don't have to take it, but consider it, and, if necessary, implement it to improve your game.

Soul-searching moment for Rich. Had to tell Lou he had listened to advice from Bill O'Reilly, *curriculum vitae* 774 first-class wickets. And, as a result, he was going to change his natural style, much of which was based on Lou's successful method — constant variety, every ball in an over different.

Fact of cricket life: Lou never played first-class cricket. Was a high achiever, but in Sydney first grade, 360 wickets. O'Reilly explained the difference: Richie, if you keep using first-grade tactics at first-class level you won't last five minutes. Forthright Bill. Advice to Rich: instead of trying so much variety, develop one pressure ball to strangle the batsman, bait the trap, frustrate him — then snap! O'Reilly said it might take four years of hard work. Pain even. It did, and there was … a bloody, chronically raw spinning finger. But Rich never looked back.

Lou inspired in Rich his great love of cricket. That it should be played in the right spirit. Lasted a lifetime. With Rene, Lou shaped Rich's character. He would develop many qualities … competitive but fair, dedicated but flexible, honest … and many, many more which are touched on in the pages following. You will be surprised by what you didn't know about Richie Benaud, my brother, a champion and a true gentleman.

THE MOST PROMISING YOUNGSTER SINCE BRADMAN

T HE final Ashes Test of 1920–21, played at the Sydney Cricket Ground, was one of the most notable in Australian cricket history, and not just because the home team completed a 5–0 series clean sweep. In the crowd for the first two days were a father and son from Bowral in the NSW Southern Highlands — George and Donald Bradman — and the 'privilege' of seeing Charlie Macartney score a superb 170 is said to have helped mould the ambition of 12-year-old Don.

Also in the Sydney crowd during that Test was one Louis Richard Benaud, a young cricketer from Penrith, a township situated 50 kilometres west of the SCG, at the foot of the Blue Mountains. Lou's parents, Richard and Nellie, had given him a trip to the Test as a 17th birthday gift. He, too, was transfixed by the great Macartney. The coincidence of these famous Australian cricket names — Bradman and Benaud — being similarly inspired is equally charming and compelling.

Cricket was in the Benaud family's DNA. At a cricket presentation night in Penrith in 1934, Lou's father told the gathering, in a speech recorded in *The Nepean Times*, 'If there is one sport that is dear to my heart it is cricket. It has been so since I was a boy.' Eleven years earlier, that same paper had reported a remarkable effort in the Nepean District B-grade competition …

The Nepean Times **(March 31, 1923):** A phenomenal bowling performance stands to the credit of L. Benaud, of Penrith Waratah CC. Playing against St Marys, he captured the whole 20 wickets of the match. This is surely a star performance of the first magnitude.

Last week we recorded the fact that in the first day's play of the match Benaud captured ten wickets for 30. That feat in itself was somewhat of the sensational, but that he should repeat the performance so far as the number of wickets is concerned on the next Saturday was something entirely undreamt of. Yet on Saturday he bagged the whole ten wickets at a cost of 35. Thus in the match his analysis was 20 wickets for 65 runs.

Lou also bowled well during the 1922–23 summer for the Parramatta High School XI and soon he was selected for the NSW Combined High School team. Then he was offered a chance by the Cumberland grade club, but his promotion to first grade in 1925 coincided with his graduation from teachers' college. After just one game with the firsts, he was posted to a tiny school at One Tree Farm, near Casino on the NSW far north coast.

For the next few years he would also teach at Warrendale School, located just outside the township of Koorawatha, near Cowra in western NSW, and then at Jugiong, 100 kilometres further south, not far from Cootamundra. He returned to Sydney and settled at North Parramatta in 1937.

Lou had met and married Irene Saville during his tenure at One Tree Farm. Lou and Rene's first child, Richie, arrived on October 6, 1930, when they were living at Koorawatha, though the birth occurred at Penrith, under the watchful eyes of Richard and Nellie, because there was no resident doctor at little Koorawatha.

The Cumberland Argus and Fruitgrowers' Advocate **(September 23, 1937):** Grade cricket will make its bow on Saturday, when Cumberland will meet University at University No. 1 Oval. The selected team contains only two changes from that which regularly represented Cumberland last season. Colin Denzel, ex-Westmead all-rounder, who has shown excellent form at practice, is back with the firsts, and L. Benaud, who has been appointed to the staff of Burnside school, has gained selection ...

Lou quickly established himself as one of the better leg-spinners in Sydney grade cricket. Meanwhile, his son was also being noticed.

Alan McGilvray (1992): I first met Richie Benaud, so he tells me, at the old Cumberland Oval in Parramatta back in the 1930s, when Richie was all of six years of age. Even then the young Benaud was something of a devotee, following his father Lou as he trundled his leg-breaks quite successfully around the grounds of Sydney district cricket. I batted a few times against Lou Benaud and knew him as one of the real tradesman bowlers of Sydney cricket. He worked long and hard for his successes, as any slow bowler must, and to Australian cricket's great benefit the trait was handed down to his eldest son Richie.

The Cumberland Argus and Fruitgrowers' Advocate **(April 12, 1939):** Richie Benaud, son of Cumberland's first grader Lou Benaud, bids fair to follow in his father's footsteps as a cricketer. Playing with Burnside in the schools competition, Richie, who is only eight years of age, has been not out each time he has batted for a total of 58 runs. He already possesses a very sound defence and a knowledge of which ball should be hit, and, in addition, is a fair bowler.

As a schoolboy, Richie led Burnside Public and Parramatta High School to premiership wins. He made his grade debut at age 11; having been given the job of scoring for Cumberland's second-grade team, he got a game when one of the regular players failed to turn up. He made his 'genuine' grade debut a week before his 15th birthday, at the start of the 1945–46 season, in third grade. His initial first-grade appearance came a little more than a year later, when he replaced Lou, who was unavailable for one game. Father and son first played together in grade cricket in Richie's second first-grade match.

Cootamundra Herald **(December 2, 1946):** District cricketers who knew Lou Benaud when he was schoolteaching at Jugiong, or who made his acquaintance elsewhere, will be interested to know that his 16-year-old son, Richie, is being hailed by critics as a potential international. Unlike Dad, who mainly made his name as a bowler, young Benaud is a class batsman. Playing for Cumberland first grade against Marrickville, he got within two of the century and handled all bowlers with ease. When in the 90s, Richie was joined by his father, and one sporting writer says that for the first time in his splendid innings the lad showed nervousness. At 98, he stepped out to a delivery by V. Collins, missed, and was stumped.

Ken Hardy ('Talking of Sport' column, *The Sydney Morning Herald*, January 28, 1947): Keep your eye on this young cricketer. Good judges are picking Richie Benaud, 16-year-old Central Cumberland batsman-bowler, as the most promising youngster since Bradman. This season he has played first grade (best scores, 98 and 89), AW Green Shield, Poidevin Shield and has made the state Second XI — a unique record. He is a born captain.

***The Cumberland Argus and Fruitgrowers' Advocate* (January 5, 1949)** Youthful Cumberland all-rounder Richie Benaud has made cricket history. He joins that small band who have been selected to represent their state at the age of 18. With Jim Burke he shares the honour of being the youngest player in Australian first-class cricket today. Both lads were members of the NSW XI in the match against Queensland at Sydney Cricket Ground.

Just a week after that story appeared in the Parramatta local paper, Richie found himself at the Melbourne Cricket Ground, batting three in a NSW–Victoria Second XI game.

HA 'Hec' de Lacy (*Sporting Globe*, December 17, 1952): I saw young Benaud first on the fateful occasion of his first big game in Melbourne back in the 1948–49 season, when NSW Second XI played the Victorian seconds. The night before the game commenced the pitch prepared was soaked and the surface lifted. Quickly a new wicket had to be rolled. New South Wales batted. The pace bowlers flew head high and Benaud was struck in the centre of the forehead by a ball from Jack Daniel.

The blow left a small crater in Richie's forehead; he was carried off on a stretcher, spent two weeks in hospital after X-rays confirmed a shattered bone, and did not play again until the following season. Remarkably, there was no permanent dent in his confidence.

AG 'Johnnie' Moyes (1962): When I watched Benaud hooking Tyson and Wesley Hall I marvelled at his courage. That tremendous blow, received at the beginning of his career, might well have caused him to flinch when the ball dropped short — or at least could have ended any desire he had to play the hook stroke. It didn't. He continued to hook — Tyson, Trueman, Hall and others — and to hit the ball with tremendous power. A man who will do that has a fighting heart, real personal courage, and indeed audacity.

Bill O'Reilly (*Sunday-Herald*, October 30, 1949): A splendid 200 partnership between Ron James and Richie Benaud was the outstanding feature of the day's play at Lidcombe Oval. In Benaud, Cumberland has a grand colt who is bound to make a name for himself in the highest spheres of the game. In stature and offside stroke play he resembles the late Archie Jackson most strikingly.

Richie scored 160 not out in 201 minutes in this match against Gordon. It was his maiden first-grade century. Lou Benaud, shrewd as ever, realised that his son's all-round abilities now needed every opportunity.

***The Sydney Morning Herald* (November 24, 1949):** There will be only one Benaud in the Cumberland first-grade XI against Manly at Lidcombe on Saturday. Lou Benaud has been chosen in the second-grade team; his son Richie will now be the principal spin bowler, as well as star batsman, in the first team.

***The Cumberland Argus* (July 26, 1950):** For the first time in its history a member of Central Cumberland District Cricket Club was selected to lead the state XI, the club's fifty-third annual report states. He is club skipper Ron James, who led NSW to Sheffield Shield victory in 1949–50. James followed up his good work by topping the State batting average ... The season also saw the passing from first-grade ranks of two veteran players who have given the club long and outstanding service both on and off the field. They are spin bowler Lou Benaud and fast bowler Lloyd Cadden. Both dropped out of the first team halfway through the season. In true sporting spirit both players considered that it was better to relinquish their places in the first XI and allow younger players an opportunity to make their debut in the higher grade.

A broken thumb, suffered in a grade game in early December 1950, just after he had been named in an Australian XI to play the touring Englishmen, kept Richie out of first-class cricket for two months and stifled any talk about him being selected in the Test team during the 1950–51 Ashes series. But a string of encouraging performances for NSW in the following summer, including his maiden first-class century (117 v South Australia at the Adelaide Oval), won him a place in Lindsay Hassett's side for the fifth Test against the West Indies, at the SCG.

In the *Sunday-Herald*, Tom Goodman commented: 'It is pleasing that one of the younger players of promise, Richie Benaud, has been brought into the Test picture.' Bill O'Reilly agreed: 'It is good to see Benaud "blooded" now.' In Melbourne, the cricket correspondent for the *Argus* was bold enough to compare Australia's newest Test cap to one of Victoria's finest: 'Sydney experts believe Benaud has greater batting assurance than any Australian cricketer of his age. They hail him as showing promise of becoming the greatest all-rounder of his type since the late Warwick Armstrong.'

Richie's Test career started quietly: scores of 3 and 19 and bowling figures of 1–14 from a single spell of 4.3 eight-ball overs. By the following season he was being lauded across the country as a future star.

Jim Mathers (*Truth*, October 26, 1952, after Richie scored 63 against Queensland): The player who most consolidated his position was undoubtedly young Richie Benaud, who stole the show from the seasoned internationals with virile batsmanship. Benaud compiled 63 in 86 minutes. He hit eight glorious boundaries with cover drives, hooks and pulls. Some of his drives must have taken the paint off the pickets with the violence of impact. If Benaud continues to develop, he might well become Australia's glamour cricketer within the next couple of years.

Hec de Lacy (*Sporting Globe*, December 17, 1952): There's another Keith Miller in the Australian field. It's Richie Benaud, 22 years, and the best white hope in the all-rounder class in Australian cricket. Benaud has the same free-swinging bat, the same crisp shots and the same determination to get his runs aggressively that has characterised the batting of Miller, the greatest pinch-hitter in cricket.

In the *Argus*, Tom Goodman was more cautious. 'Bowlers take years to mature,' he wrote, 'but if Benaud can convince the selectors he is improving his leg-spin attack he will do a lot of good for himself.'

Richie was 12th man for the opening Test against South Africa, and came into the XI for the second Test at the MCG, replacing Ian Johnson, a member of Bradman's Invincibles in 1948. Again, the returns were modest, though a fighting 45 in Australia's second innings was widely praised. He kept his place in the Test side for the rest of the season and did just enough to ensure his selection for the 1953 Ashes tour.

Lou Benaud (1953): Naturally, I am delighted with his selection. I have always taught Richie to be self-reliant and have guarded against any change in his natural style. Many young players of promise have been ruined because their style has been too drastically changed. Cumberland Cricket Club has done a marvellous job for Richie ever since he has been with them.

Previewing the tour for the Adelaide *Advertiser*, Sir Donald Bradman wrote: 'In young Benaud will be found a cricketer who could easily be mistaken for Miller as he moves lithely after a ball. Their movements, build and mannerisms are similar. Benaud is a lovely field and a batsman who can hit with tremendous power, but strangely enough in bowling he reverts to slow leg-spinners. He may easily be called upon to do a lot of work and if so will obviously enjoy it.'

However, in a squad that included two other frontline spinners, Doug Ring and Jack Hill, and fellow all-rounders Keith Miller, Alan Davidson and Ron Archer, opportunities turned out to be few.

Richie played in three Tests, averaging just three with the bat and 87 with the ball. His potential was still recognised by some experts, though, including the celebrated commentator John Arlott, who wrote: 'If his figures make Richie Benaud a Test failure it is because they cannot show in its true proportion some of the finest catching that could be wished and because as good a leg break as was bowled all season — which completely beat [Denis] Compton when he was set and going well at Lord's — appears as just another wicket.'

Richie returned to Australia to learn that Ron James had stepped down as captain of Cumberland, to give the club's Test representative the opportunity to develop his leadership skills. In the Sheffield Shield, the law was changed in Australia so that captains couldn't claim a new ball until 60 eight-ball overs had been bowled or 200 runs had been scored. Since 1947, captains had been able to claim a new ball after just 40 eight-ball overs. 'The game fell into a narrow groove,' wrote Ray Robinson in his book *Green Sprigs*. 'The frequent new balls encouraged a crop of medium-pace and fast-medium swing bowlers ...'

> **Ray Robinson (1954):** One February afternoon in 1954, Sydney onlookers saw two googly bowlers, Richie Benaud and Bob Simpson, 18, entrusted with the attack for almost two hours (a sight unknown since pre-war days when O'Reilly, Grimmett, Pepper, Ring, Ward and McCool took most of the wickets in Australia, and NSW often had three of them in one eleven). Benaud's captain, Miller, kept him bowling for 16.2 overs without interruption, except to change ends. Gradually, the young all-rounder began to look like a Test bowler ...

Richie kept his place in the Test side throughout the 1954–55 Ashes series, but not everyone agreed with the selectors. All that early promise remained unfulfilled. Having played 13 Tests by the end of the summer, Richie was still without a Test fifty or five wickets in a Test innings, though his first-class statistics were more encouraging.

His rise as a quality international cricketer began in the Caribbean in 1955, when he took 18 wickets in five Tests and scored his first Test century: 121, batting eight, in the final Test at Kingston, Jamaica. He reached three figures that day after just 78 minutes at the crease. However, Australia's 3–0 series win represented something of a false dawn, because after a promising start the team's Ashes campaign of 1956 disintegrated in the north of England, on dry, dusty pitches that were made to order for England's spinners, Jim Laker and Tony Lock.

The bright spot for the tourists came at Lord's, in the second Test, which was won by 185 runs. Keith Miller took ten wickets and Richie played arguably the best innings of his life.

Seven years later, the famous cricket writer Neville Cardus recalled meeting Richie after the third day's play, at a dinner hosted by another celebrated cricket figure, the author and commentator John Arlott.

Sir Neville Cardus (1963): There was 'something' about him which impressed me, a suggestion of latent and alluring personality. The impression was strong enough to urge me to write an article, to appear before the game was resumed next morning, in which I risked a forecast: 'Before we are much older Benaud will do something forcibly to demonstrate his natural and unmistakable gifts.'

Well, on this fourth morning, in a ticklish moment for Australia, with the day fresh and Trueman after blood with four wickets already rendering him even more than usually voracious, Benaud arrived at the ground almost late and had to rush into action at once, pads buckled breathlessly. Immediately he attacked, risking a long-armed drive. Also he hooked Trueman for six — and Trueman was the first of thousands to applaud the stroke. Benaud trusted his eye daringly. In two hours, 20 minutes, he scored 97, swinging clean round the wheel of the game in the one engagement of the rubber won by Australia.

This innings, maybe, marked the turn of his career.

The Australians did not return straight home after this tour. Instead, they remained in Europe for three weeks and then travelled back via the Indian subcontinent, playing one Test in Pakistan and three in India. It was against the Indians that Richie finally snared his first Test five-fors (7–72 at Madras; 6–52 and 5–53 at Calcutta), as he revelled in the extra responsibility that came with being a more prominent figure in the squad. Ian Johnson's best days were clearly behind him and vice-captain Keith Miller had retired after the

Ashes Tests; Richie relished bowling first or second change in all three Tests against Polly Umrigar's Indians.

> **Keith Miller (1975):** Neil Harvey is an astute judge. Neil came back from India and Pakistan and announced that Benaud could really bowl. From that point, Richie developed into a top-flight bowler. He had something of the O'Reilly touch. He could get lift off the pitch.

With Johnson retiring, critics expected the next Australian captain to be one of Harvey, Ron Archer or Richie, with Harvey the popular choice. Instead the selectors went for 22-year-old Ian Craig, part of a youth policy brought on by the retirement of Miller, Johnson and wicketkeeper Gil Langley and the decline of Ray Lindwall. Queensland's Wally Grout was the new keeper, and Alan Davidson led the attack. Benaud was also now unequivocally a senior player and he responded on Australia's 1957–58 tour of South Africa with one of the finest all-round performances in a Test series. In the fourth Test, a critical game with Australia leading 1–0 in the series, he hit 100 batting four and took 4–70 (bowling second change) and 5–84 (first change) to inspire the side to a ten-wicket win. For the series, he had 30 wickets at 21.93 with four five-wicket hauls, and he scored 329 runs at 54.83 with two centuries. 'It was on this tour that Richie really emerged as the world's best leg-spinner,' recalled Harvey in 1963.

> **Wally Grout (1965):** Richie earned this success with his sweat. He was the most enthusiastic and diligent member of the team, the first to practice and the last to leave. He was also the best spin bowler I have seen …
>
> His shock ball was, of course, his famous 'flipper', which I got to know so well that batting against him in interstate cricket never bothered me. The flipper was the ball he literally squeezed from his fingers, yet giving the impression he had spun it from the hand. When it landed, instead of turning away from the right-hander it fizzed off the pitch without a fraction of deviation. No wonder it netted him a haul of wickets.

The South African adventure was also Alan Davidson's 'breakout' series, as he took 25 wickets at 17.00. After a four-year 'apprenticeship', the Benaud–Davidson combination evolved into the best fast man/slow man bowling partnership Australia had until Glenn McGrath and Shane Warne. Richie's control was as good as any leg-spinner before Warne, and while he never spun his leg break or his wrong 'un all that far, it usually turned far enough. His high delivery generated rare bounce for a spinner and got the ball to dip and drift. Again like Warne, he disguised his flipper better than his googly.

When Ian Craig was struck down by hepatitis in 1958, Richie was the surprise choice as the new captain. Most expected Harvey, Craig's deputy in South Africa, to get the job. It was an inspired decision.

Alan McGilvray (1992): Benaud, more than any captain before him, recognised that the game had to 'go modern'. He lifted its pace, imbued it with a new, outgoing enthusiasm and opened it up to the public with an enlightened flair for public relations that was without precedent. And all of this came at a time when the game badly needed a shot in the arm if it was to maintain public support. Benaud gave it that, ushering in a period of success and prosperity to match any in the game.

Wally Grout (recalling Richie's first Test as captain): Jimmy Burke was batting to Peter Loader, who switched from bowling over to round the wicket. 'Burkie' requested that the sightboard be shifted to a position which would have obscured the view of some of the ground members sitting under the marquee, but to crusty officialdom this was unpardonable and the sightboard attendant was instructed not to comply. Burkie, after some fruitless waving, gave it away and settled down to pick Peter as well as the conditions allowed.

But he fell to the next ball from Loader, which he had lost in the backdrop of the crowd. Richie knew nothing of the sightboard incident until Jim's outburst in the dressing-room. He leapt from his seat, face black as thunder, and charged over to the members' area. I don't know what was said and probably never will, but when the next request came to move the board in front of the members, it was moved.

The series had started slowly, with men on both sides — and especially England's Trevor Bailey — batting at a snail's pace in Brisbane until Norm O'Neill played boldly for 71 not out on the final day. Thereafter, Richie's vibrant approach carried the day.

He captured 31 wickets as an England line-up that had been initially acclaimed as one of the best to come to Australia was thrashed 4–0. Then, in eight trying Tests in Pakistan and India in 1959–60, he took 47 more as Australia won both series. Yet this was all just a prelude to the main event: the 1960–61 West Indies tour of Australia. This series, remembered as the greatest ever played in Australia, was Frank Worrell's first as West Indies captain.

> **CLR James (1967):** Worrell made the tremendous decision to restore to Tests the spirit of the game he had learnt in Barbados. [He] initiated a regeneration. Benaud, the Australian captain, met him halfway and the result was the most exciting Test series in living memory.

> **Jack Fingleton (on the first Test):** In the final analysis, perhaps the two greatest men in the match were the two captains — Benaud and Worrell. There were many times on this final day when either might well have sought a foxhole, as so many before them have done. They could have played tight, shut the game up, played for a draw. But neither wanted a draw; both wanted victory; both played it that way and out of the spirit of the game came this peerless tie.

It was a series full of incidents, drama and glory, highlighted by the incredible final session of the first Test, featuring a wonderful seventh-wicket partnership between Richie and Alan Davidson and culminating in Wes Hall's last over, three wickets, a dropped catch, a missed run out, Joe Solomon's sure throw to run out Ian Meckiff, the first tied Test. Richie took his 200th Test wicket during the series. He was the fourth bowler to reach this landmark, after Clarrie Grimmett, Alec Bedser and Ray Lindwall. He had needed 24 Tests to take his first 50 Test wickets; the next 150 wickets came in 25 matches.

Prior to Australia's tour of England in 1961, Richie told reporters, 'We want to win very badly but if we lose, we want to lose playing attractively. It doesn't concern us what the opposition does. We have our policy and will stick to it.'

And this they did, resulting in one of the most memorable of all post-war Ashes series. Benaud himself was hindered by a torn tendon in his right shoulder and missed the second Test at Lord's (where Australia, captained superbly by Harvey, won by five wickets). He was back for the Leeds Test, but failed to score in either innings as Fred Trueman bowled the home team back into the series. After four days of the fourth Test at Old Trafford, Australia led by 154 runs with four wickets in hand.

Jack Fingleton (1970): Benaud thought highly of Lindwall's cricket acumen. Lindwall was a master in his analysis of batsmen and, drawing him aside from the drink in the committee room which is always a pleasant feature of Test cricket at Old Trafford at the end of a day's play, Benaud asked him to walk to the middle with him.

On the deserted cricket ground, the two famous Australians studied the pitch and particularly the marks Trueman had made at the railway end.

'What do you think of the idea of bowling slow spin around the stumps into these marks?' asked Benaud.

Lindwall pondered. 'To tie the scoring down or get wickets?' he asked Benaud.

'Well, either, depending upon circumstances,' said Benaud.

Lindwall thought again. 'I think there is merit in the idea Rich,' he said. 'But it would need to be very tight spin bowling. You don't look like having many runs to play with. I would be inclined to give it a go. But it must be tight or ...'

And Lindwall shrugged his shoulders.

Next morning, almost immediately, Australia lost three wickets to the off-spinner David Allen. But Davidson remained and, while the rookie No. 11, Graham McKenzie, held up his end, the great all-rounder produced the second of his two famous Test innings. He had made that heroic 80 on the final afternoon of the Tied Test; now he scored a brilliant 77 not out, the highlight being the 20 runs he took from one Allen over, a premeditated assault that prompted England captain Peter May to take off the bowler the Australians feared most. The last-wicket stand was worth 98; England needed 256 to win.

And for a while it seemed they'd get them comfortably, as Ted Dexter flayed the bowling. With Harvey's encouragement, Richie put the 'round the wicket' plan into action. Everything changed.

Frank Worrell (1961): Benaud bowled better than I have ever seen him bowl before, and his going around the wicket was the third vital factor on this extraordinary final day. His accuracy and direction from both sides of the wicket were fantastic.

Sir Neville Cardus (1961): In the face of Dexter's great and brilliant onslaught he [Benaud] did not flinch. In Australia's dire position at mid-afternoon he could honourably have 'put up the shutters', deployed a defensive attack and field. Instead, he played the game, bowled his fingers to exhaustion, and never lost the true sportsman's glorious vision. And the gods at last crowned him — as the gods usually do crown the man who keeps the faith.

England lost its last nine wickets for 51 runs. May was bowled around his legs for a duck by a ball that spun viciously out of Trueman's footmarks. Richie finished with 6–70, having taken 5–12 in a spell of 25 deliveries. The Ashes retained.

Bill O'Reilly (1962): Bill Woodfull, who skippered the Australian and Victorian sides in the early '30s, lost the Ashes to England once and won them twice. He was a first-rate opener who gave his team many an inspiring start in Tests, even when the Bodyline series of 1932-33 raged through the land. He knew the rules inside out.

And his team, of whom I was one, all hold imperishable memories of the solid dignity of a man whose courage was commensurate with a full pack of rugby forwards. Even with all these qualities, Bill Woodfull never captured the public imagination as Benaud has done ...

In 1961–62, Richie was joined in the Cumberland first-grade side by his 17-year-old brother John, who would go on to captain the club and his state, and wear the baggy green. NSW won the Sheffield Shield for a record ninth season in a row. However, Richie's final Ashes series, at home in 1962–63, was an anti-climax. Level at one-all after four Tests, the rubber petered out in disappointing fashion in Sydney. Harvey and Davidson retired, and Richie announced he would bow out at the end of the following Australian summer. This meant his career would end against South Africa. That farewell series would begin with the most controversial day of his entire playing career.

The Australian selectors caused surprise by recalling Victorian left-arm quick Ian Meckiff for the first Test. The legality of Meckiff's bowling action had been questioned during previous seasons and it was thought his Test days were through. Now his career was ended in the cruellest fashion, as square-leg umpire Col Egar called him for throwing four times in his first over. Richie refused to try him from the other end, explaining to the press at day's end: 'Over the years I have accepted the umpire's decision. This is one I must stand by. I will not bowl Meckiff again.'

Lou Rowan (the umpire at the bowler's end): Richie could have shifted all the blame on to the umpires, but he chose not to do that. He was prepared to accept the opinion of an expert and leave it at that. Those who saw fit to castigate Richie for what he failed to do may well have castigated him further if changing Meckiff to the other end had brought further troubles.

Richie broke a finger on his bowling hand while playing in a grade game between the first and second Tests. Bob Simpson took over as captain. When Richie returned, he suggested he do so purely as a player, given that Simpson would be leading the team on the forthcoming tour of England. In his final Test, at the SCG, Richie bowled 49 overs in South Africa's first innings, the most overs he ever bowled in a Test innings in Australia, finishing with 4–118. He retired with 248 Test wickets, 2,201 Test runs and 65 catches from 63 appearances, and would remain the only man to complete the 200 wickets/2,000 runs/50 catches treble in Tests until Garry Sobers joined him in 1971.

Most remarkably, his days as a highly influential figure in world cricket had only just begun.

Richie's first job after leaving school had been as a 16-year-old clerk in a chartered accountant's office in Pitt Street, Sydney. In 1950, he took a job in the accounts department at *The Sun* newspaper, where he stayed for six years until he approached Lindsay Clinch, the paper's editor, about a transfer to editorial. He was offered the chance to write a sports column but declined, saying he wanted to work on news and police rounds. This led to him working under Noel Bailey, *The Sun*'s legendary crime reporter. 'The finest training of all was to trail on the coat-tails of Noel Bailey,' Richie would say years later. 'It was wonderful to see and hear him in action.'

Bill Jenkings (police roundsman for the Sydney *Daily Mirror*, 1946–1979): The most famous opposition I ever had was Richie Benaud. I never had the ability to compete against him on the cricket field, but as crime reporter on *The Sun* for a brief period in the 1950s, he was a gentlemanly opponent. He was filling in for holidaying Noel Bailey at the time, but never once did I know him to try to use his position as captain of the Australian cricket XI for favourable treatment. He'd attend the daily police press briefings and, sartorially speaking, put most of us crime reporters to shame. Richie was a lively conversationalist and a debonair figure.

Richie would go on to write for a number of newspapers across the world, most notably the *News of the World* in Britain and *The Sun* in Australia. His words would be syndicated across the cricket world. He was also a columnist for numerous magazines, wrote ten books, and contributed to or edited many more.

His career as a broadcaster had its beginnings in a decision he made at the end of the Australians' 1956 tour of England, when he opted to stay in London to participate in a BBC television training course. During that Ashes summer he had been intrigued by the work of now-celebrated TV commentators such as Henry Longhurst at the British Open and Dan Maskell at Wimbledon. As part of the three-week BBC tutorial, he was given the chance to observe close-up how Peter O'Sullevan called the races at Newbury, and also learned how producers and directors and their crews went about their business. The course didn't immediately lead to a career in this new media, but it did provide a launching pad for all that followed.

'Many are called and surprisingly many are given the opportunity behind the microphone,' the great sportswriter Ian Wooldridge would observe as he paid tribute in 2005, after Richie's last Test as a commentator in England. 'Very few have served the slogging apprenticeship that makes a master cricket commentator.'

Richie spent much of 1960 in England, working as a journalist, subeditor and occasional radio commentator, and playing a little cricket, including a series of televised one-day matches. He didn't commentate on any of these games but he did make sure he was interviewed as often as possible by the BBC's Brian Johnston and Peter West. His first TV commentary experience came in England in 1963. He would work with the BBC (1963–1997) and Channel 4 (1999–2005) in the UK, while in Australia he did some stints with Seven and then Ten when those commercial channels briefly covered Test cricket, before joining the Nine Network in 1977.

Jim Laker (1979): I have the greatest admiration for Richie. He was a magnificent cricketer, in my view the best captain Australia has produced during my time, and that included Sir Donald Bradman. As a cricket commentator he is far ahead of anyone I have heard in any part of the world, and never have I met a more industrious, hardworking yet generous ex-cricketer in my career.

Alan McGilvray (1992): I admire Benaud above all others as a television commentator on cricket. His commentaries are reasoned, full of insight and experience, and sufficiently concise and understated as not to grate on the listener.

He handles his work as a commentator with all the aplomb he once showed as a captain. And the lesson of history will always be that he was one of the game's more enlightened and influential leaders.

Richie became a cricket constant during Australian and English summers, a much loved and hugely respected figure. His decision in 1977 to join Kerry Packer's revolutionary World Series Cricket as a consultant and commentator was controversial at the time, but ultimately it added to his reputation, and proved that when his father taught him to be self-reliant, he taught him well. A players' rights man from first to last, Richie backed WSC because he truly believed in it. The credibility his support gave the new venture was priceless.

The names Bradman and Benaud remain the two most important in the history of Australian cricket, not just as great cricketers and captains but also because of all they did in the decades after their playing careers ended: Sir Donald mostly as an administrator; Richie largely as a giant of the cricket media. While we know that Lou Benaud and George and Don Bradman attended the fifth Ashes Test of 1920–21, we don't know exactly where in the SCG they were as they watched Charlie Macartney's magnificent innings.

Given how the next 95 years unfolded, it would have been perfectly appropriate if they were sitting side by side.

– 1 –
A CERTAIN MYSTIQUE

'As long as cricket is played and wherever it is played, the public will always remember Richie Benaud.'

— **Norm O'Neill, 1964**

BILL LAWRY

Bill Lawry made his Test debut during the 1961 Ashes tour and was a stalwart for the next decade, captaining Australia in 25 of his 67 Tests. He scored 5,234 Test runs at an average of 47.15, and was the durable rock on which many a Test innings was built. When World Series Cricket started, Bill joined Richie Benaud in the commentary box and quickly became a fixture in the Channel Nine team. He remembers a much-loved friend and colleague who earned the respect of all who knew him ...

WHEN Richie left us, I looked back on 78 years of life and realised I had been looking up to Richie Benaud for about 63 of them. I was maybe 15 when, like all aspiring young cricketers, I first followed his deeds as the glamorous new face of first–class cricket. When I made the Australian side in 1961 at age 24, he was my captain. He had a commanding aura about him and I was just one of the young blokes down the back of the bus.

When I began my commentary career at the advent of World Series Cricket, Richie was our leader. He had nearly 15 years' experience as a television commentator with the BBC; he was the doyen and we were all novices. We all looked up to him as the cool presence that made everything work.

Even in latter days, nobody ever doubted where we all stood in the pecking order. If we left the ground together at the end of a day's play, the fans would make way for Richie with obvious respect, and he would move through them, head high and eyes fixed ahead.

Tony Greig or Ian Chappell or myself might cop some lip, but never Richie. His dignity brought the same response from fans in the 21st century as it had from the likes of us, who had played cricket with him half a century before.

Richie was cool and calculating as a cricket captain. He maintained a certain mystique about himself. He didn't talk all that much; certainly he never ranted or raved as some captains might. As a result, his words carried so much more weight. What he said was gold and that attitude carried into his commentary career.

He was also highly principled. He stuck with what he thought was right, even in the most pressured of circumstances and up against the most powerful of people. When World Series Cricket came about, it was Richie who made it work, both in siding with it at the start and giving it his credibility, then as the face of a television coverage that was quite revolutionary. He gave us all confidence. When he appeared you somehow knew it was going to be a good day. He did have to work under enormous pressure, and the professional attitudes he exuded made it better for all of us.

It was, though, a whole new ball game and even Richie was asked to make some adjustments. At the BBC he had become used to the 90-second gap after each over when he could gather his thoughts and give a considered appraisal of what had taken place through the previous over. In the new commercial world of Channel Nine he couldn't do that — just a quick score then off to an ad break. So more information had to be provided during an over.

I remember one occasion when we were on air together — Richie was economical with his words and I was a new boy content to let him lead the way. A couple of overs were played out in relative silence, and then there was a phone call from Kerry Packer wanting to know what we were doing. He informed us in very clear terms that this was not the BBC, most of the people watching didn't have a clue about cricket, and we were supposed to be telling them what was going on.

Richie wasn't going to change or in any way dilute the commentary lessons he lived by: you only spoke if you could add something to the pictures. So the next over was again virtually word-free. After that, I thought keeping Kerry onside was a bit more important, so I started rattling on. The pattern sort of stuck.

In those early days, Richie did the presenting as well as com- mentating. He didn't have the small army of commentators we see today, or a 'Cricket Show' or anything like that to help him fill the time at lunch or during other breaks in play. He would do ten minutes before play started, to set the day up, then he'd do another summary at lunch, before we crossed to the 18-footer sailing races as we did in those days. He did all the talking at tea and summaries at stumps. It was a lot of pressure, but he handled it with the same easy assurance that he had managed when he was the Australian cricket captain. Even when things went wrong, as they often did, he was in control. In tandem with a super producer in David Hill, Richie opened up a whole new era of sport on television. More cameras … and at both ends of the ground … jingles, coloured clothing, night cricket — they all came in a rush as the public got on board and the modern game started to take shape.

I remain convinced today that WSC would not have worked without Richie. Let's face it, half of the cricket community was willing us to fail, and there was so much innovation it needed a really steady hand to put it all out there. Richie did that brilliantly, bringing the game into a new era decades earlier than may have been the case otherwise.

It had been like that on our 1961 tour of England, too. Richie was the first player to bring some theatrics to the game, jumping about in celebration and generally being more lively. His background as a journalist and the fact he did a BBC-TV course way before he ever got a job there meant that he knew how to work with the media. If there was a TV or film camera around he was a natural.

Our manager on that tour was Syd Webb QC, a nice bloke who was an Australian Cricket Board of Control member back home and liked to be at the centre of things. Syd held a press conference at 10am to announce that Richie would be giving no more press con- ferences, as he had done to that point, and that Syd would be hand- ling all of that from now on. At 5pm that day, Richie gave another press conference, as was his practice. I don't think anything ever changed. Richie might have resented the attempt to gag him, but he knew the value of what he was doing, so he just kept doing it.

Another thing about Richie Benaud the captain that endeared him to everybody was that his buoyant celebrations of good performance were never countered by sharp criticism. He never felt the need to criticise, realising players were mature enough to know where they had let matters slip and that labouring the point would serve no purpose. I can remember saying to him that someone or other had got out to a poor shot, but Richie would counter, 'Yes, but it was really well bowled.' Always positive.

The outpouring from the public when Richie died — respect, I think, rather than just grief — was extraordinary. To those who knew him, he was a generous, considerate, well-loved man. But those who never met him sort of knew him too. When you think about it, for anybody 80 years of age or younger, Richie had been a part of their life for most of it.

I knew him all my adult life. I still look up to him.

DAVID FRITH

David Frith was born in England, emigrated to Australia as a 12-year-old and developed a love of cricket in Sydney, playing for St George and Paddington. As a young man, he returned to England, where he now lives, having become one of the world's pre-eminent cricket authorities and historians. Among many things, he launched and edited *Wisden Cricket Monthly* and has written more than 30 critically acclaimed cricket books.

PUSHING through just over six decades of my memory's shrubbery, I do recall my first sight of Richie Benaud. My precious and priceless old autograph book provides the evidence. 'R. Benaud', he'd neatly signed, just beneath Ray Lindwall and Jim Burke. The date, in fading red ink, is '17-2-51', which places it as the Saturday of the NSW v South Australia Shield match from 1950–51. The 20-year-old Benaud was 18 not out that evening. My hero, Lindwall, was 22 not out and that afternoon Keith Miller, whose signature I'd already bagged, had stroked a century. These were blissful days with famous cricketers close at hand, thanks to Stan Mealey, the genial SCG members' gate attendant, who let us boys into the sacred sector an hour or so after close of play.

Then, as now, I was very, very interested in what kind of people these cricketers really were. Batting and bowling averages were one thing. But what sort of men were they? Friendly? Conversational? How well did they dress? How did they speak? What cars did they drive?

We were not all that taken by our first Benaud encounter, to be honest. He seemed slightly aloof, perhaps even a touch arrogant. That padded-shouldered cream sports jacket and smooth hairstyle emphasised his resemblance to some young American film actor. There was no chirpy remark following the signature. And where did this 'Richie' come from? That's the kind of name usually given to a perky little bloke who makes mischief all the time. A Richard in those days was commonly known as 'Dick', just as Williams were all 'Bill', Roberts all 'Bob'. Imagine it: Dick Benaud.

What complicated the situation was that over the next few years, during which he made his Test debut, there were suggestions that the selectors were crazy to continue picking him. There seemed to be so many other promising young players being left on the sidelines while Benaud continued to win favour but so seldom produced the goods. In particular, there was a superb 85 by Ray Flockton for NSW against the 1951–52 West Indies which had old-timers speaking of Victor Trumper. It seemed to rub in the irrational nature of the situation.

Next summer, the poor chap had a ball slashed straight into his face. My young brother was down by the pickets and heard Graeme Hole, fielding nearby, murmur, 'Asleep again!' We considered that rather cruel. And when 'RB' could do nothing right during the 1953 Ashes series over in England, well, what future? He might have been about to disappear forever.

We now know how the selectors' unflinching faith finally paid off. Subsequent personal memories of Richie Benaud in action, 'live', on the radio and then on TV, make a stirring package: whacking Queensland fast bowler Colin Smith high into the SCG Ladies Stand, stiffening Australia's tail in Test after Test in company with Ken Mackay or Alan Davidson, that 97 against England at Lord's in 1956 alongside the miracle catch at gully from Colin

Cowdrey's fast slash, loping into the outfield in pursuit of the ball with Ian Craig alongside him, the flick back by one to the other, who then threw the ball in, being revolutionary for its time, though standard practice today.

Never was Richie Benaud the bowler seen in a better light than when he paralysed the Englishmen with leg-spin variations in the 1962–63 NSW v MCC match at the SCG. He took 7–18 that afternoon, his best ever figures in first-class cricket. Left-hander Peter Parfitt was free to pad everything away, so long as impact was outside the off-stump line. A bloke on the hill could take no more: 'Tie yer flamin' bat to yer leg, Parfitt. Ya might make a run!'

Career-best it may have been, but this performance was still outshone by what he achieved in the pulsating Old Trafford Test match of 1961. With England needing 256 and coasting nicely, Benaud took Ray Lindwall's advice offered the previous evening and tried bowling around the wicket into the rough. It needs to be remembered that this was rarely tried in those unadventurous days. Rash shots by Ted Dexter, Peter May and Brian Close soon had England in disarray and a momentous victory resulted.

Film survives and it shows captain Benaud's enthusiasm clearly. When a wicket fell he would run down to embrace the catcher — and you can see the likes of Neil Harvey and Bob Simpson preparing to run to safety. This evolutionary trend is seldom if ever credited to Richie Benaud, but the fact is that the casual nod and occasional quick handshake after the fall of a wicket were now superseded by a bit of physical expression.

Not only was it contagious but it led in time to the mass love-ins we see today and the 'ring a ring o' roses' when a match is won. I'm sure he didn't intend it to develop like this. But society has gradually moved nearer to hysteria in most walks of life — even television commentary. If only Richie Benaud were still able to take some of the moderns to one side and whisper in their ears that non-stop microphone babble is alien to proper commentary. He might have wept had he listened to recent telecasts when a commentator was regularly blitzing the ears even as the ball entered the wicketkeeper's gloves.

He had that one thing in common with Len Hutton, the Englishman who'd often teased him in their Test match confrontations. A vivid image from the old days is of Benaud trying to hit the SCG clock off Hutton's occasional and barely turning leg breaks in 1955: poor fella was bowled, but it made an ageing Yorkshireman happy in his final Ashes Test. That common trait was a strict economy with words. Some people carry on chuntering away long after they've delivered anything they had to offer that was meaningful. Not Len. And certainly never Richie. He was careful never to predict a boundary four. The ball might just stop short and he'd look foolish. Couldn't have that.

As a press-box neighbour, Richie was always there for a chat at the right time. I'd long known how much he appreciated being regarded as the shrewdest of them all. He was a clever chap.

Of the cameos remembered from many decades of Richie-watching, one more snippet must suffice: Old Trafford, 1980s, RB laboriously climbing the perilous iron staircase to the press box on high. Two Lancashire lads spot him. 'Ay! There's Richie! Yer gettin' old, Richie!'

Back came the instant reaction: 'Maybe, but at least I'm still sober.'

The cricket world mourned his passing on a truly extraordinary scale. It was natural to picture the elderly man, the cricket commentator, who had just died. But for me the vision is of the tall, cool, smartly dressed young chap at the rear door of the SCG pavilion that evening in 1951. No one could possibly have predicted such a future: world-class all-rounder, Test skipper, shrewd, unflappable commentator, just that little bit larger than life. To draw on his French blood, a *bon viveur* and *éminence grise*.

SIR TIM RICE

Known throughout the world for his work as a lyricist and author in musical theatre and film, Sir Tim Rice is also a cricket player and fan with a deep and lifelong attachment to the game. A special event for him each year is the arrival

of the players from the Heartaches Cricket Club, which he
established in 1973, for a weekend of cricket on the ground
at his home. Richie and his wife Daphne's interest in musical
theatre meant it was a 'perfect match' when they first met
Tim Rice. The friendship was strongly sustained through
the years, as Tim Rice's name and talent became associated
with more and more global successes, *Jesus Christ
Superstar*, *Evita*, *Chess* and *The Lion King* among them.

I shall never forget the first time I met Richie — at a preview of
Jesus Christ Superstar at the Palace Theatre in London in the summer
of 1972. I recognised him across a crowded foyer in the interval. I
felt rather guilty about approaching him without an introduction
but he was typically polite even before I revealed that I was in part
responsible for his evening's entertainment. The chat that followed
was a little disjointed as I wanted to talk about Doug Walters and
Paul Sheahan while Richie and Daphne were more interested in
discussing Jesus and Judas.

Thanks to that chance meeting I was lucky enough to establish
a lasting association for over 40 years. I remain extraordinarily
privileged to have known both Richie and Daphne for so long.

I particularly relish the glass of wine we shared in Tasmania
the morning I diffidently asked Richie if he would consider
becoming MCC president. I knew it was a long shot, and his
charming refusal was totally understandable, but I wanted him
to know that the Marylebone club, a conservative pillar of
the England cricketing establishment, which curiously I was
representing in 2002–03, could have imagined no greater honour
than having Richie — an Australian hero whose progressive
views on the game both on and off the field for so many years had
been so instrumental in dragging the game into each successive
modern era — at its helm. As a commentator and journalist, he
performed the same invaluable service with distinction right up
to his final day behind the microphone.

And, of course, he was a magnificent player and captain.
There are so many millions of Richie fans who must think of him
primarily as a great cricket broadcaster and writer, but while this is
an indisputably accurate description, I still think of him first as one
of the best players and leaders it has been my privilege to witness. I

only wish I had seen him play a good deal more than I did, although I am perhaps grateful that I did not see him demolish England in 1958–59.

It was a sad pleasure reading all the many wonderful British tributes to Richie, whom we regarded as an honorary Englishman, loved and missed as much in the UK as down-under.

ALAN JONES

Alan Jones is a radio broadcaster of commanding influence, a member of the Sydney Cricket and Sports Ground Trust, and a former coach of the Australian rugby team, the Wallabies. He has held a lifelong passion for sport in all its shades.

BOOKS of this kind are important. Generations are poor at seeking history, let alone understanding it. And so it is with this remarkable and much-loved Australian, Richie Benaud.

What has always concerned me about the worthy tributes paid to Richie on his sad passing in April 2015 at the age of 84 was that he seemed almost exclusively to be celebrated as a broadcaster. It is undeniable that Richie was, at his death, one of the most iconic figures and one of the most loved figures in Australian sports broadcasting. He was described by many as a broadcasting giant and indeed, to young Australians, he was the gifted, generous, forever dignified cricket broadcaster.

But to those with a greater span of history, he was a magnificent and flamboyant cricket captain, immortalised along with Alan Davidson in that famous Tied Test in Brisbane against the West Indies in 1960.

To win the Test, Australia had to make 233 runs. During the course of the afternoon, Australia were 6–92, with Richie and Davo at the crease. They took the score to 6–226. Seven more for victory.

Richie called for a sharp single. The West Indian, Solomon, hit the stumps from mid-wicket. Davidson was run out for 80. We're 7–226.

The new batsman, Wally Grout, managed a run from the penultimate ball of the second-last over. Try as he might, Richie couldn't score a single from the last ball to keep the strike. The last over of the match began. They were eight-ball overs.

Ball 1: Grout was hit on the thigh. The batsmen took a leg bye.

Ball 2: Richie was caught by the keeper for 52. Australia 8–228.

Ball 3: There was no run. The new batsman, Ian Meckiff, played the ball to mid-off.

Ball 4: A bye. The batsmen scrambled as the ball went through to the keeper. The great Wesley Hall failed to run out Meckiff, after the keeper threw the ball to him.

Ball 5: A run. Grout hit the ball high into the air. Wesley Hall dropped the catch. Australia 8–230.

Ball 6: Two runs and a wicket. Meckiff hit to the leg-side. Conrad Hunte cut off the boundary and as the batsmen turned for a third run, which would have given Australia victory, Hunte's return was accurate, low and fast and Grout was run out by a foot. The last man, Lindsay Kline, came in with two balls remaining and the scores level. Australia 9–232.

Ball 7: Kline played the ball towards square-leg. Meckiff sprinted down the wicket, but Solomon, for a second time, threw down the wicket, this time from side on. Australia was all out with the scores level. It was a tie.

When they went to tea, Richie, the captain, had gone to the chairman of selectors, Sir Donald Bradman, and said words to the effect: 'We're playing to win this.'

Well, he and Davo registered a partnership of 134 runs. They didn't win, but the captaincy of Richie Benaud was immortalised.

As a broadcaster, Richie let the pictures tell the story — coloured, sometimes, by hilarious observations. On one occasion, Glenn McGrath was out for two and Richie quipped that he was 'just 98 runs short of his century'.

The Australian opener, Justin Langer, had hit a towering six. Richie waited, because pauses were important to Richie, and then added, 'He's not quite got hold of that ... if he had, it would have gone for nine.'

In reality, there were two generations who idolised Richie Benaud. The modern generation knew the man with the grey hair and the beige or cream or bone jackets. But very few of those admirers understood the other generation who saw him as an outstanding cricketer in the 1950s and 1960s.

A magnificent spin bowler.

A dashing batsman.

A bit of a sex symbol, if you like — shirt unbuttoned to his waist, good-looking and possessed of a gentlemanly charm. And yet, in spite of all these attributes, Richie was, in so many ways, a gentle soul.

He found his true batting partner in Daphne.

And over dinner or over drinks, the conversation covered every aspect of a world with which Richie was familiar, in all its facets.

In 1954–55, when England returned to Australia, the great Arthur Morris was not made the Australian captain, despite being the incumbent vice-captain. He remained deputy as Victoria's Ian Johnson was called to the team and assumed the captaincy.

In the second Test in Sydney, when Johnson and Keith Miller were both unavailable due to injury, Arthur Morris led the team for the second and final time in Tests. But the Australian Board of Control made what was thought to be a surprising move by appointing the 'young and inexperienced' Richie Benaud as vice-captain to Arthur Morris.

Richie had been selected as a batsman and was not a regular member of the team. But typically Richie, he noted that the situation was embarrassing and Arthur Morris asked him not to be offended if he sought advice from veteran players like Ray Lindwall and Neil Harvey, who had been Test regulars for several years. Richie's turn came in 1958 when he became Australia's Test captain, following illness to Ian Craig. He remained captain until 1963–64.

He would often tell the story about the fact that his choice as captain of Australia was something of a surprise. It was either he or Neil Harvey, Richie would say, and then modestly argue that perhaps the Australian Board of Control disliked Richie just a little less than they disliked Neil.

Many stories could be told about a modest and unassuming individual, who simply let the record speak for him. The greatest innings he ever played, he would always say, was the one in which he remained not out until the day he died — with his partner, Daphne.

Oddly, it was most probably the Sri Lankan cricket writer, Harold de Andrado, who came closest to the quintessential evaluation of Richie the cricketer and broadcaster, when he wrote:

> Richie Benaud, possibly next to Sir Donald Bradman, has been one of the greatest cricketing personalities as player, researcher, writer, critic, author, organiser, adviser and student of the game.

We never lost a series under Richie's captaincy and we became the dominant team in world cricket. His legacy to young players today derives from his ruthless and relentless determination to attack, his tactical boldness, his ability to extract more from his players.

He was larger than life.

Known for his unbuttoned shirt.

Raised eyebrows.

He brought new life to Test cricket, with remarkable leadership, with his charismatic nature and with his public relations strengths. Cricket, because of Richie Benaud, was no longer boring.

And when he retired from playing in 1964, he left behind a playing legacy comparable with the very best. Indeed, in 1963, he became the first player to complete the Test double of 200 wickets and 2,000 runs.

He played 63 Test matches and 259 first-class matches, but he commentated on approximately 500 Test matches.

The most enduring virtue of Richie, the common man, was seen when he chose to end his British commentary career, which had spanned more than 42 years, when the rights to broadcast live Test match cricket were lost by Channel 4 to the subscription broadcaster, British Sky Broadcasting. Richie was a staunch advocate of cricket being available to everyone. Free-to-view TV.

Richie is gone, but the memories remain. The record stands. The broadcasting legacy will never be equalled.

And his books are a permanent and enduring record of a man who succeeded resoundingly, lived enthusiastically and was loved greatly.

JOHN HOWARD

The 25th prime minister of Australia, John Howard, has been called Australia's most noted cricket 'tragic'. A passion for the game has been a strong undercurrent throughout Mr Howard's life.

MY first recollection of meeting Richie Benaud was in the late 1950s, when he presented a talk at our local church hall, aided by coloured slides of what I think was Australia's 1957–58 tour of South Africa. As an even younger person, I had seen him play for Australia at the SCG against the West Indians in early 1952, the South Africans in 1952–53 and England in 1954–55. I particularly remember that savage late cut from a South African batsman which shattered some of Richie's front teeth.

In 1958, I recall the late 'Johnnie' Moyes heavily plumping for Richie Benaud to become the Australian captain against Peter May's touring Englishmen. This was the era of Trevor Bailey's funereal performance as an opening batsman for England, when in a Test match the spectators were lucky if a team scored 200 runs on the first day.

Benaud brought an enthusiasm to the Australian team which over time infected others. I could be wrong, but I think it was under Richie's leadership that the practice of teammates running to congratulate a bowler when he took a wicket commenced.

As it is for so many cricket followers of my age, the 1960–61 West Indian tour of Australia remains unforgettable. Under the leadership of Frank Worrell and Richie Benaud, all five Tests were played aggressively but with amazing goodwill and in an atmosphere of mutual respect and friendship. This series included the famous Tied Test at Brisbane. Australia won the series by two matches to one — the fourth Test in Adelaide was a draw.

At the end of the series, the ABC evening radio news included a report on the outcome of the fifth Test in Melbourne, won by Australia. I have never forgotten the newsreader's concluding words: 'Australia won the series 2–1 but both teams shared the greater prize for sportsmanship and adventure.' Australians loved the West Indians' approach to the game, but I have always felt that the spirit Richie Benaud brought to the leadership of the Australian team played no small part in that series being indelible in the memories of cricket lovers of a certain age.

As the years passed, I followed Richie Benaud's career as Australia's captain, talented all-rounder, regular commentator and, of course, his role in the emergence of World Series Cricket and the revolution brought to the game by Kerry Packer.

He was a man for generations of cricket lovers. My sons were enthralled by his manner of cricket commentary. His match summaries were always a lesson in understatement when that was necessary, and polite but precisely delivered criticism when that reaction was needed.

Years later still, I got to know Richie during my political years and enjoyed his gracious company and that of his lovely wife Daphne on a number of social occasions. He always had something relevant to say about current affairs. It was never cynical or carping, but rather thoughtful and reflective. One such occasion was a boardroom lunch he and I attended not long after the 1998 election. He was asked his opinion on the continuing influence of Pauline Hanson's One Nation Party, which had polled a million votes at that election. After reflecting for a moment, he said that although that party's support had probably peaked, its influence would continue for quite a time yet. It proved a most accurate prediction.

I enjoyed the privilege of playing golf with Richie on one occasion. He was kind enough to applaud those few shots of mine that encouraged one to return the following week. This was, I think, in 2004 and such was his physical condition that he carried his bag for the entire 18 holes.

When Sir Donald Bradman died in February 2001 it seemed the most natural thing that Richie Benaud should deliver the eulogy at his memorial service in Adelaide. For a number of years before his death, Richie was the patron of the Bradman Foundation, of which I became a director early in 2008. He took the duties of being patron seriously and displayed a keen interest in all its work.

When Richie died in April 2015, I said publicly that after Bradman himself Richie Benaud was probably the best known name in Australian cricket.

GIDEON HAIGH

Internationally respected writer Gideon Haigh remembers a
rare Benaud defeat.

FOR about ten years, Richie and I were members of the selection panel for the Australian Cricket Hall of Fame. Its annual meeting at the MCG, usually on the third morning of the Boxing Day Test, was an event to which I always looked forward — a selection meeting for posterity.

Richie, of course, was always superbly prepared, and we awaited his verdicts — shrewd, subtle and weighty with experience. By the end of his involvement, I think he had played with ten of the Hall's members, commentated on 11, and been acquainted with another six. At one meeting, however, we arrived at an impasse.

I made a pitch for one player; Richie made a pitch for another. After a lively discussion, we moved to a show of hands and Richie was outvoted by the narrowest margin. Looks were exchanged, and there was an uneasy pause at our going against the great man's will.

Eventually the secretary said: 'Well, that makes four–three. It's not really clear-cut.'

Richie smiled. 'Oh, I don't know,' he said dryly. 'Four–three sounds pretty clear-cut to me.'

I loved that — thought it summed up Richie's unassuming matter-of-factness in all circumstances.

RODNEY CAVALIER

Rodney Cavalier is a former chairman of the Sydney Cricket and Sports Ground Trust. In that role, he combined with benefactor Basil Sellers to develop the Basil Sellers SCG Sports Sculptures Project.

WHEN I first visited the sacred soil of the Sydney Cricket Ground in 1962 it was to see the second day's play, NSW v MCC, a Saturday. NSW was batting. Norm O'Neill and Bob Simpson were blazing. Richie was captain of NSW. His services with the bat were not required. When the game resumed on Monday, Richie ran through the MCC for 7–18. NSW did not have to bat again.

Richie was always there whether you saw him or not. When first I saw a Test later that season, first day, third Test, January 1963, Australia was fielding, Richie was captain, shirt open, very much in command. It was the image of him that day that Basil Sellers and I tried to have created in the sculpture of Richie that stands at the SCG.

Richie was always there in conversation. You did not long talk cricket as a schoolboy without Richie entering the conversation. He featured in my earliest writings about cricket, private stuff in a diary. Going over back issues of the newsletter of the Australian Labor Party's Southern Highlands branch, which I edit and in which I always find room for cricket, he appeared so often. He was on television, it seemed, from the beginning of television.

Then one day Richie moved from the field, television and debates among colleagues into my life and friendship. In writings and personal conversations, Richie took me inside a life lived in cricket and beyond.

'TIMING is one of the great things in life,' he once said. 'Timings may be your own, they may be luck, you make of them as you will.'

Richie's first sighting of first-class cricket was 1939–40, the last season before the war, when on January 13, 1940, Lou Benaud took his son to the SCG to see NSW play South Australia. They came by steam train and toast-rack tram.

From the back of the Sheridan Stand with a bottle of Blue Bow and sandwiches, two spectators in 30,400. Lou wanted his son to have a view of Grimmett, Ward, O'Reilly. In that match spinners took 34 wickets. Grimmett 6–118. At the end of the first day, which was all they were able to watch, NSW had made 270. South Australia was making its reply. Bradman was 24 not out. That was wonderful.

DURING the 1953 Ashes tour, Tiger O'Reilly cancelled dinner with Hassett to dine with Richie. That is, Bill placed advice to a coming player ahead of a night out with a friend. Bill provided Richie with advice in six points. The advice came with a warning: to achieve the levels you are seeking will require all your discipline, total dedication and four years of effort. The strictures were correct in every particular.

The O'Reilly advice Richie has shared with any bowler who sought his assistance. Books on spin bowling can take up 250 pages. Bill O'Reilly required two pages. After Warne made his poor debut in Test cricket, Warne asked to meet Richie. At their meeting Richie provided Warne with the O'Reilly wisdom, the warnings about the work ahead. Warne was so good that he mastered the mysteries in two years.

Conventional wisdom about the making of Shane Warne accords the credit to Terry Jenner. It does not diminish whatever Jenner advised to believe the difference was what Richie imparted from Bill O'Reilly. Jenner was a spinner of the second rank. Bill O'Reilly was the best there ever was.

Bill, like Richie, was a masterful writer; each wrote daily reports on the day before, accounts which saw beyond the headlines; each wrote books of memoir that stand as literature in any genre.

A line of advice that reads O'Reilly–Benaud–Warne strikes one as most likely.

Interesting that Richie never entered the contest for history. Contesting history was not Richie's way.

RICHIE'S journalism and books on the game place him in the most exalted company — among players who wrote he is up there with Fingleton and O'Reilly. *A Tale of Two Tests* is a classic work which you never tire of reading.

He was so very good at telling stories because he was so good at listening to stories. Listening, storing, distilling. A memory bank to draw from in any situation for the rest of his days. In any story I told him about politics and the SCG Trust, I did not doubt I was enjoying his full attention. An excellent memory and a wide vocabulary were reasons Richie could ride through technical and other breakdowns as long as he had a functioning microphone. No use for a cue card had he.

A signature Richie moment was recounting a story from Keith Miller about Lord's 1945 just after the war ended. Whit Monday to be precise. Richie erred on the side of precision. Why be proximate when you can be accurate? On that Whit Monday 1945 a vast crowd had turned out to be present at the resumption of serious cricket. Friends of cricket across the world were affirming life.

The story Miller told Richie was the most powerful story Miller ever told, the most poignant cricket story Richie ever heard, and it lost none of its poignancy as another retold it at a ceremony to mark the centenary of the NSW Cricket Association. We who heard Richie tell were as affected as was Richie when Richie first heard the story from Miller.

Entering the field to bat for the Australian Services side was Warrant Officer Robert Graham Williams. He had last played first-class cricket for South Australia in 1938, a broad-shouldered paceman.

In the meantime there had been a war, he had joined the RAAF, his plane was shot down over Libya, he was taken prisoner. He had spent the war in German POW camps teaching braille until his release only weeks earlier. Then he was on a plane, drafted to meet the needs of Australian cricket with no say in the matter. The London papers had picked up his story and splashed it.

He came through the gate at Lord's, broad shoulders gone, gaunt, a shadow of what he had been. Of all the moments that Keith Miller ever witnessed in cricket, this was the most powerful. The whole crowd stood and clapped him. Softly. No cheering. The crowd kept clapping all the way to the wicket. The noise was 'almost orchestral'.

Williams may have enjoyed no say in whether he played but play he did with all the pride of someone worthy of the colours of South Australia and the uniform he had worn in the skies over Europe. His presence in the Services side was his farewell to cricket. Coming in at 8–366, the applause did not unsettle him. Williams scored 53 in a partnership of 88. He also opened the bowling with Bert Cheetham and took 2–56 in the first innings, 0–47 in the second.

Richie made his first-class debut about three-and-a-half years later, on December 31, 1948. Heavy rain fell. Arthur Morris did not have to call on Richie to bowl. NSW needed 143 to win, Arthur made 108 not out. In those early days, Richie had 'three wonderful mentors' — Morris, Miller, Ray Lindwall. 'What need had I of coaches?'

He made his first-class debut at the SCG, his Test debut at the SCG and played his final Test at the SCG. Who could ask for more?

'The SCG is such a great ground,' said Richie. 'It is a wonderful thrill to walk out on it.'

Words spoken with deliberate intent as there was an ill-informed few present who advocated playing cricket elsewhere. Play hard but make sure, make absolutely sure, you maintain the tradition.

THE day of the unveiling of the Richie Benaud sculpture at the SCG, January 4, 2008, remains a special memory. He was the perfect choice to be the first subject. And we had kept the secret; only a precious few knew who the artwork depicted before it was unveiled. The man himself had not seen it.

People were everywhere on the morning of this first unveiling, including the administrative leadership of Australian cricket and a large number of former players. The cloth which covered the sculpture had caught the attention of the SCG members as they filed into the ground from 7am onwards. The stairs leading into the Ladies Stand and the overhead walkway connecting the Ladies to the Members Stand provided a fine view of the sculpture's location, as did the open windows at the back of both stands. The lawn that runs from the members' main entrance to the practice wickets is elevated, so in every direction people were watching. The media was present in large numbers, including Channel Seven because Channel Nine, the television rights holder for international cricket in Australia, had been gracious in granting all media access to the ceremony.

The governor-general, Major-General Michael Jeffery, had agreed to undertake the unveiling, but this led to a brief crisis when he advised with genuine apology that he needed to represent the nation at the funeral of the former Western Australian premier Sir Charles Court. I had rung the governor of NSW, Professor Marie Bashir, at her home immediately to apprise her of what had happened. If she was free, could she make herself available? She would make herself available whatever was on, Her Excellency answered. The selection of Richie Benaud impressed her. She wanted her office to be associated with such a significant occasion.

We had planned a ceremony in fine detail, intending to make everyone present feel that the event was memorable. We wanted proceedings to move along. The unveiling was the central moment and should proceed without delay. After my welcome, I provided an introduction to the guest speaker whose job it was to talk in general terms about the sport being honoured, maintain the suspense about the identity of the subject, spread clues (not all helpful) before announcing the name of the subject and lifting the veil.

The governor delivered a perfect speech. In the audience were Richie Benaud, Arthur Morris, Neil Harvey, Mark Taylor and Stephen Waugh, clues perhaps but not definitive, given we had made it clear the subject was not necessarily alive. When the governor announced that the sculpture was of Richie Benaud, the applause was spontaneous in every direction. We had a shroud purpose-built but the governor pulled the string the wrong way. To get it over the sculpture's outstretched arms was a challenge. The crowd renewed their applause, this time more strongly, when they saw how well done was the representation of Richie.

Basil explained his project. The sculptor, Terrance Plowright, expressed his honour at being commissioned and the pleasure of meeting the challenge. Then it was Richie.

'The first thing I want to say,' he began, 'is that I like it.'

OVER a number of years, I pieced together my knowledge of Richie Benaud in a score of conversations. Most of our chatter was at the SCG and at Lord's. The sculptures project at the SCG took me beyond casual chats into the friendship of Richie and his wife Daphne.

So it was that I, who did not ever expect to share breathing space with Richie, was invited with my wife Sally and son Nicholas in 2009 (after the Lord's Test) to be a guest of Daphne and Richie at their home in Beaulieu on the Mediterranean. Richie took us to dinner at the African Queen, a restaurant on the bay. We walked the streets of Beaulieu, we talked into a late hour, his mind eclectic, capable of reaching out to the non-tragics at the table. Next afternoon we backed up on the lawn of Basil Sellers' home at nearby Cap Ferrat — an opportunity for me to perform ever after a shameless specimen of name-dropping and place-dropping. For truly it was heaven to hear Richie recall the fourth Test, Manchester, 1961.

There was not a moment in those days and nights I did not have to convince myself I was truly in the presence of Richie Benaud.

– 2 –
EARLY DAYS

'At this stage of his career, Benaud stands out as clearly above his adolescent contemporaries as Arthur Morris did at the same age.'

— Bill O'Reilly, 1949

JON ERBY

Jon Erby has balanced a life as a family man and successful
Sydney architect with his love of cricket. A talented
opening batsman, he played 11 seasons of first grade with
Cumberland and Sydney University. A highlight was the day
he faced the fire and pace of Wes Hall at Merrylands Oval
and scored 97. In 1974, Jon was a driving force behind the
formation of the Primary Club of Australia, one of cricket's
most respected charities.

A N early memory of Richie and his fellow leg-spinner Jack
Treanor, an outstanding grade bowler who played for NSW,
is of a day in 1954 when they came down to the nets at
King's School, Parramatta. It was the first time I ever experienced the
ball actually *hissing* through the air with the spin those two guys put
on it. At times, Richie would bowl medium-paced cutters instead of
wrist-spin, in days when grade wickets weren't covered and all sorts
of difficult situations could be encountered, but when he spun them,
they really buzzed.

From around the time of that early encounter until 1956, I was
in the King's School first XI, as a right-hand opening batsman. I
played Green Shield and Poidevin-Gray with Cumberland before
trying out for grade in my last year at King's. At the start of the
1957–58 season, I found myself opening the batting for Cumberland
firsts.

Two days before the game, which was to be played at the old
Cumberland Oval, something happened involving Richie that I

would never forget. I broke the only bat I owned. Bruce Ritchie, a close friend of Richie's and a mentor of mine, said to me: 'I'll ring him. They're not too long back from the tour [the 1956 Ashes tour] and they always bring bats home with them. I'll see if he has one you can borrow.'

Richie wasn't playing for Cumberland that weekend, because the Australian team was about to fly out for a big tour of South Africa, but he told Bruce to get me to come around to his place on the Saturday morning before our game started and he'd lend me a bat. We duly turned up at his home, not far from where Richie Benaud Oval now stands, and knocked on the door. Richie wasn't an early riser in those days and opened the door in his pyjamas, with the bat in his hand.

'I cleaned it up overnight, sandpapered and repaired it for you,' he said. 'If you get a fifty, you can keep it.'

There was a challenge!

We were playing North Sydney and I found myself seeing the ball very well. The scoreboard ticked over and finally showed: J. Erby … 50. All I could think was: *I've got the bat!* One of their spinners was bowling to me and he tossed one up. I went down the wicket and launched into it … and was caught at straight hit.

As I walked off to the tunnel that led to the old, run-down dressing-rooms, I passed our scorer, Ernie Gould. 'Bad luck, Jon,' he called down. 'You got 47.'

The scoreboard operator had got ahead of himself. The applause for my maiden half-century was premature. I headed into the change-room and slumped down, with my pads still on and my head down, when Richie walked in. He was succinct in what he said, as he would be in the years ahead.

'Don't you ever do that again,' he said. 'But you can keep the bat.'

In my third first-grade game of that season, against University, I scored an unbeaten century using Richie's bat. Tired but happy, I walked into the room after our innings ended, put the bat down and noticed that the entire back of it had badly split. I could never use it again.

But I kept it, because it meant so much to me, and I still have it, a lightweight thing compared to today's big boppers. I remember its beautiful 'sweet spot'. I never had another bat as good, before or after.

Only later did I discover that this was the bat with which Richie scored his famous 97 at Lord's in Australia's second innings of the second Ashes Test of 1956, an innings that inspired a 185-run victory. And he had given it to me ... a kid out of school!

There is an addendum to this story that nearly provided an unhappy punchline. Ten years or so later and now married to Christine, I lingered one night after playing squash and had a few beers with some mates at Norths Rugby Club. I was late home and Chris clearly wasn't too happy with me. I asked her what she had been up to and she replied: 'I've been having a clean-out ... and I threw that old bat out.' I raced to the garbage bin and rescued it.

In my time with Cumberland I played a fair bit with Richie and I never played under a better captain. He certainly wasn't one who raved and ranted. He'd walk into a dressing-room and you'd hardly know he was there. His demeanour was controlled; I never saw him get rattled. He led totally by example and you always knew what he wanted you to do. I think we all had the feeling that if we didn't do what he wanted, we'd be letting him down. He was a very positive captain who always gave the other side a chance to win, which meant that we had a chance, too.

Richie was a hard-hitting batsman, although I don't believe I've ever seen anyone hit the ball as hard as his brother John. I remember a day when John hit 13 sixes against Bankstown and I ran on and told him if he hit one more it would be a club record.

'I'm too buggered!' was John's response.

When my friend Peter Howarth and I founded the Primary Club of Australia in 1974, I approached Richie and told him what we were hoping to do. We asked him to be a vice-president.

'I'll do anything I can to help,' he said.

We built a ground at Yarramalong, about 90km north of Sydney, and each year played our big fundraiser there: the President's XI versus the Twelfth Man's XI. Test players would come up and play for nothing and the crowds were big. Richie captained the Twelfth Man's team the first time the match was played, just one example of how he embraced thoroughly the ideals of the Primary Club. He delivered a major speech at our inaugural dinner and would always speak at the club's breakfast that was held during the Sydney Test match. He never missed a fundraising event. Eventually, in 2002, he became our patron (or Twelfth Man), succeeding Sir Roden Cutler.

He and Daphne were a wonderful couple, a perfect fit. Dinners at their place were a great enjoyment, with Richie the chef and his spaghetti a speciality. I have fond memories of a splendid lunch with the Benauds during the Centenary Test at Lord's in 1980, on the third day of what would be a rain-spoiled match. Daphne produced a hamper full of wonderful food and fine wine, and a group of us gathered at their car, which was parked near the lawn behind the stands at the Pavilion end of the famous ground. It rained and the lunch became a *long* lunch, with the likes of Ian Chappell and Johnny Gleeson joining the gathering.

Throughout his career, Richie famously played his cricket capless and with his shirt open, a homage of sorts to Keith Miller, whom he idolised.

Each year, I would ring him on his birthday. On the last occasion he told me the dermatologist had made him promise to wear a cap whenever he went out. Three weeks later, he rang me and announced, 'I thought you'd be interested — the specialist now wants me to wear a hat with a brim.'

BRUCE RITCHIE

Bruce Ritchie first spotted his future wife Jean (they married in 1956) while he was talking to Richie at a 'do' long ago in Parramatta. He is one of the few who can still remember the short-pants schoolboy Richie of the late 1930s. The pair met as 'little fellas', as he puts it, and became great pals, their lives circling in large order around cricket, golf and tennis. Bruce was an opening batsman good enough to make the NSW Colts team that played Queensland in 1951–52, a match in which he scored a second-innings century. In retirement, he moved to Buderim on Queensland's Sunshine Coast, far removed from Parramatta, but he retains crystal-clear memories of those happy long-ago days.

RICHIE and I met for the first time not long before World War II, when his dad Lou brought the family from Jugiong to Parramatta. Lou was a good cricketer, but he was 33 then and a lot of people thought his best cricketing days were over. But Lou was a slow bowler, so they weren't, of course.

I was born in 1929, a year before Richie, and we became the best of mates, brought together by a shared interest in cricket. As kids, we were regulars at Cumberland Oval, fetching balls for the grade teams on Saturday at the pre-game practice sessions. I recall a day when Stan McCabe and his Mosman team were there, and before they went into the rooms, Mr McCabe invited Richie and me over to have a bowl in the nets. Years later, in 1946, at a grade match at Hurstville Oval, the famous St George captain Bill O'Reilly, a great leg-spinner who would have an important link later with Richie, came and sat with me at afternoon tea. 'The last time I saw you,' he said, 'you were collecting balls on Cumberland Oval.'

Early in his sporting career, Richie was a very good soccer player — quite outstanding in fact — and he scored lots of goals in the local junior competition. But while batting for the NSW Second XI in Melbourne, he tried to hook a bumper (a favoured Benaud pastime) but missed and took the ball flush on the forehead. The result was a fractured skull and damaged sinus, which led to him having to give soccer away. The jarring of the ball as he negotiated headers proved too uncomfortable.

In the very early days of our friendship, we used to play backyard cricket every Sunday afternoon at the Benaud home in Sutherland Road, North Parramatta, near to where the Richie Benaud Oval now stands. The pitch was short, but it didn't matter. I recall a day there when I heard Richie swear for the only time in my life. Lou, a very gentlemanly character, had been teaching me how to bowl a wrong 'un, and I sent one down to Richie, who was wearing no protective gear. It failed to turn, just went straight through, and hit him in the groin. Ouch! Rich was in agony; Lou and I couldn't stop laughing. Finally, he got the words out: 'You're a pair of bloody fools!'

Richie went to Parramatta High, while I headed to Sydney Grammar, in the heart of Sydney. He played cricket on a Wednesday in the Combined High Schools competition, which gave him the chance to play grade with the men on the weekend. I played my

GPS cricket on Saturdays, which meant I didn't make my debut with the Cumberland club until later. Richie was also a very good tennis player, and I would go and watch him play. Later, as young blokes growing up, we played a fair bit of night tennis.

When Richie left school, a rising star in cricket by then, just about everyone was surprised when he took a job with a chartered accountancy firm. We all thought he would head into something to do with sport. At the time, I think that deep down he was wondering about how successful he could be at cricket and whether he could make a living out of it, so he took the accountancy option to give him a solid backup if his sporting ambitions backfired.

I have many memories of the young Richie, including happy days in Orange, playing golf and staying at the Hotel Canobolas. I recall a day when we borrowed a car from Frank O'Rourke, the notable rugby league player and a teacher at Sydney Boys High, who happened to be staying up there, so that we could squire around a couple of girls we had met. Back home, I remember carting our golf sticks on buses as we headed off for a round, because we had no other transport.

Richie was fanatically keen about his cricket and worked hard at it. But he used to have all sorts of problems with his spinning finger. It would be red raw and terribly sore after games in which he'd done a lot of bowling. In the winter months, after the wound had healed, we'd take it in turns to try to toughen the skin by working on it with emery paper. The thought occurred to us that his days in cricket could be numbered if he couldn't find an answer. The emery paper treatment helped, but it wasn't until years later that Richie found a pharmacist in New Zealand who had developed a mixture of calamine lotion and boracic acid powder that really did the trick.

I used to enjoy batting against Richie in the nets at Cumberland Oval, or on the beautiful practice wickets at the nearby King's School, where we had an open invitation. We would practise a lot and I got to know his bowling very well. One day, he said to me — he might have been talking about his flipper or his wrong 'un — 'You picked the thing better than Compton and Hutton do.'

Sydney grade cricket in the 1950s was highly competitive and greatly enjoyable. I remember a day when Richie was leading us against Mosman, who were captained by Ian Craig. With the time edging towards stumps at 6pm, Ian came onto the ground and made his way over to Richie in the field. Rich gave him a piece of paper and Ian departed.

As we walked off the ground soon after, Richie said to me: 'Do you know what that was about?'

I told him I didn't.

'I gave him our grog order,' Richie said. It was the time of six o'clock closing, when 'last orders' had to be in before six. There is some irony in the story, in that Rich and I were largely 'milkshake boys' at that time, although Richie would become something of a wine connoisseur later.

His life changed, of course, and I didn't see much of him in the years after he retired from Test cricket, though I was at his 60th birthday party in 1990 and had a lovely night. A Christmas card would arrive each year, but his career as a broadcaster meant he was enjoying back-to-back summers, following the cricket. And he was mixing with a different set of people.

I last saw him at the Sydney Cricket Ground a few years back. I probably did the wrong thing that day and intercepted him as he and Daphne were coming down the stairs. 'G'day Rich, good to see you again,' I said, and we shook hands.

'Good to see you, too,' said Richie.

We never crossed paths again.

HAROLD GOODWIN

Harold Goodwin's long association with Cumberland Cricket Club paralleled that of Richie Benaud. Harold was a robust opening batsman who headed on to a fruitful career in the pharmaceutical industry. He'll never forget that afternoon when he first played cricket against Richie.

MY first glimpse of a young blond-haired Richie Benaud came in 1941, on a cricket field outside Cumberland Oval, in Parramatta

Park. The match underway was Burnside Public School, with Richie in the ranks, against my school team, Wentworthville Public. Richie was 11. When he batted, it was startling to watch. We couldn't get him out. More than that, he never missed a ball! Burnside won the game.

The way things eventuated I would know Richie Benaud as a friend for most of his life and for a good deal of my own. I'm 85 as I write these words, and saddened that he's gone. Based on my observations over the years — playing cricket with Richie and watching him as skipper of NSW and Australia — I believe he ranks as the best captain our country has ever seen and a truly great all-rounder. He was such a fine fellow, too, good company and very sensible.

The Richie I first encountered was tall for his age. He bowled out of the *front* of his hand. Medium pace. I would discover later that he always wanted to be a leg-spinner, but his father Lou, a good leg-spin bowler with an awkward action, wouldn't let him bowl wrist-spin because of the excess bounce such bowling generated on the pitches we played junior cricket on — coir matting over cement. It wasn't until we started playing in the under-16 Green Shield in 1944–45 and shifted onto the luxury of turf wickets that Lou let Richie bowl his leg breaks in matches. Richie captained that team, as he did most of the sides he played for throughout his career.

Richie and I went to school at Parramatta High, where he was captain of the cricket team in his senior years and the most outstanding player. In 1946, we won the Sydney Combined High Schools competition — undefeated. As well as Green Shield, we played a few years together in the under-21 Poidevin-Gray competition for Cumberland and we also represented Parramatta-Granville as part of a four-man team in the inter-district Tremlett Cup. Richie was a good tennis player. I can still picture him with his old well-used racquet … and playing very well.

But cricket was his game. He reached first grade well before I did; eventually, it got to the stage where I would captain the side when Richie was away on Sheffield Shield or international duties. I came to realise that he was a far better captain than I was! And he didn't play favourites. I remember foolishly charging a Bob Simpson leg break one day, missing, and being stumped. Richie was our captain that day; next week I was in the seconds. So much for my initial game in first grade!

As a slow bowler, Richie was a genius, with an astonishing ability to 'size up' batsmen with the first couple of balls he bowled. He'd then slightly adjust the positioning of his two closest fieldsmen … and the batsman would invariably push his next defensive prod directly to one or other of them. It was remarkable. And so were his leg breaks and wrong 'uns.

Being the man he was, Richie never distanced himself from his old club, which is now known as Parramatta. Year after year, as holder of the No. 1 ticket in the 'True Blues' supporters' club, he would attend club fundraising lunches, even though he was by then a person of great standing in the cricket world, and someone much in demand. The family link to the club through Lou, Richie and his brother John is wonderful, with all three having captained Parramatta first grade.

I remember, too, a Penrith Cricket Club luncheon from a few years back, when Richie was asked what he thought about Twenty20 cricket. I'm sure there was an expectation in the room that he would be critical about this new revolution. But in his quiet way he simply made the point that there had been a crowd of about 3,000 people watching a recent Sheffield Shield final, while a Twenty20 game in Adelaide had drawn 30,000. 'The numbers speak for themselves,' he said. It was another example of how Richie Benaud moved with the times.

There was really only one time in my life when I was not very happy with Richie. It was an afternoon when I was on 95, batting against North Sydney at Merrylands Oval. I had never made a first-grade century. We lost a wicket and Richie came out to bat. I hit the next ball almost for four, but was happy with the thought of two. But Rich turned for a third … and I guess I was just a bit slow off the mark.

When I turned and saw him already halfway down the wicket … well, I just went for it. I didn't make it. I had been going along steadily against my natural instincts — which were to attack — because I was determined to get the century. As it turned out, I never did get a hundred in my first-grade career. But I was pleased with my 97 and what happened that afternoon was something that I had done myself to blokes during my career.

It was just cricket. And, after all, it *was* Richie Benaud!

ERIC TWEEDALE

Eric Tweedale is a favourite Parramatta sporting son. He played rugby with the Parramatta club on and off for 21 years, starting in first grade as a 17-year-old and finishing up as a 37-year-old captain-coach. He was among the hordes of top sportsmen whose best years were sacrificed to the war. He made his Test rugby debut on the Wallabies' tour of New Zealand in 1946 and was a member of the famously successful Wallaby team that sailed to Britain in 1947–48. He played 10 rugby Tests. Eric also played first-grade cricket as a fast-medium bowler for Central Cumberland on both sides of World War II. Among his clubmates were Lou and Richie Benaud. Still going strong at 94, he remembers a quiet boy whose boundless enthusiasm was inspired by his father's devotion to the game …

LOU BENAUD was a very good slow bowler who took a lot of wickets for Cumberland and was an important part of their side when I started playing there in the late 1930s. I hadn't played cricket at all until I was 16, and ended up playing what was pretty serious cricket with Cumberland almost by accident.

I was invited to play for Anthony Horderns in the City Houses competition, was given a six-stitcher, which I had never seen before, and was amazed at how it swung about. I took enough wickets to get into some representative under-21 sides, and was invited to attend the SCG nets.

The NSW coach then was a fellow called George Garnsey. My role became one of workhorse, bowling away at the good players like Ron Saggers and Arthur Chipperfield. But there was a little fellow watching intently who said he wanted to talk to me. It turned out to be the former Test leg-spinner, Arthur Mailey, then writing a newspaper column. He gave me a write-up the next day and told me I should play grade cricket, so I pitched in with Cumberland.

Lou was teaching at Burnside, a public school in North Parramatta, in those pre-war years and because he finished early he was always first to practice. He worked longer and harder than the others, and he would take his son Richie and pad him up so he'd have someone to bowl to before the other grade players arrived. It worked for Lou because he got a lot of practice in before the mob arrived, and it worked for Richie because it taught him some pretty good lessons at a very young age.

Richie must have been no more than nine or ten. I can remember him as a constant part of Cumberland practice, fielding the ball for anyone who wanted him to and facing up to his father's spin bowling before formal practice started.

Lou wasn't a talkative type. He'd say what he had to say in as few words as possible. It was a trait Richie developed too. You tend to listen to people like that because you know what they are saying must be important.

By the time I got back after the war, Richie was playing in the senior sides and starting to make a name for himself. My vivid recollection of him, though, is of the same kid at practice, just a bit older and a bit bigger.

His dad was still playing and they had a few games together. Richie was very much his father's son. You could tell that the same enthusiasm for the game was going to take him places.

ALAN CRAMOND

Alan Cramond first played Sydney grade cricket as a teenager in the 1930s, but his promising career on the cricket field — as an all-rounder with Western Suburbs — was knocked for six by serious injuries he suffered in Bougainville during World War II. With the war finally over, Alan moved to

Cumberland, where he and Lou Benaud became great mates,
sharing a deep love of the game. Through this friendship, he
was able to keenly and closely follow Richie's progress.

I FIRST encountered Richie when he was about 16, playing for
Cumberland under the captaincy of Ron James, a strict taskmaster
and a darned good coach who would not tolerate any mucking
around. The fact is if you haven't got the talent the only virtue in
playing under a good coach is in acquiring the knowledge. To really
benefit, you've got to have the ability — and Rich always had that.
Right from his early days in cricket, there was the sense that he was
going to become something special.

I was originally a fast bowler, but couldn't do that after I got
smashed up in the army, so I ended up bowling off-spinners. I played
seconds for Cumberland with Lou. This led to family occasions
when my wife Jill and I would visit Lou and Rene, and he and I
would sit on a bench out the front and talk for hours about tactics
and the fine points of cricket. Much of it was about bowling, about
such things as trajectory and deception, looping the ball and the
art of length and control, how the width of a cricket bat is four-
and-a-half inches and you have only to turn the ball two-and-a-
quarter inches to catch an edge. Lou loved to think about cricket
and talk about the game, and all the theories that emerged from his
discussions were undoubtedly passed on to Richie.

When I think back on the pair of them, Rich's bowling action
was so similar to his father's. There was an occasion later in his
career when I was watching Richie bowl, and I suddenly had this
strong sense that Lou had 'come back'. As a cricketer, Lou played it
tough. He would give you no quarter, but afterwards there'd be an
arm around the shoulder and words of commiseration if you'd had
an off day. He never changed, and Richie and his brother John, such
a fine player, took it all on board. The whole Benaud family put
their life and abilities into cricket. They loved the game.

Richie grew to be a man who had no airs and graces. He
talked to everybody and it seemed he got on with everybody. But
he would never push himself forward at functions. He could be
in a room and you would never realise he was there until he was
called on to speak — which he would invariably do with style. To
drive through the gates of the SCG with him and experience the

reaction to his arrival, as I did several times, was to realise how revered he was.

There was a dry, humorous edge to him, though. He could be a bit of a prankster ...

I remember playing in a country match with him many years ago, at Taree on the NSW north coast. It was an Easter weekend, so there was no play on the Sunday. Richie and Bruce Ritchie headed into town on the rest day while the rest of us finished up back in our pub, having a few beers. On the Monday morning, I wasn't too bright at all. It happened that Richie and I were batting together, and as we were walking out to resume play he said, 'You don't look too good.'

I couldn't disagree. I knew I was going to struggle running. 'Look, you've got the strike,' I said. 'Keep it for a while, will you?'

As far as I was concerned, Richie took my request on board. I expected he would stonewall for a few overs to get me through. But what did he do? The first ball he faced, he dropped it at his feet, yelled 'Yes!', and took off. I got going as best as I could, but to be honest the only reason I wasn't run out was because they had about four shots at the stumps and couldn't hit them. This was the impish side of Richie on display. It was always there, lurking somewhere just beneath the surface.

So many things cross my mind when I think of Richie and the wider Benaud family: Being with him in his office at Coogee as he dictated a newspaper story for the UK with absolute fluency, all of it off the top of his head ... His coolness in the commentary box at the SCG where I was invited at times; how relaxed he was as he sipped a cup of tea while others sweated, awaiting their turn at the microphone ... His availability to talk to young cricketers. 'When do you want me there?' he'd invariably ask when approached ... How ready he was to support fundraising activities whenever he could, the fact being that his name would draw people along ...

Richie grew up in the era of the gentleman cricketer, when the umpire's word was gospel and never challenged, and when the old traditions of the game were respected — and character-building. He lived by those old ways, as a cricketer, captain, journalist and commentator ... and as a man.

It is one of the special, fortunate experiences of my life that I have such lovely memories.

WILF EWENS

Originally from Bendick Murrell, a village near Young in
southern NSW, and then a student at Parramatta High
School, Wilf Ewens had a long and enjoyable cricket
career. For many years, he was a teammate of Richie's at
Cumberland, and in 2015 was chosen in the club's 'Team of
the '50s'. Wilf captained NSW Country teams against the
MCC in 1962–63 and 1965–66 and claims as a highlight the
first-ball duck, lbw to Freddie Trueman, he made at Dubbo
in the first of these matches. As Professor Wilf Ewens, he
became a leading figure in physical education and sports
coaching, taught in Australia and the US, worked with
the NSW and Australian cricket teams, and coached the
Canadian national side.

THROUGH the 1940s, Richie was a year ahead of me at
Parramatta High, which was the only co-educational high school
in Sydney at that time. I recall a morning there when the acting
headmaster, Mr Porter, whom we knew as 'Snakey' Porter, drew
an imaginary line from the corner of one building to another and
declared: 'To the left will be the boys' playground. To the right
will be the girls' playground.' Two days later, a thick white line
was painted on the ground, labelled 'Porter's Imaginary Line',
with the word 'Bucks' written on one side and 'Does' on the
other. The story made the local paper!

Richie and I were in the Parramatta High team of 1946 that
took out the Combined High Schools cricket competition —
the first time the school had won it in almost 20 years — and
we played a lot of cricket together after that. In early days with
Cumberland, our captain was Ron James, a NSW captain. Ron
was a strong disciplinarian and I'm sure he had an influence on us
both. 'You have to look the part,' he constantly told us. 'You have

to be attentive at all times and you have to take a cap out when fielding, in case you are facing the setting sun.'

I was in the race of the old Cumberland Oval one day and had the second button of my shirt undone. Ron looked at me. 'Where are you going?' he asked. 'To the beach?'

I told him, 'No.'

'Well, do that bloody shirt up!'

We all, including Richie, embraced this discipline. It was only when Ron retired at Cumberland that Richie began wearing the shirt unbuttoned down almost to his navel.

It's well known that Keith Miller was Richie's idol. When I picture, even today, Richie's bowling and Miller's bowling — setting aside that one was a quick bowler and the other slow — they had many of the same idiosyncrasies: the toss of the hair, the way of 'rounding' at the bowling mark.

Richie was always very precise about the things he did; he always set out to do them as well as he could. After he left accountancy and was working as a cadet journalist, he was sent out to do some digging on a pastime that was prolific on the Sydney trains at the time: what was called 'ticket scaling' — trying to get away without buying a ticket. Having boarded a train at Redfern he was pulled up by an inspector soon after he got off at Central Station. Fumbling around, he 'couldn't find his ticket'. He had purposefully used Redfern as his point of embarkation, knowing that because it was close to Central — just one stop — and therefore a cheap fare, it was the station nominated by most scalers when they were caught. The inspector steered him in the direction of the NSW Railways' security office, which was a few hundred yards away on the country platform, and it was only when they got there that Rich suddenly 'found' his ticket. He wanted to get as close as possible to the experience of being arrested for scaling, in the interests of writing an accurate story. It was typical of his thoroughness.

Richie's precision with everything — hair, dress, life generally — certainly stretched to golf. Rich always wanted to know what the yardage was, which way the wind was blowing; he could take minutes to line up a putt. One day in the early '70s, a group of us who were involved with high-level cricket coaching — Brian Taber, Peter Spence, Richie and me — headed to Kogarah Golf Club for a round. On the tee at the 8th, the 'river hole', Richie was fiddling around, taking his time before he teed off. Finally, Tabs said, 'C'mon Rich, for gawdsake, hit the ball.'

Richie swung ... and put it straight into the river. He loaded up again ... and hit his second drive in exactly the same direction. As I recall it, he didn't say a word to anyone for the next four holes.

When we played grade cricket together for Cumberland, through much of the 1950s, we usually batted at three and four, so we were out there together in the middle on numerous occasions. My fondest memory of batting with him came at Cumberland Oval in the first round of 1955–56, against Paddington, when we put on 199 runs for the second wicket. Richie opened the batting that day and scored 118, while I finished with 107. On top of his batting and captaincy, he and fellow leg-spinner Jack Treanor were the backbone of the Cumberland attack. Both took more than 200 first-grade wickets for the club during the decade. The pair of them bowled a lot in tandem, and complemented each other beautifully. Jack, a bowler more in the style of Bill O'Reilly, was desperately unlucky to miss the England tour of 1953, when he was a victim of interstate cricket politics. When Richie and Jack bowled together in Shield cricket they were, in my opinion, the best slow-bowling combination in Australia.

Another (painful) memory from the cricket field is of an afternoon at Lidcombe Oval in late 1953, when we played Western Suburbs on a horrible sticky wicket and Alan Davidson was hitting the deck hard. The ball was flying everywhere. It was Richie's first game back from the 1953 Ashes tour and his first game as Cumberland captain, Ron James having stood aside to give him an opportunity to get some leadership experience. He was batting and Davo hit him full in the groin, completely inverting the box Richie was wearing, and leaving what lay beneath black, blue and brindle.

Poor Rich was in agony and had to be carried from the field, though he was able to bat again later in the innings. I went in at No. 6, ready to adopt Don Bradman's methods in the Bodyline series, when he backed away towards square-leg and tried to hit the quick bowlers through the offside. Perhaps fortunately — at least for my health — Davo dismissed me almost immediately, and we were bowled out for 100. The next week, though, Richie hit a quick 50 in half an hour and then took six wickets as we fought back to win outright.

My friendship with Richie was just about lifelong — starting at school and not ending until his death in 2015. I would catch up with him as often as I could — including in England, when he invited me to a Lord's Test and organised through Alec Bedser to get me into the Long Room on the first day, which from what I understand is just impossible to do, unless you are an MCC member. But then Richie was always very generous. I don't believe he ever slighted *anyone.*

I recall a day that was typical — at a golf club, when some rather loud ladies spotted him relaxing after a round. Suddenly, they were swarming around him, asking for autographs at a moment when he was just looking for a quiet break. But Rich was as gracious as ever and met every request for a signature.

In a recent Parramatta District Cricket Club annual report, I summed up Richie Benaud this way:

> I enjoyed playing with Richie because his personality seemed to enthuse you to strive to higher levels. A flamboyant, confident and aggressive approach became his trademark. The unbuttoned shirt, the naked head and the exuberance for the challenge, all typified the persona: 'Richie Benaud'.
>
> The saying, 'that isn't cricket', does not apply to Richie, for he personified all the rich traditions of our great game.

THE PHOENIX

One of Richie's earliest forays into journalism came in 1944, when he was a member of Parramatta High School's first XI and penned the following send-up of his favourite sport for *The Phoenix*, the school magazine.

HOW (?) TO PLAY CRICKET

Aim: To endeavour to play cricket.

Apparatus: 1. A lump of wood shaped at one end to represent a handle. 2. A piece of round rubber, preferably without edges. 3. A plot of grass, about five acres in radius, having as its centre a rectangle 22 yards by 8 yards, with a ditch in the centre (if you are a bowler). 4. Six pieces of wood for stumps (the bigger they are the harder they fall). 5. Eleven fieldsmen. 6. Batsman and two umpires.

Method: The bowler walks or waddles to the bowling crease, delivers the ball, and endeavours to hit the stumps. The batsman, taking his stance at the wicket, endeavours to hit the ball. To the fieldsmen falls the honour (?) of chasing the ball.

Results: The ditch in the centre of the wicket is responsible for the injuries which invariably happen (most of our first-grade bowlers (?) get their wickets by means of this ditch). Also, if the batsman swipes too hard, he is liable to asphyxiate silly, silly point.

Conclusion: From this article you will see that skittles would be easier.

R. Benaud

MAIL TRAIN TO MUDGEE

On a Friday night late in September 1962, Richie Benaud, then the Australian cricket captain, boarded the Mudgee mail train at Parramatta. With him were 11 other cricketers from the Cumberland club and the team manager, owner of the local hardware store.

About the same time, an MCC team captained by 'Lord' Ted Dexter and managed by the Duke of Norfolk was preparing to journey to Australia to try to wrest back the Ashes. They would fly to Aden, board the luxury liner *Canberra*, play a match in Colombo, then start the tour in Western Australia. Expectations were high — this Ashes contest, it was said, would be as entertaining and exciting as Australia's Tied Test series with the West Indies in 1960–61.

Richie, though, had another cricket challenge on his mind. His beloved Cumberland hadn't won a first-grade premiership since 1932–33. But he'd noted a wealth of young talent now coming through the ranks, and he wondered …

Wonderment was also in the air in a small country town near Mudgee. Local cricket officials had a newly completed grandstand that needed opening, officially. They had an idea. The little town was Binnaway. Memories are distant, but you'll get the picture.

John Dwyer, slashing opening batsman: Mum and Dad drove me to Parramatta railway station, where Richie met me with, 'Hello, John, very good to see you.' I was, of course, thrilled to shake hands with Richie. It was about 10.30 at night and we were scheduled to reach Binnaway at ten the next morning. Richie told us a few stories, riveting moments from the famous Tied Test, but by the time we reached Lithgow an hour or so after midnight, a longish stop so our electric locomotive could be changed to a steam engine, he had retired to his sleeping compartment. He said he wanted to make some notes for his *Sun* newspaper column, which was called 'Come in Spinner'.

Our matches weren't anything to write home about but I remember well one incident. Our quickish left-arm spinner was bowling to a local farmer, a big man and big hitter, and he tonked a few over long-on and mid-wicket. The bowler, without consulting Richie, signalled the fielders back to the fence. Before the next delivery Richie called them all back in and the big guy kept hitting them over the top — Richie's idea of entertainment for the locals. The bowler wasn't too happy.

Getting back home was interesting. The Sunday match ended and the locals drove us 100 miles to Mudgee to catch the nine o'clock train, which arrived at Parramatta at 4.30am Monday. Not sure what Richie, on the eve of the Ashes, thought of the drive but we were doing about 90 miles per hour in the dark on a narrow road — luckily, no roos.

Bob McMillan, medium-pace swing bowler: Richie's gone now but the memories of more than 50 years ago live very vividly on. Binnaway ... not a village depicted in *Alice In Wonderland*, but a two-pub country town that at that time focused on wheat transport by rail.

To my mind, loaded with many fond anecdotes, Binnaway's biggest hallmark was abundant and genuine hospitality. The Binnaway cricket enthusiasts had encouraged, then invited our club, Cumberland, to send a troupe of 'flannelled fellas', mostly young, and a couple not so, to play two matches on a Saturday and Sunday. John Benaud and I were but 18 years old. We had played with and against each other since age 10. Richie, our tour leader, was clearly the star attraction for the locals and a big turnout presented for the start of play on the Saturday. Lashings of goodies were placed on trestle tables for lunch and afternoon tea.

I was fortunate to be chosen for the first match, with Binnaway sent in to bat by the Australian captain. Time can play tricks with our memories but I remain convinced that, being given the ball as first-change medium trundler, I knocked over the sticks of their top order, three balls in a row. The first pleased my captain, the second less so, and the third turned the show into a pantomime and created a dilemma for *mon capitaine*. At over's end, Richie approached me with an earnest look about him. Things were not going to plan and he was well known for making the play — 'proactive' is the nonsense expression we use today. My eyes were firmly fixed on my leader's face, hoping for, nay expecting, some form of congratulations. None forthcoming. Furthermore came a directive: 'If I leave you on, the match will be well over before lunch. I'm afraid it's fine-leg, son.'

I didn't know whether to laugh or cry. How many in the history of cricket have been sacked for taking a hat-trick by the skipper of the baggy green? Richie actively encouraged youth. His actions in my case appear as a contradiction but it was, as he saw it, in the best interests of the match and the promotion of the game in the bush. Country cricket the winner.

In recent times one very successful batsman was christened Mr Cricket. To me Richie Benaud was the one most deserving of this accolade. Richie gave much not only to the upper echelons of the game but to cricket wherever he could.

John Benaud: To play in a cricket team captained by Rich was perpetual work experience, enjoyable and never boring. Cricket fees? At Cumberland they were the entrance money to the greatest cricket show on earth. He was the master of mind games. He could manage his men and also manage the opponent. And, more often than not, he managed the outcome of the game.

Cumberland beat Binnaway 2–0, full house both days, cars parked doorhandle to doorhandle around the ground. Australia retained the Ashes in 1962–63. Each side won one Test. The series never matched expectations.

Cumberland went on to win the first-grade premiership in 1964–65, the squad including seven who toured Binnaway with Richie. But Richie missed the moment. As a journalist for *The Sun* he was covering Bob Simpson's tour to the West Indies, taking controversial photos of fast bowler Charlie Griffith's suspect bowling action, a worldwide scoop.

Cumberland also won the third-grade premiership in 1964–65, Bob McMillan a team member.

Another of Cumberland's young 'flannelled fellas' was Rex Flindt. He was so captivated by his brief time at Binnaway he returned as a young married man with his family. He bought and worked a farm. Tragically, he died there, crushed between a bin and a truck tray.

– 3 –
THE BENAUD ERA

'He had an uncanny way of coming up with answers that gave a new dimension to lateral thinking. Benaud may just have been the finest captain the game has seen.'

— Ian Wooldridge

ALAN DAVIDSON

Alan Davidson and Richie Benaud each made it to first-class cricket in the late 1940s. Their careers ran parallel until 1963, when Davo retired a year ahead of Richie. Davidson played 44 Tests, scoring 1,328 runs and taking 186 wickets, and he was a match-winner as a hard-hitting batsman and left-arm fast bowler. Alan and Richie first met in a school game when Richie was 14. Their friendship lasted 70 years.

I T WAS about two years ago that Richie Benaud finally apologised for running me out in the second-last over of the Tied Test. It had taken him more than 50 years and we chuckled about his belated remorse. It had probably worried him, though, because I was crestfallen that day.

I sat in the dressing-room as three wickets fell in that final over. The West Indies thought they had won. We thought they had won too, and I was kicking myself that a long partnership in which Richie and I very nearly won the day had been brought to an end in such a way.

Sir Donald Bradman saw me slumped in the corner, somewhat desolate. 'Don't be disappointed, Alan,' he said. 'Today you made history. This is the best thing that has ever happened to cricket.' Initially, I didn't know what he was on about. It took about ten minutes for the fact to sink in that the match had been tied.

The Tied Test has been talked about ever since, but Richie was a bit like me … disappointed that we had squandered a winning chance. Yet the game defined his captaincy, really, as did a remarkable series, because he was determined at every turn to 'have a go', to be positive in all he did. He preferred honourable defeat in search of a winning chance to the interminable draws that had marked Test cricket through the 1950s.

That was an extraordinary match and an extraordinary series, made so by two captains of like mind who put the game of cricket before everything else. Frank Worrell captained the West Indies superbly and was with Richie all the way in trying to entertain.

We were in all sorts of trouble on that final afternoon, 6–92 chasing 233 when Richie joined me just before tea. As we went to tea, still 130-odd behind and only four wickets standing, Rich turned to me and said: 'I think we should try to get them.' I immediately agreed. Bradman buttonholed Richie at the gate; The Don agreed too.

So we went for it. For a while it was as if we were playing vigoro ... tip and run. We took outrageous singles. By midway through the second-last over we had put on 134 and needed seven runs to win.

We agreed I should be at the batting end to face Wes Hall in the final over, but then Richie hit the ball to Joe Solomon close to the wicket and charged off for a single. Usain Bolt could not have made it and I didn't even get close.

History has it that Rich, Wally Grout and Ian Meckiff were out in that final over to leave the match tied. Pandemonium reigned. But Richie was never going to die wondering. He knew the risk of losing and he knew we could have shut up shop to just save the game. But he went for the kill, as he always did, and we all loved him for it. After that game, we pulled tables together in the dining room and all sat around, Australians and West Indians beside each other in alternate places. We swapped yarns and laughed and enjoyed. Never had Test cricket had such camaraderie.

THERE were two great influences in Richie's cricketing life. One was his father Lou, a more than useful club leg-spinner whom I played against when I first played grade cricket in Sydney. Richie was always immaculately dressed on the cricket field. He held himself to all the standards of bearing and behaviour for which Lou was renowned. In those early days, he was like a carbon copy of Lou.

The other great influence was Keith Miller, the dashing all-rounder of the Invincibles — probably the best all-rounder Australia has ever had. Richie copied everything Miller did. The attitudes, the mannerisms, ultimately his captaincy and in most respects his cricket. Miller was an adventurer and so was Richie. It made Richie the captain he was … far and away the most astute I ever ran into.

I remember as clearly as if it were yesterday the first time I encountered him. He was 14, playing for a Sydney Combined High Schools team, and I was 15, playing for the Combined Northern High School team that encompassed Gosford, where I grew up, and all points north.

It was the season after the war ended, life was pretty hard, and a lot of the kids were fairly shabbily dressed, a mixed bag of coloured shirts and shorts. Not Richie.

He faced up to my bowling already exuding the charisma of later days, blond and tall, and immaculate in creams that set him apart. Lou would have had it no other way. I bowled spin then and I remember bowling him a Chinaman … the best I ever bowled; maybe the only good one I ever bowled … and it looped and spun and caught Richie unawares. He jammed down on it and looked at me with that wide-eyed surprise that was singularly him.

We could never have known it then, but within four summers we had started our first-class careers together, and were together in NSW and Australian teams until we retired a few months apart some 14 summers later. In those early days we were the kids in the NSW team, and later the Australian team, and plenty of the Invincibles were still about. We soaked up everything they had to tell us — Miller, Morris, Lindwall and the rest — and we learned wonderful lessons.

Neil Harvey had been one of those Invincibles, but he was very young among them, more our age, and the three of us sort of teamed up when we made the Ashes tour of 1953. They called us the three musketeers … Benaud, Harvey and Davidson … because we did everything together. We would go to the theatre often, and there was a sandwich shop in Shaftesbury Avenue in London that we visited every night.

The fellow who ran it got to know us and he would load up the sandwiches with meat and stuff until you could hardly get your mouth around it.

RICHIE had some wonderful days as a bowler — especially in South Africa in 1957–58 and of course in the famous Old Trafford Test in 1961 — but the thing that impressed me most about him was his growth as a bowler, and the work he put into it. He did struggle early on, but after we were flogged in England in 1956 the Invincibles were gone and the apprentices were now the key to the team. We knew it was up to us.

Richie already was a hard worker, but he said to me as we looked forward to the next Ashes series: 'You know, those English bowlers get in hundreds more overs than us through a county season. No wonder they're so accurate. No wonder they bowl so well. We just don't bowl enough.'

It had long worried Richie that while Doug Ring and Ian Johnson were still around he got a few overs here and there, but nowhere near enough bowling to develop as he wanted. So he organised a practice routine with me. We lived in Sydney's western suburbs, so we met on the train, then rode the tram up to the SCG and vowed to bowl non-stop for two hours every Tuesday and Thursday before the rest of them got to practice. We practised until landing the ball accurately was like firing a rifle. It made a tremendous difference, and for both of us our latter years were by far our best.

AS a captain, aside from the great flair and adventure he brought to our cricket, Richie was a wonderful man manager. He could control things with a withering silence or a cold stare ... he didn't have to say much. It was a communication skill that he carried into his television commentary.

He had a computer mind. He analysed players — teammates and opponents alike — as few players could, and he seemed to retain it all. He introduced Test-eve team dinners where he called on opinions from everybody. He kept the information in his head and could always recall it as needed. But on the field there was no doubt about who was boss.

He was unflappable, in an era when banter during a game was just that. At Leeds in 1961, Freddie Trueman found a patch on the wicket that made him lethal, and in one spell took five wickets for one run. Richie got a ball that was simply unplayable, jagging a great distance to take his leg stump.

'Beautiful ball, Freddie,' Richie said as he walked past Trueman on the way to the rooms. 'Aye,' said Freddie, 'should have been a No.3.' In other words, wasted on you, Rich!

Through Richie's time as captain there were many real trials, never more than in our tour of India and Pakistan in 1959–60. In Lahore, we slept in army tents on the desert floor, with no more than a duckboard, straw mattress and blanket. In Karachi, Richie's efforts to remove a Pakistani official from the dressing-room while we had a pre-match team talk resulted in the official returning with a couple of policemen, wanting to have our captain arrested.

Sir Roden Cutler, the Australian high commissioner at the time, put paid to that. Then several members of the team were very ill with hepatitis, and at one stage we were virtually out of players, with our team manager Sam Loxton kitted up in case he needed to field. It was tough, but through it all Richie maintained a calm, steely purpose that allowed us to win both series.

I think the only time I ever saw Richie really irritated was during the 1961 tour of England, when his bent for public relations won him great favour with the press and our manager, Syd Webb — a conservative administrator more suited to an earlier time — didn't like it. He reckoned Richie was straying into matters that were board concerns. I think Rich had ventured the opinion that the north of England was very cold at the start of a tour and we would have been better off if the south had been programmed first ... and Syd 'gagged' him.

Richie was humiliated and never forgot it.

Nearly a decade later, Richie's brother John, NSW captain and a fine international cricketer in his own right, also ran foul of Syd Webb, who remained a leading NSW administrator. Syd this time took umbrage at John wearing ripple-soled boots in Sheffield Shield matches. When John refused to dump his new shoes, he was suspended. When some key officials were less than forthright about the issue, Richie responded by handing back his life membership of the NSW Cricket Association.

I became president of the NSWCA the following year and did everything I could to get Richie to take back his life membership. I made sure John's suspension was immediately ended — it was ridiculous in the first place — and I pleaded with Richie year after year to reverse his decision. He wouldn't. He was fiercely loyal to his brother and to him it was a matter of principle.

I suspect, too, that the experience of the gag in England and the high-handed nature of cricket administration at that time led Richie to his ultimate support of the World Series Cricket breakaway when the revolution came in 1977. Today's players who are making a fortune out of the game have a lot to thank Richie for, since his intervention at that time had much to do with the ultimate success of the World Series concept and the great modernisation it brought to the game.

It was crazy that players were treated the way they were by administrators who simply could not change with the times. We used to get two pounds a day for a Shield match and 50 pounds a day for a Test. For the second day's play of the fifth Test against the West Indies in 1960–61 we had more than 90,000 people at the MCG, yet the match payments for the entire team totalled a paltry 600 pounds.

Richie could see change coming. We had some tough times through all of that. As president of the Cricket Association I was on one side and Richie was on the other, and I know Richie was hurt that he was put in a sort of purgatory by many cricket officials. Sir Donald Bradman, for instance, wouldn't talk to him for a long time.

The battle did enormous damage to establishment cricket. NSW Cricket had to sell Cricket House in Sydney, and some units we had as well, just to pay the legal bills. In the end, we could all see the inevitability of what that revolution brought. Richie just saw it before most of us. Our friendship never wavered, though. Richie had been a huge part of my life since my teens. He remained that way for 70 years. He had an enormous influence on Australian cricket … and on the many people whose lives he touched. I was just one of them.

NEIL HARVEY

Neil Harvey first made the Australian Test team as a 19-year-old against India in 1948, scoring a century in his second Test. He toured with Don Bradman's Invincibles later that year and was Australia's premier batsman through the 1950s, finishing his career in 1963 with 6,149 runs from 79 Tests. At the time, only Bradman among Australians had made more. Harvey made four Ashes tours and with Alan Davidson formed a friendship with Richie that lasted from their first Sheffield Shield game together until Richie's death.

I WAS vice-captain of Australia for four years under Richie Benaud. Many people thought I should have resented that. I didn't. I had been vice-captain under Ian Craig before Richie was made captain. I probably felt a bit more aggrieved when Ian was made Australian captain, given that I was leading Victoria at the time and my experience went back to the Invincibles of 1948. I was the favoured candidate on both occasions as far as press and public were concerned, but I never got the job.

I was disappointed, of course. Being captain of Australia is an honour lots of players strive for and my great mate Sam Loxton had given up the captaincy of Victoria so that I could have a go at it. He was more disappointed than I ever was that both Craig and Benaud beat me to the top job.

When Ian Craig fell ill in 1958 and they gave the captaincy to Richie after we'd enjoyed a very successful tour of South Africa, I knew that it was the end of any captaincy ambition for me. I had expected to get it, I won't deny that. But these things have a way of working out and the time I had as vice-captain to Richie was one of the best periods in my career.

I congratulated him when he got the job. We didn't say much. I committed myself to supporting him, we embraced and we got on with it. Looking back, it was a wonderfully successful time. I determined I would be a good vice-captain and I think as a team we worked very well.

Richie was a man for his time. He was aggressive in his captaincy, prepared to gamble when the occasion warranted. He was also a wonderful diplomat off the field, with a real flair for public relations. It was a time when the game had ground down a bit and Richie was just the man to put a spark back in it.

The first time I ran into him was a game in Melbourne in 1950–51, back in the days when Sheffield Shield games were big-time and if the NSW-Victoria match was played over Christmas it would draw 30,000 people. And I remember he got me out in one of the first games we played, caught in the deep as I was having a flay at everything. I don't think Richie would ever have argued, though, that he had a flying start in first-class cricket.

He had a lot of potential and was clearly a worker who never stopped trying to improve his game. But he didn't spin the ball much and a bit of perseverance was required early on to get him to the stage he eventually reached. He was at his best on firm, bouncy wickets. He worked hard at developing his flipper, which gave his bowling a much sharper edge. His accuracy and his ability to work batsmen out were his big pluses.

Batting against him, I always treated him with respect, though I was quick on my feet and I didn't really have much trouble with spin bowlers generally. There was one occasion, however, that I remember taking to Richie. It was early 1957. I was captain of Victoria and we were playing NSW in Sydney.

Ian Craig was the NSW captain. He had just been appointed captain of Australia for a tour to New Zealand, and I was a bit upset about that. We had named Bill Lawry, a regular opening batsman, as our 12th man and were going with Colin McDonald and Len Maddocks as openers. We tossed and Craig sent us in. I returned to the dressing-room to be told that McDonald had been hit in the nets and was off to hospital with a broken nose.

Sam Loxton was our vice-captain and he knew exactly what to do. 'Go and tell Craig what's happened, and tell him we want to change the side,' he said. That would allow us to put Lawry in and give us two openers. So I traipsed through the members' bar to the NSW dressing-room, put my request to the NSW captain, and was flatly refused. My blood was boiling. I grabbed the pads and said to Maddocks: 'Come on, Lennie, I'll open with you.' It was nearly five o'clock when I got out ... for 209. Richie bore the brunt of that. He got a bit of stick.

As a captain, Richie was a trendsetter. He was the first to have regular team meetings. I think the only team meeting Bradman ever had in 1948 was on the boat on the way over, which was hardly the place to start analysing opponents. Richie began doing it regularly, discussing how we would bowl to certain players, how to handle certain bowlers. It is now a routine within Australian teams.

He also developed a different atmosphere within the team, celebrating successes and generally making it all a lot more lively. We certainly needed some life when he took over. The first Test of his captaincy was that dreadful Brisbane Ashes Test in 1958–59, when Trevor Bailey batted throughout the fourth day for practically nothing and England scored 106 runs in the day. Richie set about fixing all that, culminating in the wonderful series against the West Indies in 1960–61. He really set international cricket on a new path.

Richie had a very determined streak in the way he approached his cricket, and a stubborn streak as well. They were both on show on that famous day at Old Trafford in 1961 when he took six wickets to scuttle England, just when they looked like taking us to the cleaners. It was certainly the best I ever saw Rich bowl, and he was under some duress, too, from the bad shoulder that had forced him out of the Lord's Test a month earlier.

We were in all sorts of trouble on that last day. England were 1–150 chasing 256 and Ted Dexter was in his 70s and belting us. The pressure was on. Richie and I put our heads together and I suggested it was time he tried to do something with the big hole in the pitch that Freddie Trueman had made while bowling during our long second innings. The hole was just outside the right-hand batsmen's leg stump. Such a strategy involved bowling around the wicket, something Richie never did. It was an idea he had discussed with Ray Lindwall the previous evening.

He decided to give it a go. Dexter was out almost straightaway, then Peter May came in and was out second ball, bowled around his legs. Richie had found the middle of the hole Freddie had dug for him and the ball spun sharply, clipping May's leg stump. It was so gentle May didn't even realise he was out. I was fielding at leg slip. 'Hey, Pete,' I yelled. 'You're out.' He looked at the square-leg umpire and, sure enough, up went the finger. Suddenly we were in with a chance. That's where Richie's stubborn streak took over. By the time he had six of them he thought he could do pretty much anything. They still needed 50-odd, Richie was looking at a seventh wicket, but I was getting jittery. The new ball was due.

'Let's take the new ball and finish it,' I said to him. He kept going. I was fielding at cover point, the ball came to me and I threw it across the pitch for four overthrows. Not the right thing to do, perhaps, but I needed to make the point. Richie relented, brought Alan Davidson on with the new ball, and four balls later Brian Statham's stump was out of the ground and we had won a great victory.

Way back in 1950, at that first game in Melbourne, I quickly hit it off with Richie and Davo. We were on opposite teams but at that time the game was more social. On the Sunday rest day I invited the pair of them home for lunch. We have been great mates ever since, right up to Richie's passing.

I roomed with Rich on two tours. I got to know him as the total gentleman he was, loyal and generous, with an impish sense of humour that was so understated it was hard to get used to. In every way, a champion.

COLIN McDONALD

Colin McDonald made his Test debut in 1952, in the fifth Test against the West Indies, alongside Richie Benaud. He played a total of 192 first-class games in which he scored 11,375 runs, 3,107 of them in Tests, before a wrist injury forced his retirement soon after the 1961 Ashes tour. He was noted for his resolute defiance against the fastest bowlers. In later years, Colin was an admired radio commentator with the ABC.

Above left: Rene and Lou Benaud at Ballina in the late 1920s, not long before their move to Koorawatha and the birth of their son Richie.

Above and left: Richie in the studio and at Jugiong, already showing poise in front of a camera.

Above: Jugiong Public School
in 1935. The school's teacher,
Lou Benaud, is standing at far left.
His son Richie is by his left elbow.

Right: Young Richie stands proudly in
front of the Benaud family's car of
the '30s, a Chevrolet National Tourer.

Below: Another image from the
days at Jugiong, this one with Richie
holding his pet dog Nipper with his
right arm and another dog, Peter,
with his left.

Right: Richie, aged 15, in the
backyard of the Benaud home in
Sutherland Road, North Parramatta.

The undefeated Parramatta High School first XI of 1946. **Back (from left):** Gordon Wilkins, Keith Lego, Ian Black, Doug Milner, Warwick Dunn, Wilf Ewens. **Front:** Harold Goodwin, Kevin Quinn, Mr PN Tester (coach), Richie Benaud (captain), Ray Caterson, Ken Kirkness.

Left: 'There has never been a finer worker for any club than Sid Teale,' said Richie in 1952 of the long-serving secretary of the Rangers Cricket Club. Richie played his junior club cricket for Rangers.

Right: In October 1963, a 'Golden Jubilee Reunion Cricket Match' was held as part of Parramatta High School's 50th anniversary celebrations. Richie led his 1946 team against the school's first XI, captained by Peter McDonald.

The Australians at Worcester at the start of the 1953 Ashes tour.
From left: Jim de Courcy, Richie Benaud, Gil Langley, Colin McDonald,
Ron Archer, Jack Hill, Keith Miller, Lindsay Hassett and Arthur Morris.

Richie tries to stop a straight drive from Tom Graveney during the second Test of
1953, at Lord's.

Left: Richie at Worcester in 1956, on his way to 160 in 195 minutes, his highest first-class score in England.

Below: The Australian captain is surrounded by reporters, including (front, at left) V. Venkateswaran and GK Menon, during the tour of India in 1959–60.

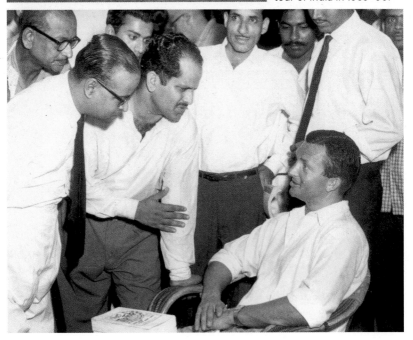

The location of the Richie Benaud sculpture at the SCG was for many years a site where famous team photographs were taken, such as the group shot for the McCabe-O'Reilly testimonial match in 1956–57. 'The positioning could hardly be better,' Richie quipped at the sculpture's unveiling in 2008. 'That is the spot where I always used to park my car.'

Richie in 1958–59, his first summer as Australian skipper.

TO establish my credentials as a past cricketer of some standing I often say to a questioner: 'I debuted with Richie Benaud.' I have never had anything other than a favourable reaction to these words. On my retirement some 47 personal Test matches later, and on our third tour by sea to England together, Richie was my captain and perhaps the greatest Australian Test-match captain ever. He was a man of the utmost integrity, a cricketing brain without peer, an excellent batsman, a wonderful fieldsman and the only 'over the wrist' spin bowler to not suffer by comparison with the great Shane Warne.

In my soon-to-be-published book, *Taking Strike*, I have selected my best Australian team since World War II. I excluded Don Bradman, whom I consider a pre-war player. The team is: Arthur Morris, Bill Lawry, Neil Harvey, Greg Chappell, Steve Waugh, Keith Miller, Adam Gilchrist, Richie Benaud (captain), Shane Warne, Dennis Lillee, Glenn McGrath, Ray Lindwall (12th man).

Australia has been blessed with the leadership qualities of its captains. Richie therefore is in exalted company when I place him at the top of a list that includes Lindsay Hassett, Steve Waugh, Mark Taylor and Allan Border among others.

Richie's feats on the cricket fields of the world have been well documented, but it is not so well known that he suffered two serious injuries, both occurring in matches in which I was playing. I shall never forget either incident: the first occurred on the MCG in a state second XI match between Victoria and NSW in January 1949; the second in Sydney during a Test match against South Africa in 1952–53. I record them here as recounted in *Taking Strike*:

> The NSW second XI captain, Brian Dwyer, was a medical doctor, as was the Victorian wicketkeeper, my brother Ian. They were both destined to play their part in a professional sense. Jack 'Dasher' Daniel was also to be involved in an unintended fashion. The scores were of no consequence in this account, suffice it to say that Richie, batting as a nightwatchman, survived the first day's play and resumed for a brief stay on the second. On that morning I was fielding close in at point as Daniel, a fiery and accomplished bowler, delivered a bouncer at Richie, a ball he considered eminently suitable for hooking. Perhaps it was, but Richie missed.

Helmets were still 30 years off. I had given up hooking short, head-high deliveries because of this lack of protection. Not Richie. The ball hit him in the forehead above his right eye. My brother was first on the scene and I was not far behind. It was not necessary to be a doctor to know Richie had suffered a massive fracture. He had a hole, obviously the shape of a cricket ball, in his head. The horrible noise of bone splintering was equalled by the visual image.

All the fieldsmen rushed to the scene. By the time he had been carried from the ground all the swelling had completely obliterated the visual evidence. It was just a matter of getting him to hospital and having him X-rayed to find out the extent of the damage. The X-rays showed no fracture. My brother informed Brian Dwyer, in some detail, of the visual evidence and Dwyer made sure that Benaud would seek further X-ray examination in Sydney. Fortunately, that further examination revealed what many of us already knew. The thought of him walking around Sydney with an undetected hole in his head was unsettling. I have stated that Richie was the best captain I played under. It was a near thing that he had the opportunity.

I was a fellow fieldsman when Richie was struck at the SCG. By January 1953 we had both graduated to Test cricket. We were enjoying the pleasant experience of playing in the company of Lindsay Hassett, Arthur Morris, Keith Miller, Neil Harvey, Ray Lindwall and Bill Johnston, 'Invincibles' all. The occasion was the first day's play of the third Test against South Africa and the series was square at one-all. The unheralded and underestimated South Africans were becoming embarrassingly competent and confronting. They had won the toss and even though batting on a greenish, lively pitch, Jackie McGlew and Johnny Waite had advanced the South African cause by seeing off the initial fast and penetrating overs delivered by Lindwall and Miller. Indeed, the first wicket to fall resulted from a run-out.

Hassett, the Australian captain, had decided that it was time for a change of pace and brought Bill Johnston into the attack. Richie Benaud, never anything but highly enthusiastic in the field, perceived an opportunity and moved from his position in the gully, closer and closer to Waite: a slower spinning delivery might find the edge of Waite's bat and a catch result. Richie had not counted on a shorter, much faster delivery from Johnston — one good batsmen pounce upon and square-cut, often to the boundary. Waite was an extremely good batsman and executed the perfect response to such a delivery. From point-blank range, the ball flew straight into Richie's mouth.

I was fielding nearby at point, and again witnessed the result. Richie asserted that he instinctively spat the 27 pieces of fractured denture into a handkerchief. Some missed, as I have a vivid memory of flying teeth. It was not the most pleasant sight, but it remains vivid as the years pass. Richie recovered quite well, but he was lucky. The ball was travelling much faster than the Daniel bouncer. A fractured cheekbone, jaw or skull would have been far worse. He actually batted on the third day, but understandably did not trouble the scorers.

I will remember Richie with admiration and affection for the rest of my days.

Oh, and I only ever hit one six on the MCG. I hit Richie over the long-on fence.

PETER THOMSON

It can be argued that the distinguished Peter Thomson is Australian golf's parallel to Richie Benaud. Friends for more than 50 years, the pair were gentlemen of the games they played — albeit robust competitors. There is also the mutual territory of journalism, with both having written extensively on their chosen sports. Here, Thomson recalls the first time he saw Richie Benaud in action in England, during the second day

of the Australians' game against Hampshire on Richie's second
Ashes tour. What the great golfer does not mention is that
just three days earlier at Hoylake, he had won his third straight
British Open. He would win two more, in 1958 and 1965.

MY first sight of Richie on tour was in early July, 1956. I was a guest of Fred Thatcher, president of Hampshire County Cricket Club, and the Australian team, who were under the captaincy of Keith Miller that day. Regular captain Ian Johnson must have given himself the game off. The match was being played at Southampton, between Test matches.

I was honoured to be the only 'outsider' allowed in the Australian dressing-room. This occurred after Australia finished their first innings and before Hampshire began their reply. Keith addressed the team in no uncertain terms, admonishing them to 'get the bastards out so we can get back to London'. His social agenda loomed large in his life!

As my memory has it, Richie bowled and bowled. In my mind, too much, but then he was young and obeying orders, so I was told by Bill Dowling, the Australian team manager. It was not the most memorable of matches, and finished in a draw, but it was my first glimpse of Richie's talent and I was treated to a feast.

Such was my enjoyment of that first day, it will remain forever crystal clear in my mind. In the years that followed, my wife Mary and I spent many happy hours in the company of Daphne and Richie, who were the quintessential 'ideal couple'. We have always been so fond of them and together with Daph, shall always cherish the memory of Rich.

GORDON RORKE

Gordon Rorke was a tearaway fast bowler who made his
Test debut in Richie Benaud's first series as captain, against

England in 1958–59. He was the subject of much controversy,
triggering a change in the no-ball rule to counter bowlers
who dragged their back foot. Gordon was blindingly fast,
and though his bowling was legal according to the law of the
time, batsmen complained that because of his 'drag' he was
too close to them by the time he let the ball go. He played
only four Tests. His progress as an international bowler was
stymied by serious illness, contracted on a difficult tour of
Pakistan and India.

KANPUR, situated on the banks of the Ganges in northern India, holds some pretty grim memories for me. It was the scene of our second Test against India on the tour Richie Benaud led in 1959–60. The city was known as Cawnpore in those days and it was where I was waylaid with amoebic dysentery and hepatitis. I was the first of a string of players to fall ill on that tour. We toured Pakistan and India and the team won both series, overcoming conditions that were, to say the least, pretty dreadful. I ended up in a leprosy hospital, with dirt floors, and the team doctor told me years later he did not think I would survive. Thankfully, he was wrong.

I played the Test in Kanpur … some of it, anyway. But I was not feeling well, and I managed only three first-innings overs when we bowled. By the time we were batting out the fourth innings I was bedridden back in our hotel, feeling very washed out.

India had an off-spin bowler named Jasubhai Patel, who was sending them down at medium pace on a newly laid pitch that was like plasticine. He'd taken 9–69 in our first innings, and was on his way to becoming the first Indian bowler to take 14 wickets in a Test. I don't know what I was thinking, but on the last day I had it in my mind that I had to bat in an attempt to save the match, and I somehow got myself out of bed and down to the ground. When the ninth wicket fell we still needed 120 runs to win, and apart from me there wasn't a person on earth who would have considered my batting capable of providing any help at all.

Richie, of course, was our captain and he was horrified when I turned up. He organised a taxi and sent me straight back to the hotel. As soon as the game was over he came back to my room and lay on the bed next to me. He stayed there for hours, just reading a book, keeping an eye on me, keeping me company. I have never forgotten the empathy he showed me that day. It was the way he was so often with the players of his teams. He truly cared.

My health just got worse. They shipped me off to a leprosy hospital — the only hospital available apparently — until the Salvation Army captain who ran the hospital got me out and took me back to his home. I had a bed there until he ushered me out of it in great haste. 'Sorry,' he said, 'but my wife's having a baby, and she is having it in this room.'

I was shipped off home not long after that. The team ultimately was so ravaged by illness that by the end of their eight Tests (three in Pakistan and five in India) they were struggling for players. It was a measure of Richie's coolness under pressure that he was able to manage all of that, and still have the team perform the way they did. We won 2–0 in Pakistan and beat the Indians 2–1.

I read not long ago how the great American golfer Arnold Palmer revolutionised his sport, just by the strength of his personality. Golf had always been regarded as fairly elite, a bit above the crowd, until Palmer brought a more relaxed approach, a friendly bent for public relations that won over the masses. If Palmer revolutionised golf in that way, Richie certainly revolutionised cricket. I was fortunate to play in the Ashes series of 1958–59, when Richie took over the Australian team. Immediately, attitudes changed. Richie was demonstrative in the way he congratulated us for our successes. His shirt was unbuttoned, he had a huge grin on his face and there was much backslapping. But, importantly, he rarely said anything when a mistake was made, or somebody failed. He knew they knew, and reasoned there was no need to make it worse by rubbing it in.

I made it into that series for the fourth Test as a late replacement for Ian Meckiff. The Cricket Association secretary Alan Barnes rang to tell me only the day before the game that I was in, and it was a matter of getting to Adelaide in great haste. No time to be measured for blazers and such. Richie rang me soon after. He told me he would bring one of his old blazers and jumpers for me to wear. He also made the moment special, by underlining the importance of it. 'Your life will never be the same now,' he said. Representing Australia at cricket does change a lot of things.

I bowled a lot of overs and did well in that fourth Test, which we won. We won the last Test as well, when I was the fourth fast bowler in the team, alongside Ray Lindwall, Alan Davidson and Ian Meckiff. The English press stirred up a lot of trouble on that tour, particularly in regards to Meckiff and myself. They wrote of suspect actions and 'dragging', and generally objected to the pace attack we mounted. Our bowling put England under a lot of pressure. The press reaction put our team under a lot of pressure as well.

But Richie Benaud never let pressure worry him or anybody connected with the team. He was calm and cool about it all. He never mentioned any of it to me as far as I can recall. In the end, the criticism only added to the motivation. Richie had a wonderful way of managing all those things and of looking after his players above all else. He was a great cricketer, but he was an extraordinary captain.

NEIL MARKS

Neil Marks, aka 'Harpo' and 'Marksy', has been a positive force in and around the Australian cricket scene for more than 50 years. His own career of bright promise as a talented left-handed batsman was cut cruelly short in the early 1960s by a rare and serious congenital heart defect. Scorer of a century in his first two Sheffield Shield matches, he seemed destined for a glittering career. Instead he fought for his life but came through, against the odds, thanks to delicate surgery performed at the Mayo Clinic in the US. Doctors were amazed at his sporting achievements, one likening him to a 'nine-cylinder motor that had been running on six cylinders'. Neil's first-class career ended abruptly, but his love for the game never did and he went on to score more than 11,000 career runs for his beloved Northern District in Sydney grade cricket. Along the way, he became a renowned storyteller and raconteur in the cricket community. His five books contain some of the funniest and most poignant stories ever written about Australian sport.

WHEN, as a kid, I first became aware of him, he was 'Ben-ode'. That's how the commentators and many others around cricket wrestled with his name. Quickly, they got the pronunciation right, but by the time I was playing, the name had moved on again via the parlance of the dressing-room and he had become 'Benord' or 'B'nord'. He remains that to me and many others in the cricket world, although Ian Chappell always made it a plural, calling him 'Benords'.

It was in 1947 or 1948 that my father, Alec, managed a NSW Cricket Association team of young players of potential on a country tour. Included on a trek that lasted two or three weeks was R. Benaud of Cumberland. Already a sports-fanatic youngster by then, I remember asking Dad when he got home who out of the team he reckoned might play for Australia. He came up with a few names: Richie and Graeme Hole, who both went on to play for Australia, were among them, as was John Kershaw, a player of great natural ability who never realised how good he was.

My oldest memory of seeing Richie goes back to when he was playing for Cumberland with his father Lou, who also bowled leg-spin. I remember Jim Sullivan, the old groundsman up at Waitara Oval, telling me he reckoned Lou was the better bowler of the two — not an unreasonable view at that stage considering that Richie was still learning the leg-spin art. When he came into the spotlight, Richie was a great batsman who could bowl a bit. In the years that followed, he got better and better as a leg-spinner, while perhaps his batting faded a little. I always thought his 'toppy' was his best ball, though on a wicket giving some support he could really turn his leg break. He had two wrong 'uns — one of them disguised and the other that didn't turn as much and was pickable by all (except Pommy batsmen). And he could bowl a good flipper.

Years after that first sighting, I went away with Richie on a trip to the bush with one of Jack Chegwyn's touring teams. We were playing at Parkes. They were a pretty fair country side and scored around 200, then had us five for about 50, at which point Alan Davidson and B'nord got together and saved the day. However, the main entertainment came in the locals' innings. It centred around Gordon Rorke, who could be the fastest bowler in the world, although you never *quite* knew where he was going to bowl 'em. On this day he was all over the place and Richie took him off early and put himself into the attack. After a couple of deliveries, the batsman went *whack* and the ball flew up in the air.

Rorkey tore in from out near the fence, but ran too far and the ball went over his head. Soon afterwards, the same bloke got onto another one but this time Rorkey, still out on the boundary, lined it up … and the ball donged him on the head and ricocheted over the fence for six!

'Sorry B'nord,' said Gordon at the end of the over.

'Rorkey, I didn't mind you misjudging the catch,' Richie replied, his bottom lip making an appearance. 'And I didn't even mind you knocking that second one over for six. But what I *am* dirty about is that it hit you on the head and wore all the shine off the ball!'

After the final wicket had fallen, Cheggy came into the dressing-room, beaming. 'Thanks, fellas — well played,' he said. 'It was a good game, most enjoyable.'

And Rorkey chipped in, 'Thank *you*, Cheggy, for inviting me. I've had a terrific trip!'

B'nord glanced across from the bench with one of those dry looks of his. 'You must be easily pleased, Rorkey,' he quipped. Then he paused …

'You must be easily pleased.'

Then there was the day when we (Northern District) were playing Cumberland on their home track and we knocked them over for 72. Jim Burke, our captain, said, 'We'll get the runs as quick as we can and then I'll close and we can stick 'em back in.'

I came in at No. 4 that day, joining Burkey in the middle. We were just a few runs short of the 73 needed. With the scoreboard on 72, I nudged one for a single and immediately Jimmy turned to Richie and said, 'That'll do us, B'nord — you have a go.'

'Are you closing, Burkey?' Richie asked.

'Yep.'

But there was a problem. The kids on the scoreboard had got it wrong. As we walked off, our scorer, Bob Fraser, was yelling out, 'Go back! Go back! You haven't got 'em yet.' Their scorer, Ernie Gould, was shouting, 'It's a tie! It's a tie!'

Burkey had to go to Richie and say, 'I think I've made a mistake here, B'nord.'

'No you haven't,' Richie replied. 'It's a tie. This is what cricket is all about! It's perfect. We've both got points.'

'No, your board was wrong,' Burkey responded.

'It's not our board,' chipped in Cumberland player Wilf Ewens. 'It belongs to Parramatta Council.'

B'nord strung Burkey along for about five minutes, as the banter among the players continued and Jim got dirtier and dirtier. Eventually, Richie let him off the hook with a smile and we went back out there to get the extra run we needed. That done, as we walked from the field, B'nord turned to Burkey and with tongue firmly in cheek asked, 'Have you checked with the scorer?'

There was a fair bit of cross-pollination between baseball and cricket in the late 1950s and early 1960s. One season, B'nord suggested we should organise a cricketers' baseball team and play three or four games. Freddy Bennett, a good cricketer who had coached baseball at a senior level and who would go on to become chairman of the Australian Cricket Board, agreed to manage the team and guide us.

Before our first game, coach Bennett was giving us our signs. 'My signal for a steal will be if I touch my cap on the second pitched ball after the pitcher has thrown a ball,' he explained. 'My signal for a hit run with a man on third, I'll do so and so ...'

Freddy obviously thought it was the World Series. On and on he went, until eyes glazed over.

Finally, B'nord stopped him. 'Freddy, Freddy,' he said. 'How about this ... for a hit and run, you take your cap off, throw it on the ground and jump up and down on it. For a steal, drop your daks and ...'

Freddy got the message. 'All right, you blokes,' he said. 'Do what you want to.'

Again, it was that dry Benaud humour. But underlying it all was an abundantly generous spirit and a willingness to help out whenever he could. I had experience of this during the 1960–61 season, not long before I got sick.

'What are you doing tomorrow night?' he asked out of the blue one day. 'Would you like to come over to dinner?'

I went and we had a long talk about my run of outs that season. We discussed possible solutions and he came up with a few suggestions. I remember, too, a baseball trip to Lithgow with him and Kevin 'Crazy' Cantwell that showed how unaffected Richie was by status. He just happened to be Australia's cricket captain; I was pretty much a nothing, just a young bloke doing his best. Anyhow, B'nord picked Crazy and me up in his little car and we headed off to Lithgow. It was bloody freezing once we got into the Blue Mountains and when we finally arrived and walked into the dressing-room someone called out, 'B'nord, you look like you've been to Antarctica.'

'Oh, it was the trip up,' he said offhandedly. 'Marksy had the window down the whole time.'

'Why didn't you tell me?' I said to him.

'Don't worry,' he said. 'You wanted it open.'

I can only wonder how many other Australian captains would *not* have demanded that the window be closed.

Fragments of memory of the remarkable B'nord will stay with me. There was a comment he made after his first season as a television commentator, how he was convinced that the important thing about TV broadcasting was not what you said, but what you didn't say. And there were enjoyable golf days and how he was determined to stay on his single-figure handicap (he played off nine for a time). B'nord loved his golf.

As a cricket captain, he was exceptional, very, very clever. He also benefited, undoubtedly, from the advice Neil Harvey gave him as vice-captain. If Harv made a suggestion, it would always be done. The B'nord I will remember is a modest, decent and dryly funny man. He was fundamentally reserved, but a leader. He had a deep bond of loyalty to the game and to his fellow cricketers.

He never sought the limelight, but he lived with it and handled it supremely well through his years as cricketer and broadcaster. When the end of play came for him in 2015, his quiet departure epitomised the man. Not for B'nord would there be the fanfare of a state funeral.

He would not have wanted all that fuss.

SIR GARFIELD SOBERS

Sir Garfield Sobers is popularly accepted as the greatest all-rounder cricket has known. A spectacular batsman who scored 8,032 Test runs, he also could bowl left-arm medium-fast, left-arm orthodox spin and left-arm wrist-spin to great effect, making him a unique player. He took 235 wickets in his 93 Tests for the West Indies over 20 years, 1954 to 1974.

AS captain of Australia through that remarkable Tied Test summer of 1960–61, Richie Benaud had an amazing capacity to get on with people. Personally, I found him to be a fierce competitor, but a charming and intelligent man. We all considered him a friend, then and certainly in the years that followed.

I had three seasons with South Australia in the Sheffield Shield competition after that tour, so I had the chance to see a bit of Richie in Australian domestic cricket, and whenever he came to Adelaide for Test matches. A good example of his easy-going relationship with those he played against, and his concern for his players, was a discussion he had with me prior to the fourth Test against Ted Dexter's English team in 1962–63.

'Sobey,' he said, 'I wonder if you might have a word with Normie O'Neill. He's finding it hard to get runs and he's down in the dumps.'

'Sure,' I said.

I sat down with Normie and we had a long chat about batting and all the things that can get in your head to make it hard. Norm was a nervous type who took things very seriously. He'd had a good series against us two years before, hitting a brilliant 181 in the first Test and getting two or three half-centuries. But he had scored hardly any runs in the first three Ashes Tests.

It seemed to me that the pressure was getting to him. He was pushing and prodding, or doing silly things trying to hit himself back to form. Normie was normally an aggressive player, and when he tightened up he struggled. The crux of what I told him was just to play his shots, to play his natural game.

It seemed to work. He turned the corner brilliantly to get a hundred in that Test match, and he thanked me for my input. He might more especially have thanked Richie, since it was Richie's understanding of Norm's problem, and his insights into how I might help, that did the trick. Ironically, Norm's century kept him in the side and might well have cost my South Australian teammate Ian McLachlan selection — but I enjoyed helping in that way. To me, it was a further example of the bond that had been built between the teams who had played in that wonderful series that began with the Tied Test. There was a unique spirit in that series, and Richie Benaud had a particular talent for making it so. Richie and our captain, Frank Worrell, were just marvellous people, and between them over that summer they turned cricket on its head.

Sir Donald Bradman had challenged them at the start of the series to mount a sort of rescue mission, because he was genuinely worried that Test cricket was dying. 'It doesn't matter who wins but make the game attractive,' he told them, and that was the way it was played. The two teams mixed so well we were like family. We stayed in the same hotels, we had drinks together, and many of us became lifelong friends.

My first encounter with Richie was on the 1955 Australian tour of the West Indies, when I was a very young man, new to Test cricket, and Richie was still finding his way as a Test player. I did not get to know him on that tour really, but I certainly did when the 1960–61 series unfolded in Australia. I found Richie to be a great sportsman.

He was always friendly and polite. When I played for South Australia and came up against Richie in Shield cricket he would welcome me to the wicket with a 'Morning Sobey, how are we today?' He would look at me, but not really look at me. You knew that however nice he might be, he would still do whatever he could to get your wicket. He was not a great turner of the ball — not like Shane Warne and others — but he was very accurate and he would keep at you, and he gave very little away.

Richie, of course, was a big part of the Brisbane Tied Test, which will always remain to me the greatest game in which I played. When

Wes Hall started the final over, Australia needed just six runs to win with three wickets in hand and we looked like we were gone. Frank Worrell said to Wes, 'No matter what, don't bowl a bouncer because we don't want Richie hitting a six.'

After Richie and Wally Grout managed a leg bye from the first ball, which got Richie on strike, Wes tore in and let fly the fastest bouncer you've ever seen. Richie indeed tried to hit a six, but succeeded only in getting a top edge and was caught behind. Wes was delirious with delight and ran to Frank, who was none too pleased.

'I said no bouncers,' Frank said. 'What if he had hit a six?'

Poor Wes was a bit deflated.

Two run-outs closed it out. Joe Solomon threw down the wicket from side on to run out Ian Meckiff for the final wicket. I was fielding at leg slip hoping the ball wouldn't come to me, because the tension was stifling. The scores were level, although none of us knew that. Some of us thought we had won, some of us thought they had won. A tie had never happened before and such a result just didn't occur to us. But it was somehow fitting. Both sides had given everything for a win, when either of us could have closed it up to avoid defeat. It was the way that series was played.

I was grateful to be there and to meet some great men. Richie was one of them. So was Alan Davidson, whom I found to be a great bowler and a lovely person. Richie had him tabbed, though. If Davo was getting wickets, you couldn't get the ball off him, but if he had gone for a few fours he seemed to develop strange ailments that needed some time in the field.

Richie never fell for it. 'One more over, Al,' he would say, and Davo would keep plugging away. It was always a good example of Richie's motivational skills and the understanding he had of the people he played with and against.

It is only a year or two since Richie and Daphne were in Barbados, and we had a wonderful lunch … half-a-dozen of us from that marvellous series. As we talked and laughed and remembered, it only emphasised again just how special those days were. And nobody ever was in any doubt of the part Richie played in all of that.

FRANK MISSON

Genial Frank Misson was a fine fast bowler who played
his cricket vigorously and with a sense of enjoyment,
representing NSW from 1959 to 1964 and Australia in five
Tests — three during the 'Calypso Summer' of 1960–61
and two on the 1961 Ashes tour. It was his NSW teammate,
Warren Saunders, who came up with Frank's nickname —
one of the most creative in sport — during practice one
day at the SCG No. 2. Dispatching players to various nets, a
ground official, Mick Burt, called his name loudly as 'Frank
MY-SON', to the glee of fellow players. Saunders instantly
tagged him 'Strepta', as in streptomycin, an antibiotic of the
time. Among his mates from that period — of whom he has
many — he would be Strepta forevermore.

IT was in the season of 1958–59 that — as an unsophisticated
20-year-old, not long out of school — I was first picked for NSW.
It was a Sheffield Shield game in Perth. Richie was our captain and
I was totally in awe of the whole experience. It was hot over there
in the west, as it can be, and before long in Western Australia's first
innings I cramped up really badly — in my legs and my hands. I
went across to Richie.

'Mr Benaud, I can't bowl,' I said, and I explained my dilemma.
'We'll fix that,' he answered.

Richie called the drinks man onto the field, and asked him to
bring a couple of salt tablets. Well, they fixed me, all right — pretty
much straightaway — and I thought, *Gee, this guy knows something!*

Well, of course, Richie knew plenty. But it's worth putting on
the record that a few years later I did *him* a favour, via an event that
took place early in the 1962–63 season, something which neither
of us ever forgot. Our first Shield game of that season was against
Queensland in Brisbane. Back then, we didn't play on Sundays.

Guys would generally play golf or go to the movies on the Sunday, but on this occasion we met in the breakfast room and Richie announced there was the option of a trip to the Gold Coast, to spend the day at what was then the hotel of choice down there: Lennons at Broadbeach, near Surfers Paradise.

Lennons had a nice pool and grass surrounds, and as a keen swimmer from Coogee this arrangement suited me just fine. Four or five of us went down for a lazy day beside the pool. It was typically warm Queensland weather, with a hot sun beating down, and for Richie, always a sun-lover, it was perfect. He was drifting on a li-lo soaking up the rays and I was not far away, poolside, reading the Sunday paper. All of a sudden, I looked up and Richie's off the li-lo ... and going down. I thought, *That's a bit unusual ...*

I knew Richie didn't like to get his hair wet. He came up spluttering for a few seconds and then he was heading towards the bottom again. *He's in trouble here!* I jumped in and grabbed him and got him to the side of the pool. He clambered out and said to me, 'That's the first and last time I'm ever going for a swim!'

Richie told me later that in his younger days, when his dad Lou was a teacher in NSW country towns, he had never learned to swim. The story of the Australian cricket captain in trouble at the bottom of Lennons' pool never got out publicly, although I could envisage the headlines: 'Teammate Saves Aussie Captain'. Richie and I used to joke about it in the years that followed. In more recent times, when I was trustee of Wylie's Baths at Coogee, I'd sometimes see Daphne and Richie on their morning walk and I'd sing out, 'C'mon in, Rich, the water's beautiful!'

His answer was always roughly along the lines of: 'No way, you bugger.'

Early on the Ashes tour of 1961, I chanced to be batting with Richie in a match at Hove, against Ted Dexter's Sussex side, when the strange sea fog the locals call a 'fret' came in and covered the ground to the extent that you couldn't see the other end of the pitch. Then the wind came and blew it away, and we got going again. I was at the non-striker's end and Richie hadn't scored as yet. On the first or second ball he faced after the resumption, he went for a huge cover drive and missed by a mile, but the ball deviated off the pitch to the bloke at first slip, who caught it. There was a muffled appeal. I knew Richie hadn't hit it and turned and walked back to the crease, where the ump gave a quiet, 'Not out.'

Then I turned around and saw that he was halfway to the pavilion. *What's going on here?* I thought. I ran over to him and said, 'Rich, you didn't get within a bull's roar of that. The umpire has said not out.'

He stood there for a moment, then said, 'Aw, bugger it, I can't come back now.' And he walked off. I spoke to him about it later and he answered with words to the effect: 'I'm very proud to be Australia's captain and the last thing I want on this tour is to have some sort of controversy where the Australian captain walks and then comes back. I thought in the circumstances it was best to keep going.'

I sort of understood. The first Test was coming up and the responsibility of the captaincy was no doubt weighing heavy. Not too many would have done what he did that day; for me, it was an occasion that said a lot about him as a captain ... and as a man. Adding to the moment, it was his second duck of the game. He told me later it was the first 'pair' of his career.

The tour climaxed two months later, when we won the fourth Test at Manchester to retain the Ashes. The final day was one of Richie's greatest, as he took 6–70 in England's second innings, his leg-spin wizardry bowling us to victory, but there was a little-known happening in the Aussie dressing-room that also played a part in the victory. England had won the third Test at Leeds by eight wickets, levelling the series, and the pressure was really on. In our room at Old Trafford, Richie drew the attention of the players to a newspaper cutting he'd pinned on a wall — it was a story written by the Sydney *Daily Telegraph*'s Phil Tresidder, who happened to be one of Richie's best mates in the press. Phil's article suggested in strong terms that the Australians had dropped their bundle after the third Test defeat and were a dispirited lot. My suspicion to this day remains that the story was something of a ploy, reflecting Richie's shrewd thinking. In later years, I asked both Richie and Phil whether my suspicions had foundation. Neither denied it outright, making me think I am probably on the money.

He could be hard on the field. When the Englishmen, captained by Ted Dexter, were out here in 1962–63, there was something of a psychological battle in progress between Richie and 'Lord Ted'.

In the MCC v NSW match, I split the webbing in my left hand fielding a hard-hit cut shot and I had to go off so the resident team medico, 'Doc' Anderson, could stitch me up. Back on the field, Richie put me at mid-wicket, with Dexter batting. The wicket was taking some turn and before long Dexter got down the pitch to him and thumped a ball which was heading over the top of me ... but possibly reachable.

A quick flash came to mind: *Should I take it two-handed and possibly split the webbing again or go for it one-handed?*

I opted for the latter and ... bang! ... it stuck. Beauty! Almost instantly, Richie wheeled around and said, 'What the fuck are you doing?'

'Look, Rich,' I spluttered. 'I didn't want to split the webbing again.'

He wasn't convinced. 'That was a real show-off act!' he said. I defended myself — and that was the end of it. I suspect that his stern response had a lot to do with the fact the England captain was the batsman involved.

Richie's objective when he was bowling was always to get wickets, but he'd really get pissed off if he gave away more than two runs in an eight-ball over. He was a tight bowler. On the tour of England he used to put me at square-leg or backward square. He knew I had a good arm and he would deliberately drop one short, which the batsman would often drag around in my direction. It was all part of a ruse to set batsmen up for the flipper, which would be short again but which would hit and spit. When he got it right, the ball often skidded through for an lbw. He had a lot of success on that tour with the flipper.

One thing that always amazed me about Richie was the way he handled the public speaking part of being captain. The first week of an Ashes tour was a big one — keeping with tradition, there was the first practice at Lord's, followed by a black-tie dinner that night and other events following. Invariably at these big functions, the Poms would roll out one of the most prestigious after-dinner speakers in the land, to which Richie had to respond. He always did so impressively, with an Aussie touch. When the 40-year anniversary of the Tied Test was celebrated in Brisbane in December 2000, there were a couple of occasions when Richie spoke. I took particular notice ... you could have heard a pin drop.

He had the gatherings enthralled; it was a skill he'd honed over a long period of time.

My final deliveries here concern two matches from Richie's final season in big cricket: 1963–64. The first involves the arrival in Australia that summer of a 19-year-old South African left-hand batsman named Graeme Pollock, who would, of course, go on to perform some wonderful deeds.

In NSW's game against the South Africans in Sydney, before the first Test, I was bowling when Pollock came to the wicket. Richie came up to me for a serious talk. The bottom lip was out. 'I've got mail from South Africa that he's susceptible to a ball cutting away, on or outside the off stump,' he said. 'Try hitting that line.'

So I did, and three balls later Pollock was 12 not out after hitting three magnificent cover drives to the fence. After delivering the third ball and watching it scream to the boundary, I followed through. Richie was fielding in the slips.

'Are you *sure* that mail was right?' I asked him.

'I don't think it is,' he muttered wryly. Quickly, we learned that to have any hope of keeping Pollock sort of quiet, you had to bowl at his pads, try to cramp him.

A couple of months later came the only time I ever saw Richie being thrashed by a batsman. It also happened at the SCG, this time in a Shield game when South Australia's Les Favell really took to him. Les and Richie knew each other from way back, from Green Shield days in Sydney, and on this occasion Favell, an audacious batsman with a cavalier approach, pounded him all over the ground. It was 'Favelli' at his devil-may-care best, but rather than taking himself off, Richie kept bowling.

Afterwards, I was talking to Alan Davidson and I asked him why Richie had persevered even though he was being pummelled. 'That's the worst beating I've ever seen him take,' I said.

'Oh well,' said Davo, 'it was Favelli.'

In other words, they were just a couple of old mates having a crack at each other. Richie wasn't going to back away. Neither was Les. They really enjoyed the contest and the crowd got their money's worth, all right …

Richie *always* liked that.

BRIAN CORRIGAN

Dr Brian Corrigan is a sports medicine pioneer in Australia.
He was medical officer for the Australian Olympic team
over two decades from 1968 and had long involvement with
soccer, rugby league and cricket. He was the medical officer
on Richie's 1961 Ashes tour and in the early days of World
Series Cricket. Corrigan also served as chairman of the Drugs
in Sport committee of the Australian Sports Commission and
as chairman of the Australian Sports Drug Agency. He was
inducted into the Sport Australia Hall of Fame in 1999.

MANY things made Richie Benaud the special sportsman he was. He was a great communicator and a wonderful captain. He had a very sharp mind and was the sort of person who got on with everybody, especially all the people with whom he played cricket. But to me one thing that really stood out was his courage.

You hear all sorts of heroic stories about footballers and boxers and the like who compete when they are hurting. But I know more than most just how much pain Richie had to overcome, more or less throughout his career, to achieve the things he did. The leg-spin that Richie bowled put enormous strain on the body. It took a lot of skin off his fingers and it sorely tested his right shoulder.

The best example, but certainly not the only example, was Australia's 1961 tour of England that Richie led, when he mounted a superb bowling spell to win the Manchester Test and retain the Ashes. I was the team doctor on that tour and I don't think I'm breaking any doctor-patient confidentiality when I state the obvious: the damage to his shoulder as he faced up to that game was such that he should not have been playing, let alone trying to let leg-spinners rip. Yet he bowled 32 overs and took 6–70 in the England second innings to win the game. The pain must have been excruciating.

Richie had done the damage in the first game of the tour, against Worcestershire. I think it was Tom Graveney he was bowling to, but he ripped a wrong 'un that also ripped his shoulder, doing a lot of damage underneath the rotator cuff — an unusual injury that makes the shoulder very painful. He missed some cricket, of course, including the Lord's Test, but he also insisted on bowling through a lot of games when he should not have. He didn't bowl very well under such a handicap, at least not until he got to Manchester for that crucial fourth Test, when he bowled the spell of his life. The Old Trafford result was just reward for a lot of courage.

It wasn't the only time he battled on in pain. Richie spent a lot of his career nursing a spinning finger that was worn and bloodied. I remember one club game at Mosman Oval during his final season, when he dug his finger into the ground going for a catch and broke it. The fact that he was playing a club game the week before a Test was remarkable enough — you wouldn't see modern players committing themselves like that — but the lengths he went to so that the finger injury was manageable when he played his final Tests against South Africa was another thing.

He stayed up all night after the Mosman match, holding a cricket ball and working the hand so that, broken finger or not, everything else worked well enough to let him return to the field of play as quickly as possible. He bowled 57 eight-ball overs in his farewell Test, 49 of them in the first innings, in which he took four wickets.

It was a privilege to be around Richie and the Australian cricketers of that time. It seemed to me that from the very first ball of Richie's captaincy a certain magic took over the team. They worked hard at being very good, but they also worked at enjoying themselves. The atmosphere was wonderful. Richie could take a joke, too.

One thing he did like to do as soon as the seatbelt light went off in an aircraft was to have a cool glass of wine. He was not a particularly good flyer and the wine no doubt was a settler. Before one of those big trips I wrote a letter to Qantas suggesting that Richie should not be offered alcohol on the flight. The letter, of course, was read as doctor's orders.

Richie, predictably, asked for the wine as soon as the flight was underway. The hostie apologised … no wine. Richie waited a while and asked again. Same result … 'Sorry sir, we can't give you any.' Eventually, the frustration was too much and Richie demanded to see the captain. The pilot explained, with profuse apology, that he had been instructed not to allow Richie any drink 'on doctor's orders'.

'The doctor's name would not by any chance be Corrigan, would it?' Richie enquired.

Great mirth all round. Richie got his wine. And I don't think he ever got me back. We remained friends in all the years that followed. He was simply a great man.

TED DEXTER

'Lord Ted' Dexter was the total aggressor as a cricketer: a batsman of extraordinary power and an imaginative captain who played 62 Tests between 1958 and 1968. He and Richie were like minds and the dynamics of their early rivalry grew into lifelong friendship.

BACK in the early '60s, news did not travel so fast as it does today. For instance, there was no television coverage in Britain of the great Australia v West Indies series, including the Tied Test. It was only later on that I saw some grainy footage of Wes Hall at full tilt, with the keeper leaping to take the ball way above his head … and still going up! But somewhere in the background the name of Richie Benaud was starting to gain resonance — perhaps no more than the odd murmur to start with but growing perceptibly.

Fast-forward to the 1962 season in England, with the normal press coverage, as always, skewed towards the coming MCC tour to Australia. One of the stranger strands of news centred round the reappearance of David Sheppard (by now Reverend David Sheppard) on the county scene. Not only was he taking a summer's sabbatical for some rest and recuperation from parish duties, it was soon clear that he had an eye on a tour place — and indeed the captaincy.

The most likely candidate for the top job was Colin Cowdrey and the distant outsider of three was Edward Dexter, if only because he had been entrusted with a tour to India, Pakistan and Ceylon in 1961, and had emerged with at least a modicum of credit.

Which is where the Richie Benaud factor came into play. Richie's reputation as a forceful and dynamic captain had gained a momentum of its own. Added to that was a sense that his public relations expertise was a formidable part of his leadership.

Note the initials MCC ahead of 'tour' in a previous paragraph. The Marylebone Cricket Club had not entirely relinquished its world administrative role at this time. Teams selected to play overseas were expected to represent the very best traditions of the great club and indeed of the nation. The MCC committee had a strong say in selection.

Thus, whatever the counter-arguments might have been, the surprise announcement was made that it was the outsider, Edward Dexter, who was selected to face up to the Richie Benaud-led Australians in 1962–63. So I really have Richie to thank for this sudden elevation from the ranks — a definite leg-up for the Dexter career image. But I knew that it was up to me to face Richie down whenever the opportunity arose.

I wonder whether either Cowdrey or Sheppard would have accepted an invitation to join Richie in one-on-one discussions and commentary after each day's play in the Tests. I doubt that any pair of captains in modern cricket would agree to such public proximity on a daily basis. But it was at Richie's invitation and to say 'no' would have given him the edge he wanted. The net result was that we played a drawn series, with much good cricket on both sides, and began a friendship that was to last a lifetime.

It was Richie more than anyone who helped me establish a system of cricket rankings in the 1980s. Many other journalists and broadcasters were unwilling to give credence to a new (and infinitely better) statistical measurement of performance — perhaps because they disliked a sponsor's name attached, giving the rankings a mildly commercial element.

Richie Benaud, the cricketer and communicator par excellence, was more far-sighted and he lived, like me, to see the confirmation of the rankings principle when it was adopted by the ICC and became the official standard of comparative ability and achievement.

In recent years, we shared an appreciation for the health benefits of time spent in the south of France. We were welcome visitors to his sunny flat in Beaulieu and vice versa to our apartment in Nice. To say that we were sparing on the delights of vin rosé would be less than truthful.

The only area where Richie and I never quite saw eye to eye was over golf. I always asked him about his game and was given blow-by-blow accounts of his latest swing instruction, equipment, etc, etc. He never once enquired the same of me. Perhaps he feared the same in return. Ah, well! Nobody is perfect!

BRIAN BOOTH

Brian Booth played 29 Tests for Australia. An elegant strokemaker and known to his mates as 'Sam', he captained the team in two Tests during the 1965–66 Ashes series in Australia. A strong mutual respect existed between Richie Benaud and Brian Booth, reflected in the Benaud family's request that Brian lead the service at Richie's private funeral.

IN all, I played 11 Tests with Richie Benaud and for eight of those he was our captain. I played first-class cricket with him for nearly a decade, all of it in the same side. It was a successful period, mainly because we had Richie Benaud and Alan Davidson in our team at both Test and Sheffield Shield level. They were the difference between NSW and the other states, and also between Australia and everybody else.

As a cricketer, Richie was a wonderful all-rounder. As a captain, he established an attitude within his teams that changed the game. But to me his real success was as a person — as a man capable of understanding the people around him, of caring about their welfare, and of ensuring that they were all comfortable in the roles they had to fill.

I played my first Shield game in the 1954–55 season, as a fill-in for injured players; I was dropped after my first game, but was recalled as a late replacement for the NSW game against Len Hutton's MCC touring side. 'Late replacement' hardly covers it, really. I was already at work, teaching at Hurlstone Agricultural High School, when the call came. By the time I caught a train to the city and then dashed to the ground, the match was half an hour old and NSW were three wickets down. I scored 74 not out, which suggested some sort of a future for me.

I played six out of seven NSW matches in the next season, but my record was modest. Keith Miller was captain for most games, and with men of the calibre of Jim Burke, Sid Carroll, Bob Simpson, Ian Craig, Bill Watson, Alan Davidson and Richie in the team, I did not really feel part of it.

It all changed in the match against Victoria at the SCG, when Miller was injured and Richie replaced him as captain. Before the game, Richie sidled up to me and said, 'Sam, I want you to go out there today and score a century for me.' To me, that was a career-changing vote of confidence. I fell 87 runs short of the ton, but that didn't seem to matter. Here was my captain telling me I had the ability to make such a score, and that I could handle the responsibility that came with being a top-six batsman. From that point, I felt part of the team.

I can recall many examples like that where Richie seemed to read people's minds, to know what they were feeling and what was needed to lift their confidence. He could also make a strong point in the most inoffensive way. In the NSW match against Ted Dexter's MCC side in 1962–63, I went in at No. 4, after Bob Simpson and Norman O'Neill had each scored centuries, and the score was 2–250. By tea, I had hit a careful 20 not out.

'Brian, I don't mind you taking time over your innings so long as you go on and make a good score,' Richie said to me at the break. 'But if you use up a lot of overs and don't get a good score you make the task of following batsmen that much harder.'

In other words: 'Play for the team, not yourself. Get on with it, or get out!'

It was all part of Richie's modus operandi — keep it interesting, look for a declaration, chase a result.

For those of us who shared our time in cricket with him, memories of Richie came flooding back in the weeks and months after he died. There was the second Test against England at the MCG in 1962–63, for instance, a Test England won handsomely. When the scores were tied and England still had seven second-innings wickets standing, Richie threw me the ball. 'I'm going to give you the privilege of bringing this Test match to a close,' he said. And so I got to bowl in a Test against England.

Colin Cowdrey was the batsman on strike, a half-century already under his belt. My first ball was medium-pace of respectable length. Colin played defensively, looked up and said with that gentlemanly air of his, 'Well bowled, Brian.' Second ball was pretty much the same. This time Colin stroked it effortlessly to the boundary for the winning runs. My Test match bowling analysis against England thereafter remained at two balls for four runs. But I had bowled in an Ashes Test, thanks to Richie.

The fourth Test of the 1963–64 series against South Africa provided a great example of just how commanding Richie could be, with a minimum of fuss. Peter Burge had been run out just prior to lunch and soon after he returned to the dressing-room a discussion with Norman O'Neill, the other batsman, ensued. It was friendly enough to start with, but it slowly became more robust.

Richie rose to his feet, pulled on his blazer and announced to all and sundry, 'I'm going down to lunch and when I come back I don't want to hear any more about that run-out.' Silence. A ceasefire was immediately called. Everybody pulled on their blazers and followed Richie. No more was said. Richie was in his final season and by this time had handed the Test captaincy to Bob Simpson, but his aura and his command remained intact. He had made a clear point about the danger of a team defeating itself from within.

Retaining the Ashes on the 1961 tour of England was perhaps Richie's pièce de résistance, and it was no fluke. From the very start, he was meticulous in the way he planned it, and when he finally clinched that series — almost single-handedly through his 6–70 in the fourth Test — it was a brilliant piece of imaginative cricket.

We were the last team to travel to England by boat, and the long sea voyage could be both a trial and a benefit. Richie made the most of it. He appointed Graham McKenzie and myself to conduct calisthenics for the team every day, and with Neil Harvey and the third selector Colin McDonald he spent time planning every detail. He made it clear to us from our first team meeting that we were there to win, but that we would do so playing attacking cricket.

The fourth Test brought my first Test selection. Richie said to me at the nets the day before the game: 'Congratulations, Brian, you are in the team for tomorrow. How does it feel to be playing your first Test?'

I replied that it was an honour, but I would try to treat it as just another game of cricket.

Richie looked at me quizzically. 'I wish you well with that philosophy,' he said.

I was soon to find out that Test cricket, especially against England, was not just another game of cricket. This was especially true of the game I immediately found myself in. It was the most remarkable match I ever played in — we did not look like getting out of it until after tea on the last day, when Richie turned on his magic 'round the wicket' spell that won the game.

I scored 46 in our first innings and only nine in our second as we battled for runs. I was feeling pretty down. Richie sat down beside me and said in his quiet, deliberate way: 'Disappointed? Forty-six in the first innings and nine in the second is 55 runs. If all our batsmen had contributed in this way we would not be in the trouble that we are at present.' I was encouraged by that. History has it that Davo and Graham McKenzie put on 98 for the last wicket, and that Richie turned the game Australia's way on the last afternoon when all seemed lost. I was standing nearby when he had the critical conversation with vice-captain Neil Harvey where they resolved there was no hope of saving that game … we had to try to win it.

When we played Western Australia in Sydney early in the 1963–64 season, WA scored 420 batting first, then Richie declared the NSW first innings at 1–425 after Bob Simpson had scored 247 and Grahame Thomas 127. After Western Australia batted again we were left to chase 262 in less than four hours to win. Richie asked me during the lunch break on the final day whether I would like to open the batting in our second innings. I told him I was easy, that I didn't mind where I batted. 'Well,' he said, 'if you don't open you might not get a bat at all, and if we are going to win the Shield we can't do it on just two people's performances.' I finished up 169 not out, and we got the runs we needed for the loss of only one wicket. I got his point on both counts.

Richie's last first-class game for NSW was against South Australia in Adelaide that season. He had a great farewell, scoring 76 and 120 not out, and taking five wickets in a game that we eventually won by six runs after Simmo declared our second innings at 5–390, setting them 321 to win. It was my very great pleasure to bat with Richie in his final innings, in which we compiled an unbroken partnership of 221, and as we left the field I told Richie what a privilege it had been to bat with him that day. I had much to thank him for — his mateship, his captaincy and the many lessons that he had taught me about the game, especially the spirit in which you should play the game and the value of teamwork.

When Richie died in April 2015, Daphne and the Benaud family asked me to conduct the service at his cremation. It was a private and moving occasion. I said there that Richie had touched and enriched my life — and the lives of countless others — in more ways than he would have known.

His legacy will endure.

IAN MECKIFF

Ian Meckiff played 18 Tests for Australia between 1957 and 1963, taking 45 wickets. A left-armer of good pace, he was particularly effective against England in 1958–59, taking 6–38 to scuttle England for 87 in their second innings of the second Test. His success created a storm among the visiting journalists, who accused him of throwing. Ian's career ended in the first Test against South Africa in 1963–64, at the Gabba, when umpire Col Egar called him four times for throwing in his first over. Richie declined to bowl him

again, and Ian retired at the end of the game. Claims of
conspiracy were rampant — that Ian had been set up as a
public relations scapegoat — but the Victorian accepted his
fate with good grace and remained firm friends with both the
umpire and his captain.

THE first time I shared a cricket field with Richie Benaud was a
Sheffield Shield game in Melbourne over Christmas in 1956, and
the match finished in the competition's first ever tie. Seven of us
on the field that day — Richie, Alan Davidson and Norm O'Neill
from NSW and Neil Harvey, Colin McDonald, Lindsay Kline and
myself from Victoria — were at the Gabba four years later, involved
in the first Test match tie as well. I have always looked upon that as
an amazing historical coincidence, more so for me because I took
the final wicket to tie the Shield game, and I was last man out in
the dramatic final over in Brisbane.

Shield games between NSW and Victoria were no holds barred
in those days, but my first impressions of Richie set him apart from
most of the other players. I was very young and I remember him
being very welcoming to young players coming through, no matter
which side they were on. And he was always good-humoured.

I scored 55 in our first innings of that first game — top scored,
actually — but my batting was never especially commanding, and
I got most of my runs with spooning shots that just managed to get
over the fieldsmen's heads. Richie told me with a smile that I had
'the best nine-iron shots in the business'. By modern standards, it
would perhaps be considered a sledge, worthy of glares and stares
and sharp words in response. In those days, it was pleasant banter.
We both laughed.

I made the Australian team not long after, first for a short trip to
New Zealand and then for a Test series in South Africa. Ian Craig
was made captain for both tours, somewhat controversially, but
Richie and Neil Harvey were looked upon as senior players and
to newcomers in the team like Lindsay Kline, Bob Simpson, Wally
Grout and myself they were great mentors.

Richie had first made the Test side in 1951–52, but it was at
about the time of my arrival that he really started to dominate. Most
of the established men of the early 1950s — Keith Miller, Lindsay
Hassett, Arthur Morris, Bill Johnston and the like — had retired

and Richie, Neil Harvey and Alan Davidson became the core of the team. Neil was my Victorian captain at the time and I knew how much he knew about cricket, but when he teamed up with Richie they were unbeatable as a leadership team. Neil helped Richie a lot, a fact Richie always acknowledged.

Richie assumed the captaincy in 1958–59, the season Peter May's England team came to Australia. Much has been said about how adventurous he was, and how he inspired attacking cricket, and that is certainly true. But I always thought a real key to that series was the resentment felt by men like Benaud and Harvey, Jim Burke and Colin McDonald, who had been on the 1956 tour of England and felt dudded. Off-spinner Jim Laker took 19 wickets to rout Australia in the Manchester Test of that series, on a disgraceful pitch that the Australians considered had been deliberately prepared to make them fail.

Richie was always wary of pitches in foreign fields. When we went to India and Pakistan in 1959–60 we had to play two Tests on mats. They promised us a turf wicket for the first Test in Dacca, but Richie had been misled about pitches often enough and accepted their assurance with a 'We'll see.' When we got there the 'pitch' was a yellow strip of hard-baked mud. We would be playing on a mat, so Richie sent 12th man Lindsay Kline to the ground at 9am every morning to ensure that the mat was laid tight, without ripples to help their seam bowlers.

That was a hard tour. I think the PM, Bob Menzies, had cooked it up as diplomatic fare for still-emerging nations. When we played at Karachi, again on a mat, the American president Dwight Eisenhower turned up. He was also on a diplomatic mission. We had slugged away all morning without taking a wicket, but as soon as the president arrived three fell quickly. He was only scheduled to stay a couple of hours, but when Richie met him he asked him if he could stay a bit longer, given the difference his appearance had made to our wicket haul.

We played eight Tests on that tour — three against Pakistan and five against India — and by the end of it we had only 12 fit players. A few had returned to Australia, ill with hepatitis. I had roomed with Lindsay Kline and relied on him as my morning wake-up call. By the last Test against India he was on his way home too, and it was only a late call from Gavin Stevens that got me out of bed. I dressed hurriedly and raced to the ground, but I was still about an hour late.

Nobody had missed me in the foyer as they headed for the bus. Nobody had missed me in the dressing-room. When the players took the field the ball was left on the turf for me to bowl the first over. It just sat there until it dawned on our captain that he had only ten players. When I did arrive, Richie was surprisingly light on admonishment. 'Meckiff, you can bowl,' he said. And bowl … and bowl … and bowl. He kept me on for the rest of the session.

I played in the Australian team on and off for seven seasons. There was pressure along the way, given the way the English press attacked me over my action when I took wickets against them in 1958–59. Throwing was a bit of a cause célèbre at the time, with a string of players in a number of countries under pressure. I was one of them.

Richie never stopped supporting me through that period. He told me that he had no problem with my action. His responsibility, he reckoned, was to keep the team focused, working together, and he would have defended any of us against outside attack. But when my situation came to a head in the Brisbane Test against South Africa in 1963 the trends were pretty clear. After I had been called the third time, he came to me and said, 'I think we've got a problem.'

I told him I sort of knew that. 'Just get through the over, finish as you want,' he said.

Richie wore some flak afterwards for not bowling me from the other end and testing the second umpire. But he had his principles. An umpire had made a call and he was not going to question that. I think we all knew the die had been cast anyway. The dramas of that afternoon in no way affected my relationship with him. Whenever I bumped into him in later years he was always on for a chat. We had a big lunch in Melbourne for the 50th anniversary of the Tied Test and I asked him down for that. He gave a wonderful talk.

Richie was a man who knew what players needed. He also knew what the public wanted. I think his experience as a journalist was a big part of that. It was reflected for years after his cricket finished in his role as a commentator, where that deft combination of knowledge, appropriate silence and a quirky sense of humour made him the best there's ever been.

BARRY JARMAN

Barry Jarman represented Australia between 1957 and 1969.
For much of that time he was understudy to Wally Grout,
but he did play 19 Tests and captained Australia in the
Headingley Test of the 1968 Ashes series. Jarman appeared
in 94 first-class matches for South Australia from 1955 to
1969, made three Ashes tours and played Tests against
England, India, Pakistan, South Africa and the West Indies.
He later became an ICC match referee.

IT'S a while ago now, but there was a time when Richie and I dabbled in horse racing. We did have some modest success, but it is also fair to say that we had some rotten luck. It started in the early 1960s when Jack 'Slinger' Nitschke, who had been a handy cricketer for South Australia about the time of Bradman and played a couple of Tests, set us up with the lease of a gelding. Richie, Norm O'Neill, Ray Steele, who had been the treasurer on our 1961 Ashes tour, and myself had asked Slinger what he could find for us, because Slinger was a top breeder and he knew about these things.

'Geez,' he said. 'Pity you didn't ask me a week ago. I had a beauty.'

The beauty we missed out on was a filly called Proud Miss, who won ten races in a row and finished up favourite for the Golden Slipper and ran second. That was our first bit of bad luck. Never mind, we finished up with a gelding called Sleep Walker, trained by Colin Hayes, who won a Coorong maiden handicap at Tailem Bend and an improvers' race at Balaklava before breaking down. While we had a lot of fun picking up the Coorong trophy, Richie was certainly never going to get rich on it. A fiver each way was about his limit.

Richie might not have been the most lavish punter but he loved the races, and when we worked out Sleep Walker wasn't going to set the world alight we started looking for something else. A bit later we got hold of a stayer we called Trent Bridge. We ran it in a meeting at Gawler and thought it ran a reasonable fourth. But when the jockey got off it he told us it was no good and suggested we send it back to the owner in Perth. So we did. That was our second piece of bad luck.

In Perth the following year for a Sheffield Shield game, I looked through the paper for some form and found Trent Bridge was the top weight in the main race of the day. Further enquiry suggested not only was it a good thing, but that since we'd sent it home it had won seven races and was rated the best stayer seen in Perth for ages. We also discovered that when it had come fourth at Gawler, so offending our jockey, the second-placed horse was Galilee, who went on to win the Caulfield-Melbourne Cup double in 1966. When Richie found out he just grunted. Never did use a lot of words.

We had a dabble, too, during the 1964 Ashes tour. I was reserve wicketkeeper on that tour and Richie was there as a journalist, having retired from first-class cricket earlier that year. The leading Victorian jockey Ron Hutchinson was riding in England at the time and he organised a lease for us of a thing called Pall-Mallann, which was by the sire Pall Mall, owned by the Queen. Richie had to be recorded as the official owner, because we cricketers on tour could hardly be seen to be racing horses on the side.

Now we had a bit of fun with Pall-Mallann. We raced it in green-and-gold silks that I'd brought from home, because they were the colours we always used and because they were the colours of Woodville, my Adelaide cricket club. We thought they were lucky and they were. Pall-Mallann won a race at Newmarket, which was pretty good, but unfortunately we were playing Yorkshire at Bradford at the time. The race was at 2.30 and Normie O'Neill was next in, so we sent a message out to Brian Booth and Peter Burge, as I remember it, not to get out before then, so that Normie could hear the race. When Pall-Mallann duly won there was a great hullabaloo from the dressing-room, which confused the crowd and the bowling side, but was great fun for us. Of greater moment was the disaster that befell Richie Benaud. He had promised to put a bet on for the trainer, Sid Dale, but forgot. Rich faced a difficult negotiation to placate poor Sid.

Flushed with success, we then decided to have a go at leasing a greyhound. It was called Social Mac and its owner was Colin Cowdrey, a great English Test batsman for more than 20 years, who liked the dogs and the races. Colin's second wife, in fact, was a horse trainer who later on won a Caulfield Cup with a 66–1 long shot, helped considerably by an Irish jockey who knocked half the field out of the way in running, but managed to salve the pain of a hefty suspension with the fruits of victory. Anyway, Social Mac won a race at Catford in London and Richie was delighted, as we all were. We felt our racing adventures had been well worth the punt, as it were.

On the cricket field, our luck had always been similarly fickle, coming and going in erratic fashion. There was the time, for instance, when Richie and I were batting at Edinburgh in a match against Scotland in 1961. It had drizzled all day, as it often did, but we played anyway and we were going along nicely when Richie lofted one into the outfield. We had crossed as the ball headed for the rope, and when we saw it jump over the rope we stopped mid-pitch for a chat. Somebody threw the ball back, the keeper broke the wicket, and we were informed with great glee that Richie had run himself out.

Then there was the matter of the lucky tie. When I started as a kid with South Australia, it sort of got to me that the heavyweights in the team, like Ian McLachlan and John Lill, would always come to the game in their old school ties, as was the way of it with the lads of colleges like St Peter's and Prince Alfred. My old school was Thebarton Technical High School, which was not quite so highbrow, but I figured if I could get a tie from there I would be part of the crowd. So I went to the school and asked the principal for a tie. He got me to talk to the boys and then sold me a tie for seven shillings and sixpence.

I took that tie to England and when we were in big trouble in the Old Trafford Test, nine down in our second innings and only about 150 to the good, I took the tie and hung it around a light hanging down in the dressing-room and said, 'That'll change our luck.' Straightaway Davo hit a six, and he and Garth McKenzie put on 98 for the last wicket. That allowed Richie to work his magic in England's second innings, taking six wickets. England were all out for 201 and we won by 54. Richie grabbed hold of me at the end of the game and said I was never to come to another match on tour without hanging the old Thebby Tech tie with due ceremony. It was lucky, he said.

Mind you, Richie and I were due some good luck. Aside from the racehorses, we had some shocking luck — or at least I did — right at the start of my career, when we were on tour in New Zealand in 1957. During our final game in Auckland, Richie was batting at practice and I was to be the next batsman in the nets. They called 'last two' (meaning Richie would receive two more deliveries), and I bent down to grab my bat just as Richie decided to finish his net with a flourish against our left-arm spinner Lindsay Kline. He smashed the ball straight to where I was getting ready to have a hit, Lindsay yelled 'look out' and I lifted my head just in time to see the ball about two feet in front of my right eye. The result was four facial fractures, several days in hospital and for Peter Burge the new experience of wicketkeeping in a first-class match. Richie was devastated and came to see me in hospital each night after the day's play. And when I got home he wrote me a lovely letter in which he promised never to bat in the nets again when I was in the vicinity.

Richie was a great captain and a fine man. I had a mate, John 'Squizzy' Taylor, who was a budding leg-spinner, and early on — I must have been about 20 — I took him to the Adelaide Oval on the morning of a Shield match against NSW and asked Richie if he could have a look at him. It must have been not much more than 15 minutes before the game, but Richie came out to the nets and watched Squizzy for about ten minutes. Then he spoke with him and generally made him feel very important and much more enlightened about the mysteries of leg-spin. Richie was that sort of bloke.

I consider myself very lucky to have known him.

NARI CONTRACTOR

Australia played Test matches in India on two tours during Richie's career, in 1956–57 and 1959–60. One man who appeared in both these series was Nari Contractor, who

scored 108 in the third Test at Bombay (now Mumbai) in
the first week of 1960 and then went on to captain his
country in 12 Tests. The two men who dismissed Nari most
often (six times) in Tests were the West Indies' Wes Hall
and ... Richie Benaud.

WHEN one talks about the great all-rounders in the game, Richie
Benaud can't be too far down the list headed by Sir Garfield Sobers.

I am not going by statistics. Mere figures don't do justice to
Richie's batting, bowling, quicksilver fielding, astute captaincy and
overall flair. I saw all these qualities from the field of play over three
Test matches in the 1959-60 season at home.

However, the first time I saw Richie play was on the Ian
Johnson-led Australia tour of India in 1956–57. They landed in the
subcontinent after their disappointing 1956 Ashes series — matches
in which Benaud did not exactly set the Thames on fire with his
leg-spin bowling.

I played in the last Test of the 1956–57 series, in Calcutta, and
while Richie took a number of wickets, there wasn't anything in his
performance to suggest that he would go on to become a *great* all-
rounder. I say this even though he trapped me leg before wicket for
22 in the first innings. I thought he bowled far too many loose balls
and some of our batsmen played rash shots. But we were aware that
Keith Miller, among others, felt he was a star in the making.

When Richie returned to India in 1959–60 as captain and
the side's premier all-rounder, he was an absolutely different cup
of tea. His accuracy had developed manifold, his faster one was
really quick. We had thought our leg-spinner, Subhash Gupte, was
uniquely accurate but Richie was now equally spot on. He was also
remarkably consistent for a wrist-spinner. Great bowler that he was,
Gupte could be brilliant one day and benevolent to the opposition
the very next.

Richie must have worked endlessly to perfect his art. This
labour, I am sure, was the reason he was now a completely different
bowler from the one I saw in 1956–57. He could bowl the ball that
he wanted to bowl in whatever situation he found himself in, and he
kept getting wickets. Of course, he was always a very good fielder
— we in India had all read about his stunning catch in the gully to
dismiss Colin Cowdrey at Lord's in 1956.

Many years later, I read about the advice Richie got from Bill O'Reilly, which I'm sure was pivotal to his future success. In 1953, on Richie's first tour to England, O'Reilly told him to concentrate on a 'fiercely spinning leg break'. O'Reilly added that it would take him four years to see the results. Was Richie's performance on the 1959–60 tour to India a result of that advice? It could well be, but let's not forget that he had to be good enough and dedicated enough to successfully implement O'Reilly's instruction.

I believe the same advice was passed on to Shane Warne when he approached Richie for some tips in the early 1990s. Of course, as Richie was glad to report, Warne took only two years to reap the rewards.

In the first Test at Delhi in December 1959, after enjoying figures of 3–0 in the first innings, Richie emerged as our tormentor-in-chief in the second innings. My opening partner, Pankaj Roy, was on 99, when Richie noticed his discomfort against the left-arm spinner Lindsay Kline. He stationed himself at short-leg, where Pankaj was caught off the very next ball.

As much as he fostered team spirit in his own side, Richie was always willing to appreciate the efforts of the opposition. I remember the Australian team's applause near the pavilion after Jasu Patel and Polly Umrigar (4–27) bowled us to victory in the Kanpur Test. Jasu had followed up his 9–69 in the first innings with 5–55 in the second and Polly took 4–27 as we won against Australia for the first time. Richie and his teammates came to our dressing-room to congratulate us. There was that genuineness about it and no 'put-ons' just for the camera. 'There was not the slightest doubt within our team that we had been beaten by a better side and it was a matter now of organising ourselves for the next game,' he wrote later in his autobiography, and I know from having been there that he meant every word of that.

That was the first and last time we won a Test in that series. And while we may have beaten the Australians in Kanpur, it shouldn't be forgotten that they bowled us out cheaply on the first day. Richie started it all by getting the first two wickets of the innings — Polly Umrigar and myself before lunch. From 38 for no wicket, we slumped to 152 all out.

Richie was invariably very polite and endearing to the opposition after play. If you asked him a question, you could be assured of an honest view, which was a different response from that of other opposition captains we encountered. There was no issue-ducking where Richie was concerned.

We kept in touch after 1959–60 through New Year's cards and letters. I met him in person for the last time near the commentary box at the Wankhede Stadium in Mumbai during the India v Australia World Cup match in 1996. I loved his commentary and summaries. He was always precise in his observations and to the point, he never praised anyone without merit and he did not indulge in unwarranted criticism. He played with a straight bat. In his passing, Australian and world cricket lost an icon. And I lost a friend.

BOB SIMPSON

Bob Simpson was one of a number of young cricketers who followed Richie into the NSW and Australian teams of the 1950s. He would also succeed Richie as Test captain. He played 52 Tests between 1957 and 1968, and then returned in 1977–78, at age 41, to lead Australia at home against India and on a West Indies tour after many of the country's best cricketers joined World Series Cricket. Bob coached the Australian team with much success from 1986 to 1996.

I WAS 17 years old when I first played Sheffield Shield cricket with Richie Benaud. It was NSW versus Queensland at the Gabba in November 1953. I'd played a couple of Shield games the previous season when the Test players were away, but this was my 'debut' with the full-strength team. It was also my first experience of Keith Miller as NSW captain.

Queensland won the toss and batted on what was a dry pitch. Ray Lindwall and Jack Clark, a right-arm fast-medium bowler from the Paddington club, opened the bowling. Then, after just five overs of pretty uneventful cricket, Keith suddenly brought Richie into the attack.

'But Nugget, the ball's still new,' said Richie.

'Don't worry about that, it'll soon be old,' Keith shot back. 'Just think about the field you want.'

The look on Richie's face betrayed the fact that he wasn't convinced, so Keith added, 'It's all right. It'll spin like a top for an hour. We've got a great chance to bowl 'em out.'

It took no time at all for Richie to prove that Keith had read the wicket exactly right, and soon my captain was walking over to me with the ball in his hand. 'Your turn to bowl, young Bobby,' he said.

Somewhat shocked, but delighted, I got through my first three overs. But then Keith walked over and enquired, 'Why am I yet to see your excellent wrong 'un?'

'I seem to have lost it for the time being,' I replied.

'In that case,' he said dismissively, 'you can piss off until you find it.'

So it was sadly back to first slip for me, from where I saw Richie take five wickets before lunch.

Richie was a good bowler in those days, but a fair way from the great leg-spinner he'd become. The turning point, I'm sure, came in South Africa in 1957–58. I can still picture him at the Wanderers Ground in Johannesburg on that tour, bowling in the nets for hours on end, trying to land his spinners on a handkerchief he'd positioned on a good length. Richie would bowl 10 or 12 deliveries and then a local schoolboy would duck into the net, gather up the balls and return them to him so he could aim at that handkerchief again.

For the rest of his career Richie was renowned for his accuracy. He turned himself into a magnificent bowler. His strength was his length, which was relentless. I imagine there are very few wrist-spinners in the history of Test cricket who have conceded fewer runs per over.

He was quicker than most leg-spinners, with a good arm ball and a good flipper, which sometimes made it hard for me at first slip because I liked to stand as close as possible to the batsman on the basis that it is better to drop a catch than for the ball to not carry. Occasionally, when a batsman slashed at his quicker one, the ball struck me hard in the chest and I had to grab the rebound. I remember catching Garry Sobers off Richie's bowling in this way during the second Test of the 1960–61 series.

Of course, Richie — as our captain and, with Alan Davidson, the leader of our bowling attack — was pivotal to the Australian team's success during the 'Benaud era', but he was not a one-man band. The team was full of famous names — Davo, Neil Harvey, Norm O'Neill, Colin McDonald, Jimmy Burke, Bill Lawry, Ian Meckiff, to name a few. Two of the unsung heroes, who both had big influences on Richie, were Ian Craig and Wally Grout.

Ian was our captain in South Africa. He'd been a controversial choice ahead of Harv and Richie, but he did a superb job. Ian was a very astute on-field skipper and a great public speaker; each of us felt very proud to be a member of a team led by him. He was very encouraging of all the players in our squad, as Richie would be after him. Both men genuinely cared about how the team was travelling, and nothing was too much trouble for them. A lot of people think the revival of the Australian team of the late 1950s came about under Richie, but that's not strictly true. Ian Craig was in charge when we stunned South Africa 3–0, and Richie then built on what his predecessor had started. They were both good and kind men, and great leaders.

The best wrap I can give for Wally Grout is to say that I can remember all the catches he dropped. There were very, very few. Wally was a masterful wicketkeeper, especially up to the stumps, and he had this amazing ability to make difficult catches look easy, which often masked his skill. When you watch the film of the crucial catch he took off Richie's bowling to dismiss Ted Dexter on the last day at Old Trafford in 1961 it looks pretty simple — until you take into account the fact that the pitch was turning, Richie was bowling around the wicket, it was his quicker one and it wasn't really pitched short enough for Dexter to cut. Wally gloved it with no fuss, threw it a few yards in the air and Dexter, the dangerman, was on his way. It could only have helped Richie's self-confidence — which was already strong — to have such a genius behind the stumps.

Wally gave enormous support to Ian and Richie as captain, and he was the same with me when I replaced Richie during the series against South Africa in Australia in 1963–64. The circumstances of my taking over as skipper were a little unusual in that we knew Richie was retiring at the end of the season but then he broke a finger in a grade game and had to miss the second Test. Initially,

I was appointed as a 'caretaker' captain but then Richie suggested that because he was giving it away it would be best if I stayed in charge, with him continuing as a senior player. I must admit that at first I wasn't sure this was going to work: one, because I thought I'd stress about whether I was giving him a fair go; and two, because it can be hard to back your own instincts when your former boss is right behind you. I thought it would be like a student taking over while the teacher sat in the front row. But Richie was brilliant, very helpful and always happy to share his knowledge without ever forcing it upon me. As a bowler-captain, he'd had the happy knack of neither over-bowling nor under-bowling himself; now, as a former captain, he always seemed to know the right time to offer an opinion. And he was as enthusiastic as ever.

Though he never said anything to me, I will always think that Richie played a part in my appointment as Australian captain. He was close to Sir Donald Bradman, who was hugely influential in those days, and he was also a man of firm opinions. In this regard, he was just like Keith Miller. If Richie had genuinely thought I wasn't up to the job, he would have said so.

Richie was also, beyond question, a man of courage. I saw that many times on the cricket field, and I saw it again after he retired, when he covered Australia's 1965 tour of the West Indies as a journalist. Moving from the field of play to the press box is not always easy — suddenly you are placed in a position where you have to pass judgment on former teammates. But Richie was always fair in his criticisms. I can't recall a time when a story written by him upset me or anyone in the Australian dressing-room.

In the Caribbean, he wrote some articles, supported by his own photographs, that questioned the legality of the bowling action of the West Indies' paceman Charlie Griffith. For Richie, reporting the facts as he saw them was a matter of principle, and I thought he showed plenty of guts in running with the story. I know it put him offside with the local fans and pressmen, and he was also criticised by some powerful people in West Indies cricket, including Sir Frank Worrell. But the game needed people of conviction like Richie to highlight that there was something happening on the field that needed fixing. Gradually from this point, the problem of throwing disappeared from international cricket, at least for a couple of generations.

On a personal level, I appreciated the fact that he never put me in a difficult situation by discussing the articles with me or tipping me off that they were going to appear. A comment from the Australian captain might have added to the story but he never sought it. We were, at the time, in the middle of a Test. Even at a stressful time like this, he was as considerate as ever.

SAGA OF THE BOOTS

Richie Benaud always took great pride in his shoes. Gucci was a favoured provider and from his days as a young man, whatever the brand, he always kept them polished to a military shine. Of course, this — and the fact he liked to place them so he could slip straight into them after he'd showered and changed at the end of a day's play — proved something of an invitation to irreverent teammates.

For years, Richie sought a confession from the miscreants who nailed his shoes to the floor at the end of a Test at the SCG back in the early 1960s. He challenged Frank Misson only a few years ago, to 'nail the blame' as he put it. Misson allowed only that he was an accomplice, and that blame might more justifiably be sheeted to a lanky Victorian of jovial disposition. As the stories were told after Richie's passing, Bill Lawry finally owned up:

> We've heard a lot about how Richie thought before he spoke … he did everything in slow motion. Well, that's wonderful when he's broadcasting or writing for the papers, but not so wonderful when you're at the end of the game waiting for the bus and Richie would always be last.
>
> I must admit at the time I was making a few runs — it was not the sort of thing you'd do if you were out of form — but there was some building going on at the SCG, so I picked up a hammer and two three-inch nails while Richie was having his shower and I nailed his shoes to the floor.
>
> All my teammates, courageous as they were, ran off. And Richie comes out, puts on his underpants … his shirt, his tie and everything … checks the Brylcreem and the lips … has a bit of a walk around [in his socks]. Finally, he's dressed and he puts his feet into his shoes … and he can't move.
>
> And he turns around and says, 'Bloody Frank Misson!'

It was not the only time Richie's shoes became the target when teammates were getting mischievous, and practical jokers were looking for a laugh. Alan Davidson recounts a tale from the 1961 Ashes tour, when Richie was being Richie:

Richie had seen a picture of Bradman at the toss at Lord's in 1948, and Bradman was not in cricket boots, but wore a pair of fancy brogues. It so impressed Richie he took himself off to Simpsons of Piccadilly and paid 40 pounds, huge money in those days, for a pair of brogues, just so that he could wear them at the toss as Bradman had done. Richie decided to give them their first hit-out at Lord's, as I remember it, in a match against the MCC. They sat on the dressing-room floor as Richie went through his painstaking dress routine, ready to be slipped into ...

Now, here's where another great mystery has grown surrounding Richie's shoes. Davo recalls them getting the nail-to-the-floor treatment, too, although his fingered villains, Lawry and Misson, will own up to one nailing scandal, and one only, and that was in Sydney. But as Davo tells it, whatever happened to those fancy brogues triggered remorse in Richie's teammates ... once the laughter had ceased, of course. He continues:

Richie said nothing. Just put on his cricket boots and went out to toss. The shoes were wrecked, so we raided the team fund to buy him a new pair. He was undoubtedly furious, but he never let on. It was an age when we always knew when fun was fun and when respect within your team, and for the opposition, was genuine and seen to be genuine.

– 4 –

IN THE PRESS BOX

'Few former Test players have been so generous about the
abilities and attitudes of the next generation of players.'

— Christopher Martin-Jenkins

JOHN WOODCOCK

John Woodcock first toured Australia as a BBC cameraman with Freddie Brown's 1950–51 MCC team. He graduated to cricket correspondent for *The Times* in 1954 and retained this position until 1988. He was editor of *Wisden* for six years, and is renowned as a brilliant and principled writer, and one of cricket's true gentlemen. Dubbed the 'Sage of Longparish', in his 90th year he penned these recollections of Richie.

I HAVE any number of friends who are proud to boast, and never miss a chance of doing so, that they batted in partnership with Richie or held a catch off his bowling. That it was in a village match is of no significance. What matters is that somewhere there is, or was, a scorecard on which appears the magic words: c Muggins b Benaud. I know a little of the feeling, having stumped someone once off the equally great Bill O'Reilly during the England tour of Australia in 1950–51, when things were much less rushed than they are today, and time was made for the press to play the occasional cricket match.

I used to raise a side each year to play against Longparish, the Hampshire village 65 miles south-west of London where I was born and still live, and no one entered into the spirit of the occasion more readily than Richie. Among other Australians who came and played, when they were teaching, coaching or holidaying in England, were John Inverarity, Ian McLachlan, Ian Redpath and Paul Sheahan. Longparish were a good enough side to win, from a field of more than 500 villages, the national village knockout competition, the final being played at Lord's.

So the cricket, played on a lovely ground with a thatched pavilion, was of a decent standard. 'Invers' never fails, whenever I see him, to ask after 'that blacksmith [not that he was one] who kept hitting me out of the ground'. His analysis that day was 9–1–82–1, prompting the headline in the local paper: 'Aussie Star Humbled!' On another occasion, when Graeme Pollock was in England playing for a World XI, Richie joined him at the wicket when we were 8 for 3. It was probably the only time they played on the same side, and they added 149.

Richie and 'Daphers' did some of their courting in Longparish, as Ian and Christine Redpath did, and very welcome they were, too! The village is on the banks of the River Test, the world's most famous trout stream, and Richie and Redders both loved fishing, wading up the river side by side and casting a dry fly like a pair of spin bowlers in action. Anything they caught would be smoked by Daph, to be had for supper with a glass or three of something white and still.

Oh! The great days, in the distance enchanted …

PHIL WILKINS

Phil Wilkins became chief cricket writer at *The Sydney Morning Herald* in 1967, succeeding the legendary Tom Goodman. He was cricket correspondent for *The Australian* for 11 years and finished his career with a return stint of 16 years as the *Herald*'s chief cricket writer. He also served as Australian correspondent for *Wisden Cricketers' Almanack*, Agence France-Presse and London's *Daily Telegraph*. At heart, he has always been a country boy who never lost the heroes of his youth.

GONE, and never forgotten … the man in the mind's eye, the face, the voice, the stride, the figure in coat and tie. From 60 years past he emerges, with Keith Miller and Lindy, Griz Grout and Slasher Mackay, Ninna Harvey and the Little Fave, Johnny Martin … mirages of youth and the game of decades beyond, disappearing, seen from the boundary, of feats and heroism past, memories gleaming like brass buttons on a trench coat, flashes of light in encroaching mists, men of our youth, men who made our lives, men who delighted us, crushed us, inspired us.

From the radio and the crackling voices of Alan McGilvray, Vic Richardson and Arthur Gilligan, calling the nation from England and South Africa, the words of Bill O'Reilly and Jack Fingleton, relating stories, painting the picture, day into night.

From Tasmania and the dying tin mine to the Hereford beef country and gold reef never found in the New England ranges, to the mining sands and dairying fields of the far north coast, we listened to them and their accounts of play. Richie seemed always to be there, the all-rounder not so supreme, at least early on in the eyes of the national selectors.

They were wrong and we, the army of Benaud men and women, knew they were wrong. We were proved correct, watching and listening to the feats of the tall all-rounder from the Cumberland club, son of Lou, the middle-order batsman and bold striker, artful leg-break bowler, sometimes quick through the air, as Tiger fiercely advocated, sometimes over the eyes, the splendid gully fieldsman. And when he was struck in the face that day, the Benaud horde recoiled with him, bled with him.

And as Richie advanced, climbing the first-class ladder, so did the boy from the scrub move into grade cricket, every game fashioned on the hero, from when Lismore Norths played Mallanganee in a trial with Jack McLean and Len Henley, to calamity at the hand of John McMahon at Riverview Park. And the patriots realised Richie was part of a long-term plan for Australia to regain its standing, its glory, when they sent him to South Africa in 1957–58, Benaud and the broad-shouldered bull of an all-rounder from the Lisarow bush on the Central Coast, Alan Davidson. And the horde was proved right.

Ian Craig's Australians won 3–0. And what a team South Africa had: the batting might of 'Jackie' McGlew, Trevor Goddard, Russell Endean and Johnny Waite, and the attack of the fast-bowling fiends, Neil Adcock and Peter Heine, and the spin of Hugh Tayfield. Then we knew we had a team.

Later that summer, in the Broadway foyer of *The Sydney Morning Herald*, there he was, quiet, distinguished, lost in another world, not in creams but dressed for work, as police roundsman for *The Sun* afternoon newspaper, always impeccable, never dressed casually, never, as of more recent eras of the journalistic class, resembling something the cat dragged in. He entered the lift and alighted on the editorial fifth floor and the cadet followed him out and watched him walk away, and remembered he had forgotten to breathe.

When the majestic Peter May led his England team to Australia for the summer of 1958–59, Richie Benaud was Test captain. Australia won the Ashes back, 4–0. They had been conceded twice by Ian Johnson's teams through the bleak '50s, a period darkened by the storm clouds of Frank 'Typhoon' Tyson and Brian Statham and the mystique of spinners Jim Laker and Tony Lock.

In 1960–61, the dawning broke through into full sunlight. The West Indies replaced wicketkeeper Gerry Alexander as captain with the young, vibrant Barbadian, Frank Worrell, and in a glorious conspiracy, Worrell and Benaud brought the game shining into every cricket household in Australia. As the first Test entered its last day at the Gabba, and with cheerful optimism the Australians confronted the formality of a 233-run chase in just over five hours, so the tide turned on Newcastle Harbour.

Belief began turning to trepidation, nerve ends were disintegrating and tremors quaked across the nation. With every wicket that fell, the crowd grew around the little transistor radio outside the cabin on the Stockton ferry. With every passing over, the passengers inside the cabin emerged, until every person on board was there, listening, tilting the vessel precariously, a difficult thing to do on a flat-bottomed punt. Even the skipper was involved, one eye on the waterway, one ear against his cabin windshield.

'Turn it up! Turn it up!'

Even then, with the second-last ball of the final over, when Joey Solomon's throw struck the wicket from side on, nobody really knew, at the Gabba or on Newcastle Harbour, who had won the game and who had lost it. Even the ABC broadcasters were momentarily flummoxed. Then the penny dropped: a tie! The first tied Test!

But when, weeks later, the final ball was delivered in Melbourne for Australia's two-wicket victory and 2–1 Test series success, many in the sunburnt country would gladly have settled for a series-levelling draw by the West Indies, if not another tie. No, not the Gabba again. That was too damaging to the nation's nerves, whatever we thought later and whatever the rest of the world thought of the game's eternal inspiration.

It's the little things that count, that make the suit fit the man, the little things you remember. The Nawab of Pataudi led the Indians to Australia in 1967–68. It was Christmas Day and Adelaide's churches were doing a brisk business and the restaurants were closed tight, every one of them.

By midday, the Indians were starving. We were all booked into the 'Little Travelodge', players and journalists alike, and no food was available, not by customary means, anyway. Richie and Daphne and the journalist's wife, Jeanette, stormed the manager's office, obtained the key to the kitchen and raided the larder. An hour or so later, the Indians were gorging on the best food in the house.

In 1972, returning to England as cricket correspondent for the *Herald* for Ian Chappell's campaign to regain the Ashes, the Ashes lost in Australia in 1970–71 to the battle-scarred warrior, Ray Illingworth, it was a pleasurable privilege to share the John Fairfax car with Richie and Daphne, experiencing the once fabulous travelogue of counties between the five Tests, sometimes necessitating long overnight journeys on the motorways. Richie would occasionally sit in the back seat, assembling his thoughts and dictating newspaper copy to Fleet Street.

On those trips, when he was driver, generally on isolated back-road byways, he had the curious practice of beeping the car horn with not a car in sight. It was only after a number of experiences of this perplexing nature that it dawned on the co-driver: Richie was warning the sparrows and other birds feeding on the roadway of the car's approach. Dear old bird-lover Benaud.

It was on one such car trip that the co-driver began having an inkling of what might come. In the privacy of the car, Richie sometimes mused out loud, almost daydreaming, not seeking confirmation from a whippersnapper, merely bouncing ideas around in his head.

Somewhere after Dennis Lillee's early-tour side strain at the Lord's nets, translated as a back-joint injury, and before Bob Massie's injury in his second over of the MCC game at Lord's, leaving David

Colley heroically shouldering the pace attack, Richie said before the Old Trafford first Test: 'We'll be all right, I think.' And he lapsed into silence.

It became so prolonged that the co-driver eventually prompted: 'What's all right, Rich?'

'Lillee's bowling better now. If he's fit, we'll be okay.' Silence, and then: 'What do they call him — FOT?'

'Flipping Old Tart.'

'Him and Massie, they're a good pair.'

'Fergie — as in Massey Ferguson, the earthmoving company, tractors and so on.'

Long silence. The co-driver tossed a coin in the pool: 'What do you think of those Bankstown blokes, Thomson and Pascoe?'

'They're no value here. They're back in Australia.'

'True. But they're both quick — and they're definitely mad, mad as meat axes, actually.'

'Good. It helps.'

Bob Massie took no part in the first Test. He'd torn abdominal muscles and watched his Western Australian teammate rattle through England's batsmen in the second innings at Old Trafford, finishing with 6–66 from 30 overs, and eight wickets for the match.

But Australia's batsmen could not handle the cold, greasy Manchester conditions against John Snow, Geoff Arnold and Tony Greig, and went down by 89 runs.

Massie was fit for the second Test at Lord's, and it was Massie who went mad.

In a strange, still befogged Test, the splendid Ross Edwards made his Test debut, Greg Chappell hit a hundred and Massie took 16 wickets in the game.

Lillee bowled just as well as at Old Trafford and claimed the other four wickets. Australia won by eight wickets to level the series, and drew the third Test at Trent Bridge. Then came Headingley, Leeds, and the Australians were greeted with a strangely mottled pitch. No one had seen its like before. A grass disease called fusarium had riddled the strip.

Derek Underwood ran amok, captured ten wickets and Australia lost by nine wickets. Justice was done at the Oval, Kennington, when DK Lillee satisfied all that Australia had bred another champion, capturing five wickets in each innings. Both Chappell brothers, Ian and Greg, struck first-innings hundreds and Australia thundered home by five wickets to draw the series, two-all.

And all the way through the tour Richie's thought in the car kept ringing like a bell: 'I think we'll be all right.' Over the next four years, truer words were never spoken.

Then television took him away. Locked in the commentary room behind the arm, rarely sighted in the press box, he became a near-ghostly figure, passing in the corridor with a cheerful smile, always brisk, always busy, striding somewhere else.

And now he has gone. Will we remember him? Always. Can we forget him? Never.

NORMAN TASKER

Norman Tasker started writing on cricket when Richie Benaud was captain of Australia, replaced him as *The Sun*'s cricket correspondent, and saw close-hand how he operated in press boxes around the world.

RICHIE BENAUD always looked upon the time he teamed up with Noel Bailey as one of the luckiest breaks of his life. Richie graduated to the role of Australian cricket captain in the time he worked with Bailey as a crime reporter on the Sydney afternoon paper *The Sun*. Bailey was old school, a hard-nosed reporter with a keen news sense and the ability to grab a phone and quickly dictate a story with clarity, straight off the top. Richie learned the lessons and always considered himself a journalist first, a commentator second. It was his choice to learn the newspaper business from the bottom up.

My career in journalism began at Frank Packer's *Daily Telegraph* in 1959, at 16 years of age and straight out of school. One of my first jobs as a copyboy was to monitor the police radio in the police rounds room, and I was listening in when Kevin John Simmonds and Leslie Alan Newcombe made their escape from Long Bay gaol. They killed a prison guard and the manhunt that followed was one of the biggest Sydney had seen.

My shift was ending in the early hours of the morning and the senior reporters invited me along for the ride as word got out that the escapees had been sighted in the northern suburb of Frenchs Forest. The chase was on. That's where I first saw Richie Benaud. He was standing in for Noel Bailey, was Australian captain at the time, and he cut a dapper figure among the hard-bitten reporters and coppers on the job.

I remember thinking even then how evident was his work ethic, despite the fact that this was a time before the high-end professionalisation of sport, when champions still needed ordinary jobs and real work was something everybody did. Richie was just one of the boys, interviewing policemen, notebook in hand, filing his words, keeping the early editions of the paper well fed.

The following year I was transferred to sport and my first serious cricket job was to cover a Sheffield Shield match between NSW and Queensland at the SCG. Frank Worrell's 1960–61 West Indians were playing South Australia in Adelaide, as they worked their way around the country towards Brisbane and the first Test, and the *Telegraph*'s lead cricket writer, Phil Tresidder, was reporting on that match. NSW batted first. Brian Booth scored 51, Ian Craig 146. At stumps Neil Harvey was 210 not out and NSW were 2–424. A good day's play, I thought, and I wrote with enthusiasm. I thought I had done okay, commanding the back page of the paper.

Back at the office the sports editor bellowed at me: 'Do you have quotes from the captain?'

'Well, er, no,' I responded.

Talking to the captain of Australia was not something a teenage novice did easily. 'Well, get some,' he ordered.

So I had to ring Richie at home, with great trepidation. As I announced myself, 'umming' and 'ahhing' and wondering what to say, Richie picked up on my floundering nervousness.

'Perhaps,' he said, 'you could ask me this.' He then suggested a question to ask him. 'If you asked me that,' he went on, 'I would answer like this.' He then gave me an answer. The questions were no Dorothy Dixers either. That went on for four or five questions until I relaxed. I included them in my story and everybody thought

I was very clever and had done a fine job. I wrote about cricket on and off for the next 55 years, and I never forgot that initial kindness.

By the time of the next West Indies tour of Australia, in 1968–69, I had joined *The Sun*, principally as their rugby writer. Richie was specialising as *The Sun*'s cricket correspondent. The newspaper world had gone through some serious upheaval the previous year, with a major journalists' strike and a settlement that redrew the grading system under which journalists were employed. Richie, looking for new opportunities anyway, objected to the new rules. He redefined his role at *The Sun* to write specialist columns and I was conscripted into the day-to-day role of cricket correspondent. Through the Tests of that summer Richie would ring me each morning to discuss how we would attack the first edition. He would often volunteer to write about the toss. It never ceased to fascinate me how much knowledge he could put into discussing the toss of a coin and just what it would all mean to the outcome of the game.

Knowledge was one thing, but the real success that Richie achieved through those early years in the media came through his work ethic. Whether he was rattling away on an ancient typewriter or running to a microphone somewhere, he never seemed to stop. I remember a Test match in New Zealand in 1974, when he was doing radio work that required a connection in the big open stand at the Basin Reserve. It was bitterly cold as an icy wind blew in off Cook Strait. Richie got himself a sheepskin coat that looked like something Shackleton might have worn in Antarctica and cut a lonely, forlorn figure at the front of the stand as the Chappell brothers went about hitting 646 runs between them.

I can remember him too at the WACA Ground in Perth, when his schedule required press filing on one side of the field and radio reports on the other, and he seemed to be lapping the field every ten minutes as he worked his way through the day.

By the 1990s, I had started a cricket magazine called *Inside Edge*. I called Richie and asked if he would write a column each month. He agreed, with the proviso that his material was carefully subedited and that we were especially careful that there should be no split infinitives in his material. Such was his concern for the English language. He never missed a month and became a centrepiece of the magazine for a decade or more.

Richie finished up a legendary commentator and a celebrity with an international presence, but he always saw himself as a working journo and everything he achieved was achieved through hard work, relentless preparation and a determined eye for detail. He was, when all is said and done, the ultimate professional.

MIKE COWARD

Mike Coward is an internationally renowned cricket writer, author, commentator and filmmaker. He was chief cricket correspondent at the Adelaide *Advertiser* and *The Sydney Morning Herald*, cricket columnist with *The Australian*, and has contributed to a range of international publications. He has also applied himself to the continuing benefit of the Bradman Museum and International Cricket Hall of Fame, and to the leading cricket charities, the Primary Club and the LBW Trust.

AS a trenchant 14-year-old critic I blamed Richie Benaud for not interceding on my hero Les Favell's behalf when the selectors chose to leave Les out of the Australian team for the 1961 tour of England. In those days, and like so many South Australian teenage boys, I only had eyes for Favell, who played the glorious game in the manner Sir Donald Bradman demanded at the start of what was destined to become the first series for the Frank Worrell Trophy … the unforgettable summer of 1960–61.

Why should Favell be deprived of the opportunity to realise his dream of playing in England? After all, he had been good enough to tour the West Indies under Ian Johnson in 1955, South Africa with Ian Craig's party in 1957–58, and Pakistan and India with Benaud in 1959–60.

The fact Favelli, as his peers called him, failed in each innings of the fourth Test at the Adelaide Oval at the very moment he could not afford to fail did not mollify me. From my position behind the pickets on the eastern boundary, he could do no wrong even when he fell for four and one — hooking and cutting to the very end of his 19-Test career. He was in a class of his own.

Twelve years later, in the front-row corner of the old press box at Lord's during the second Ashes Test, I was battling unforgiving deadlines as a reporter for Australian Associated Press when Benaud suddenly appeared at my side. We were barely on nodding terms at this point in my career in sports journalism, yet such was his capacity to care and mentor that he wanted to make sure I was managing the pressure as swing bowler Bob Massie decimated the flummoxed England batsmen. With characteristic quietness, he offered a hand if it was needed.

I have never forgotten the generosity of this gesture and, of course, in an instant I emphatically absolved him of any guilt in the axing of Favell. As summers passed and I became entrenched as a cricket writer and commentator, I had the great fortune to work with both Benaud and Favell and to learn of their great respect for each other. Both were amused when I somewhat self-consciously recounted my boyhood railings and frustrations.

In 1972 I did not dare to dream my career would enable me to associate with Benaud and so many luminaries of the cricket community. A voracious consumer of all media but with an abiding love of newspapers, Benaud quietly monitored the writing of aspiring and emerging cricket scribes and, at times, gently made criticisms and suggestions. He was generous with his time and always offered encouragement and perspective.

Later, as a senior member of the cricket writing fraternity, I had the good fortune to conduct long interviews with Richie for ABC-TV's *Cricket History Series* and for the precious archive at the Bradman Museum and International Cricket Hall of Fame at Bowral, which he served as patron. A stickler for accuracy, he was as renowned for the thoroughness of his research as he was for his precision in recalling times, people, places and events. He was considered in his opinions and utterances; sage-like as the doyen of the international cricket commentariat.

Always self-contained and self-protective, Richie possessed a delightful if restrained sense of humour often evident when he was in conversation before an audience with whom he could interact.

Whether he was doing a mate a favour at a cricket or golf club dinner or making his annual guest appearance at the chairman's lunch at the Sydney Swans Football Club, invariably he shared a pearl of wisdom or a pithy observation with his myriad admirers.

I also had the pleasure of witnessing first-hand his philanthropic work with the Primary Club of Australia and the Bradman Museum and International Cricket Hall of Fame and had the privilege of introducing him when he delivered the third Sir Donald Bradman Oration at Government House, Hobart, in January 2005.

I will long value my association with Richie and be forever thankful for his spontaneous and gracious offer of help when Bob Massie so famously ran amok at Lord's in June 1972.

MAX WOOLDRIDGE

Max Wooldridge is a freelance journalist and author. His stories, mainly about travel and music, have appeared in many of Britain's leading newspapers and magazines. His memories of Richie go back to his early childhood.

WHEN you're a child you are too obsessed with playing with wheeled toys or if Mum is making mashed potato for dinner to realise you're in the presence of greatness.

Richie was a close friend of my father, Ian Wooldridge, the late, decorated British sportswriter who died in 2007. In a touch of gentle sledging that still makes me smile, they addressed each other by their surnames, 'Benaud' and 'Wooldridge', throughout their 45-year friendship.

Of course, as a kid I didn't see Richie like the majority of people did, as 'Richie Benaud, the Australian cricket legend'. He was just 'my dad's friend, Richie', a welcoming and amusing visitor to the family home in west London. He and Dad would chuckle over glasses of wine, their witty banter imbued with pearls of wisdom.

An early childhood recollection is a personal tutorial Richie gave me in the art of leg-breaks and googlies, using an orange bowled across our lounge-room floor. I never kept the piece of fruit. Sadly, I probably consumed it soon after my masterclass.

It was a memorable encounter, but it wasn't until my teens, when I started to grow up and learn more about cricket, that I became aware that Richie was such an unwavering icon of sport. Much later, when I started to make my living as a travel writer, I was lucky enough to fly to Australia on several assignments: daring rodeo school, dusty cattle drives, even crazy outback pub crawls by helicopter. It was on these trips that I learnt of the tremendous affection with which Richie was held in Australian hearts.

If you're a Brit travelling around Oz, the sport of cricket inevitably comes up and naturally whoever currently holds the Ashes will usually raise the subject. A few times, probably after too many bottles of Coopers Pale Ale, I mentioned that Richie was a longstanding family friend and one of my father's great mates.

The reaction was always the same. The cynical, third-generation squints of drinkers bored with dodgy politicians and overconfident reality TV stars suddenly became bug-eyed stares. Their hearts warmed at the mention of a true hero and I was afforded new status by association, instant elevation from being just another soft Pommy bastard to a good bloke.

This is pretty much the highest accolade any British male can hope for down-under. Warm embraces and back slaps were accompanied by 'Good on ya, mate' and 'Get this guy a beer!'

I worked with Richie only once. In 2012, I interviewed him for a short documentary about the 1960 Tied Test for the BBC World Service's *Sporting Witness*. The series producer was a big cricket fan and was aware my father and Richie were close.

As I knew he would be, Richie was marvellous to work with. One morning, the producer and I sat down and devised a long list of carefully thought-out questions. We needn't have bothered. After the opening question, Richie launched a beautiful delivery: a continuous, fascinating recollection from more than half a century earlier.

As he spoke, we began to tick off our questions one by one until there were none left. Richie answered every question without any interference. The producer and I swapped glances that said, 'Wow, what an utter pro.'

I did nothing that day except turn up. Richie did everything. I had witnessed another personal masterclass from Richie, this time as a broadcaster.

GEOFF ROACH

For many years variously editor and sports editor of Adelaide's newspapers — *The News, Sunday Mail* and *The Advertiser* — Geoff Roach was also a long-time sports columnist with a passion for golf. Richie and Daphne were involved with the international golf circuit for many years through their work with the head of the International Management Group (IMG), Mark McCormack, so their paths crossed often. Geoff looks back on some epic encounters.

OKAY, I admit it. As far as can be verified, I am the only imbecile ever to have sacked Richie Benaud. From anything. Yet if, because this is supposed to be a chronicle of justifiable praise for the life and times of a truly splendid man, you are now anticipating some sort of fulsome apology for so doing, forget it! The truth is I will always regard that action, and its outcome, as one of the best, most fortunate decisions of my life.

Perhaps, though, it might help allay your gathering contempt if I *explain* the circumstances — and consequences — that provoked such a reckless deed.

It so happened that back in the mid-1970s Rupert Murdoch made one of his rare mistakes by appointing me editor of *The Sunday Mail*, a position I neither sought nor wanted but was persuaded to accept for fear of otherwise getting the flick. No sooner had I done so, my worst fear was confirmed.

Apart from a few seasoned operators and contributors, the paper — then an unholy joint venture of *The News* and *The Advertiser* devoted to gleaning advertising revenue from the burgeoning real-estate and furniture entities — was what might charitably be called sparsely staffed and with a budget that gave no possibility of enhancement in that area.

What transpired was a review of all existing arrangements, one which revealed 'DE Benaud and Associates' was in weekly receipt of a D-grade journo's salary as part of a News group contract for Richie's column.

Now have no doubt that like most of my generation, I revered Richie and all he represented and wrote. But as a callow editor bereft of any youthful troops, I couldn't help but consider the output which might eventuate from hiring an enthusiastic D-grade recruit. Hence the fateful decision was made to 'let go' the Benaud column, at least for the time being. Trouble was I then had to communicate this to my idol, a deed eventually done by phone after an afternoon's consumption of suitably bracing liquid. To my utmost relief, the news was taken with equanimity.

However, it was then suggested, I might not perhaps be fully aware of the scope and opportunities encompassed in the current arrangement — a situation that might be remedied if we were to meet for dinner when he and Daphne were in Adelaide a week hence.

The initial contact point was a motel on Hindley Street, which at that time hosted most of the city's visiting celebrity cavalcade. And there, lying impressively bronzed and resplendent among a sizeable crowd on the pool deck, was the great man himself.

Now at any other time, there is no doubt Richie would have been the focus of the gathering's scrutiny. But not this time. For just a few lounges away sat an exquisitely formed female clad in the most fetching of bikinis. One immediately identified her as Miss Britt Ekland, in town with her latest beau, Mr Rod Stewart.

Now it is entirely possible, of course, that Richie was already well aware of her presence and would not have been averse to a meeting with her. But sensing a rare and stupendous opportunity, I asked if he would consent to a photo with the Swedish bombshell. Permission was swiftly granted, a photographer summoned, and the picture — of Richie watching appreciatively as Britt strolled by — made a huge hit on the front page of the following Sunday's *Mail*.

Suffice to say that when dinner followed, a chord was struck, one based chiefly around joint passions for journalism, golf, cricket, consumption of Yalumba's Pewsey Vale wine, horse racing and Daphne's ethereal loveliness.

As a result, the Benaud arrangement was not only restored forthwith but a friendship evolved that would not merely enrich my life for the next 30-plus years but influence many of the decisions I later had to make.

Golf was very much the fulcrum around which we revolved, both as participants and correspondents at the great tournaments around the world. Richie's ardour for the game knew no bounds. During Adelaide Test matches, I would pick him up at 5.15am and we would hit off in the dark at Royal Adelaide or Kooyonga. We would be back at the Hilton for breakfast by 8.30.

On one occasion we were joined by the redoubtable News Corp golf writer Tom Ramsey, who was the instigator and organiser of many of our excursions. As we walked from the 18th tee, Richie suddenly let out a cry and stood frozen with one leg in the air as a large black snake slithered at speed past him.

He remained thus as we continued on, until Ramsey looked back and called, 'Come on, Richie, keep up. The snake was more frightened than you.'

The Benaud head was raised, the look produced and the answer firmly given: 'No it wasn't, Tom.'

At incomparable Royal County Down in Northern Ireland for the first time, Richie accepted a traditional Ramsey bet (con) that he could not break 100 from the back markers and without a caddie. On the blind fifth tee, Tom had the honour and drove in one direction. I, following, drove in the opposite.

'How droll, gentlemen,' Richie responded.

Then, after a moment's pause, he correctly followed my lead. Asked how he came to that decision, he explained that as Tom got his supply of golf balls free but I hated to lose one, it was a logical conclusion. Sadly, it didn't help. Much to his dismay, his 100th shot came on the 17th hole.

In England, our favoured venue was stately Woburn Golf Club, to which we travelled — on the rare occasions it actually started — in Richie's navy Jaguar that was the UK equivalent of the infamous Sunbeam Alpine he drove in Sydney. On one such occasion, I somehow managed to go six up after six holes and smugly suggested we adjourn to the clubhouse for a glass of wine.

Instead, the lip pushed forward, the glare was produced and Richie played the next 12 holes in one over par to win on the 18th. I was never in the rooms after a Test match, but I doubt that Richie was ever more visibly jubilant after victory than on that day.

'Perhaps you might like to have that wine now,' he declared.

Fine food, wine and company were Benaud constants. I was never more privileged than one year at Wimbledon when Rich and Daphne hosted luncheons in the Nine Network marquee. My fellow table guests included luminaries such as James Hunt and his ever-present dog, Imran Khan and an English beauty, Tim Rice and Elaine Paige.

It was a sublime occasion until the notoriously irascible Nine boss Sam Chisholm walked past, glared and loudly demanded to know: 'Why are we feeding one of Rupert's men, Richie? Can't he afford a sandwich?'

'Don't worry about it, Sam,' Richie instantly replied. 'It's part of our charity programme and fully tax-deductible.'

What turned out to be our last meal together took place not far from where we had enjoyed our first. This time, we were at Adelaide's Georges restaurant as guests of Yalumba's Rob and Annabel Hill Smith, who had assembled an international group of friends.

The restaurant had in fact been booked out for a 40th birthday party, but room had been found for us and we were seated in a discreet outer area.

Even so, we were spotted by a fellow with whom I was vaguely familiar. He came over and asked if it would be possible to have a very brief word with Richie. Consent was given, the exchange took place, Richie smiled, nodded a couple of times and the chap departed.

A moment later, this same fellow could be heard on a microphone, delivering a paean of praise to the birthday boy and telling his audience how he had agonised over the choice of a suitable present for him.

'Then it struck me,' he said. 'David loves his cricket. So I got in touch with Richie Benaud and he readily consented to come here tonight to mark the occasion.'

The elation which followed as Richie appeared and said a few suitable words would have sent the Richter scale soaring. It was followed by David proposing to his girlfriend and ordering French champagne to flow for the remainder of the night.

'I think that went reasonably well,' said Richie when he returned to our table.

A typically understated appraisal, I am thinking now, of his own magnificent life.

DAVID NORRIE

David Norrie became the rugby correspondent for the *News of the World* in London in 1979 and the cricket correspondent seven years later. When he left the newspaper in 2007, the UK Sports Journalists' Association paid tribute: 'Norrie has always been a prolific writer, ghosting a library's-worth of sports books, most recently the official biography of Darren Gough, as well as working with commentary legends Richie Benaud and Murray Walker, former England rugby captains Will Carling and Roger Uttley, and with cricket skipper Michael Atherton.'

WHAT a pleasure and a privilege it was to enjoy Richie's friendship for nearly 30 years; had it been just 30 days, it would still have been a pleasure and a privilege. I can't help wishing we could sit down at Langan's in Piccadilly for lunch just one more time.

I was a brash, opinionated upstart of 32 with an extremely limited knowledge of cricket when I was given the ultimate journalistic colleague in 1986. When I took over as cricket correspondent of the *News of the World*, Richie had already been the paper's cricket columnist for over a quarter of a century.

What with the phone hacking, Old Bailey court cases, editors on trial (and one going to prison) and the *News of the World*'s closure in 2011, there have been times recently when I've wondered whether it

'How are you feeling?' Prior to Australia's tour of England in 1961, Richie spent a few days in hospital after having his tonsils removed.

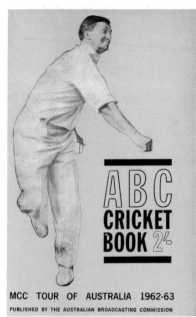

The captains feature on the covers of these two season guides published for the 1962–63 Ashes summer. Richie appears on both, and he is joined by England's Ted Dexter on the front of the *Mirror* publication.

Below: Richie, bowled by Garry Sobers at Bridgetown, fourth Test, 1955.

Right: Sobers, caught Simpson bowled Benaud, at the MCG, second Test, 1960–61.

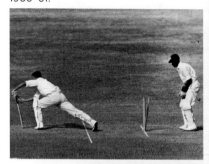

Richie and Daphne raise a glass to Sir Garry, the second man (after Richie) to complete the 2,000 runs/200 wickets double in Test cricket.

Richie with Sir Donald Bradman (above) at the Gabba during the Tied Test, and two months later with Frank Worrell and the Frank Worrell Trophy (below) at the MCG after Australia won a thrilling fifth Test by two wickets, to clinch the series.

Four images from the
fourth Test of 1961 at Old
Trafford, Richie's greatest
day in Ashes cricket.
Opposite page: With the
Test slipping away, Richie
went round the wicket, a
move that quickly resulted
in the dismissal of Ted
Dexter, caught behind by
Wally Grout. **Above:** Peter
May is bowled around his
legs. **Right:** Richie, at slip,
catches Fred Trueman off
Bob Simpson.

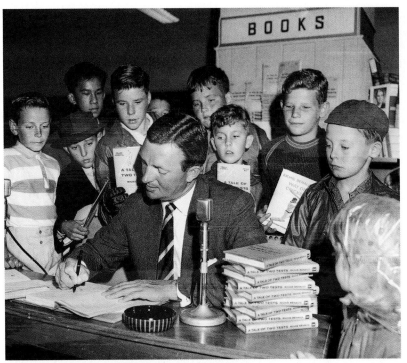

Richie at David Jones in Sydney during the 1962–63 summer, signing copies of his recently released book, *A Tale of Two Tests*.

Young South Australian batsman Ian Chappell is caught by Richie for 55 at the Adelaide Oval in February 1964. This was Richie's final Sheffield Shield match.

The captain stands back as Neil Harvey and Alan Davidson walk onto the SCG at the start of their final day in Test cricket, Sydney, 1962–63.

Richie's final ball in Test cricket, to South Africa's Eddie Barlow, fifth Test, SCG, 1963–64.

CENTRAL CUMBERLAND D.C.C. 1ST XI PREMIERS - 1964 / 65
Back Row: H. Goodwin,   D. Timmins,   R. Shepherd,   B. Woolmer,   J. Benaud,   D. Hartman,   J. Dwyer,   K.D. Walters.
Front Row: R. Flindt,   R. Aitken,   J. Aitken,   M. Godfrey,   D. Smith.
Absent: R. Benaud (Captain) - in West Indies,   J. Chadban,   J. Parkinson,   S. Teale,   W. Brisby,   D. Good,   W.E. Gould.

was all worth it. Richie answers that in a split second; he was still the paper's cricket columnist when it was closed.

I had departed four years earlier, shortly after 'my' award-winning sports story regarding Andrew 'Freddie' Flintoff's pedalo escapade in St Lucia. I did know that Fred had been out late and drinking after England's World Cup defeat by New Zealand, but those water antics were as much a mystery to me then as they are today. When I couldn't get a straight answer about the story's source, it was time to move on.

Richie was the first person I spoke to about leaving. Invariably, when there was a decision to be made, his counsel was my first port of call. Richie might have been known as the voice of cricket around the globe, but he was a great listener; no rushed judgments, just considered common sense and observations. Occasionally, when I eventually reached an obvious conclusion, he would smile with the look of slight bemusement as to why it had taken me so long to get there.

We seemed to hit it off from our first lunch, when the *News of the World* sports editor, Bill Bateson, brought us together. I was on a summer's trial and Bill kept me on tenterhooks until the end of that period before confessing that I'd had the job after a few weeks when Richie reported, 'He'll be fine.' He'd added that my contacts' book was already about the best in the business; complete tosh, of course, but yet another example of Richie's generosity of spirit.

There was another test to pass that summer: being accepted by the Benauds — not just Richie, but also Daphne. Theirs was a cricket partnership as productive, complementing and successful as Lillee and Thomson. Daphne, like Richie, showed me great kindness and friendship from the very start.

Although Richie spent his time in the commentary box and I was in the press box — often at opposite ends of the ground — we kept in touch by phone during Test matches. On a Saturday, I would wander round before play and at lunchtime; we'd discuss the topics of the day so there was no duplication in our copy.

After the day's play, we would meet up in the facility hosted by the Test sponsors, Cornhill Insurance, to raise a glass or two. One night, I was approached by Raman Subba Row, then chairman of the Test and County Cricket Board (TCCB), explaining there was something serious he wanted to talk to Richie about. They were soon locked in conversation, but it didn't last very long. Richie explained that Raman was worried there was far too much Test cricket being played and wanted to know what could be done about it. 'Play less' had been Richie's solution, although this simple approach seemed to confuse Raman.

One memorable series was the return of South Africa in 1994 for their first tour to England in the post-apartheid era. The first inkling of the Michael Atherton 'dirt in the pocket' incident came from South Africa, where the live television images were being shown. In the UK, the cricket was sharing the BBC's Saturday afternoon coverage with horse racing. Richie rang me and the office to say we were about to see some pictures that needed explaining and might just be the story of the day.

How right he was. That night at Lord's, after several hours of hanging around, a statement from match referee Peter Burge was read out, ending with the usual: 'The match referee will be making no further pronouncements. The matter is now closed.'

I rang Richie and gave him the good news. 'Oh, they think so, do they?' was his verdict. He had seen it all before and, lo and behold, there were further statements the following night after England had been bowled out for 99 and lost by 356 runs. Atherton was fined £2,000, there were calls for him to resign, and the fallout rumbled on for weeks.

Atherton answered his critics with a battling 99 at Headingley in the next Test, then claimed a century would have been the perfect riposte to the 'gutter press'. Richie did not take kindly to being described as such and let Atherton know that prior to dinner on the first night of the third Test, at the Oval. Bollocking over, Richie carried on as before and was a great champion and supporter of Athers when he moved seamlessly into the commentary box.

Athers did not dine with us that night, but Sir Tim Rice did. In his typically modest way, Sir Tim handed each of us a copy of a yet-to-be-released CD that he had just finished for Disney with Elton John. 'I think it's turned out okay,' he said.

Sir Tim wasn't wrong; *The Lion King* is still going strong!

Richie and I played a lot of golf in the early years, at Woburn, at the RAC in Epsom and in Australia. I recall turning up to play at Adelaide at the crack of dawn without any clubs. Richie was not best pleased, but he handed me a four-iron, a wedge, his spare putter and three golf balls, with the clear message to keep my ball in play, not forgetting his usual, 'Go well.'

Eventually, the golf matches and our time together in press boxes ended, but, fortunately, the lunches and dinners continued, as did trips to the theatre. In the early days, we would lunch with the *News of the World* editor and sports editor to welcome Richie over for another English summer, and there was always dinner with the ladies to mark the return to Australia. The Benauds moved from Pont Street in London to Beaulieu-sur-Mer in the south of France and there was more fine dining.

Richie bowed out of the commentary box in England after perhaps the greatest Ashes series of all time in 2005. I vacated the press box midway through the summer two years later; that's about the time the Benaud lunches at Langan's gained a momentum of their own. The arrival of Richie and Daphne's England itinerary was the starting point. Several dates would be suggested and firmed up.

Richie would leave the guest list to me, although Daphne laid down some ground rules. After one rather chaotic meal when we waited a couple of hours for a guest who never appeared, it was decreed that Richie must raise a fork no later than 30 minutes after raising the first glass.

Early in 2013, I listened to *Desert Island Discs* and learned of the amazing life and career of the castaway Sir Sydney Kentridge QC. Then 90, Sir Sydney had been part of Nelson Mandela's defence team in his treason trial and lawyer for the Biko family at Stephen Biko's inquest. He had then moved to England. He was also a cricket nut and his father had taken him to a South Africa-England Test at the Wanderers Ground in Johannesburg in 1928. I wrote to his chambers, inviting him to one of our lunches and a few weeks later Sir Sydney and Richie were in deep conversation discussing the finer points of cricket and the law.

A regular dining companion was the great racecaller Sir Peter O'Sullevan, who had been Richie's broadcasting mentor and inspiration. 'The most organised man I have ever come across,' was Richie's verdict. Their friendship began in 1956 when Richie was on a BBC training course, which included 'shadowing' Sir Peter at a race meeting to see how the commentator operated.

O'Sullevan was clear: 'I don't want to hear a peep out of you. Just make notes and we will sit down at the end of the day over a glass of wine and chat.' That suited Sir Peter and it suited Richie. It seemed to work, too.

Their relationship extended more than 50 years. At one lunch, the actor Stephen Mangan, another cricket fanatic, was delighted to point out that not only was he sitting between Sir Peter, the voice of racing, and Richie, the voice of cricket, but that he had just signed up to be the voice of Postman Pat in a new movie!

It was Nigel Wray, the owner of probably the finest sporting memorabilia collection in the UK as well as Saracens rugby club, who reunited Richie with a match ball from the famous Tied Test at Brisbane in 1960.

From a collection of more than 7,000 items, this was Nigel's favourite and 52 years down the road, Richie's signature was added to Frank Worrell's, Gerry Alexander's and Wes Hall's at Langan's. After Nigel headed for a taxi, Richie asked the remaining guests how we thought Nigel might react when he got home and discovered his most treasured item was no longer in his possession. It was now languishing in the breadbasket!

Theatre trips with Richie and Daphne in recent years included *Waiting for Godot* with Ian McKellen and Patrick Stewart, *The Queen* with Helen Mirren and *The Sunshine Boys* with Danny DeVito and Richard Griffiths. I liked the plays to be a surprise, but one night the best-laid plans went amiss after a flash flood delayed our arrival at Victoria Station. I had arranged to meet the Benauds in Her Majesty's Theatre, which was across the road from the Haymarket where we were actually going. Daphne saved time by getting the programmes; there were some confused looks as we walked in to see *Waiting for Godot* with programmes for *The Phantom of the Opera*.

The Benauds' renowned organisational skills only failed once as far as I'm aware — or perhaps they were just too good. The date we had chosen for a Benaud visit for lunch in 2013 just happened to be the same day as the Prudential RideLondon cycle event to the Surrey Hills, which are very close to our home, south of London. The city's bridges were closing at the crack of dawn but Richie, or more likely Daphne, got to work, planning their journey with all the precision of the D-Day landings to beat the various obstacles that were being placed in their path.

That was the background to taking a call from Daphne at 9.15am. A few minutes later, the Benauds had set a new record for the earliest-ever arrival for lunch. We had a great day. Richie visited Newdigate Cricket Club, on the Surrey-Sussex border, to open a new artificial pitch before making a presentation to the club's best youngster, in which he explained that whenever someone in the Benaud family received an award they had to make a speech. Seconds later, the lad was making his first ever public utterance. Everything was done for a purpose.

The highlight for me, though, was Richie's adoption by a team of plasterers who were on tour in Sussex. Their Sunday game had been cancelled and Newdigate were helping them out. Their shouting and comments were rather loud and earthy until they finally realised that it really was *the* Richie Benaud just a few yards away. A couple of minutes later, he was in the middle of this group, posing for pictures they will treasure for a lifetime.

They are not the only ones!

DAY OF THE SHIPWRECK

In the immediate aftermath of his retirement from cricket, Richie Benaud worked as the cricket correspondent on *The Sun*, an afternoon paper in Sydney. *The Sun* was fighting a full-scale circulation war with the *Daily Mirror*, Rupert Murdoch's first Sydney base and an early platform for his assault on the world media market. The *Mirror*'s cricket correspondent, and thus Richie's direct competition, was Robert Gray, a flamboyant character and a brilliant journalist. The pair became lifelong friends.

In many ways they were an odd couple: Richie immaculate and measured; Gray extroverted and knockabout. But they had personalities and a sense of humour that clicked. Bob made Richie laugh.

Ian Chappell's first-class cricket career started just before Richie retired, so he was a contemporary of both men. Chappell marvelled at their escapades and delights in recounting them. The most dramatic was the saga of the shipwreck, when a planned day out in Gray's cabin cruiser turned to disaster. It was 1981. Gray had long left journalism to set up a business in sporting apparel, but the friendship continued and a day out on Port Hacking, suitably fed and watered, was the sort of thing that appealed to them.

To set the scene for the sort of relationship that Benaud and Gray had, their working demands at the start of the MCC's 1965–66 Ashes tour of Australia are a good starting point. The tour began with a Combined XI game in Perth, where the deadline demands of Sydney afternoon papers required copy for the first edition to be dispatched prior to 5am, Western Australian time. Bob and Richie worked a system where they would file at night, either before or after dinner. On this particular occasion they decided they would eat first.

The dinner was a good one. The wines were fine, the conversation stimulating and time flew. When time came to file copy, Richie opted to do so straight after dinner. Feeling a little diminished by the conviviality of the occasion, Bob decided to take a nap first. After Richie sent off his piece, he tried to wake Gray so that he could do likewise. Waking him proved impossible, so Richie did the right thing and filed his copy for him, alerting the

Mirror to a significant change in the condition of injured Australian fast bowler Graham McKenzie.

Next day Bob was grateful, the Sydney *Sun* sporting editor less so. He rang Richie as soon as the *Mirror* appeared, complaining vociferously that he had been scooped and demanding to know why he had not known about the McKenzie story.

Move forward 16 years. Gray and his wife Grace have invited Richie and Daphne to a lovely afternoon on Port Hacking in Gray's cabin cruiser, cheekily christened *Pissed as Newt*. Ian Chappell sets the scene:

'Bob's boat was moored out from the beach, requiring a short trip in a rowing boat with a small outboard motor attached to get there. Bob was all set, in shirt, shorts and thongs. Richie was a bit more formal in cashmere sweater, slacks and Gucci shoes, and Daphne had packed a picnic basket filled with all sorts of delicacies. Once aboard the runabout, a challenge in itself, Gray gunned the motor. Then he made his only mistake, but it was a big one.

'He turned right when he should have turned left. The runabout headed for the wharf, which it climbed spectacularly, sending the bow spiralling into the air and throwing all aboard and their provisions into the water ...'

Such was the magnitude of the disaster, Richie wrote to his insurance broker Warren Saunders, a former NSW teammate said by many to be one of the finest batsmen never to play for Australia. Under the letterhead of DE Benaud and Associates, the letter read:

October 16, 1981
Mr Warren Saunders
Warren Saunders (Insurances) Pty Ltd.,
3 Forest Road,
Hurstville.
NSW. 2220.

Dear Mr Saunders,
    My name is Benaud, a partner in the firm of Benaud and Associates (a division of Cesana Pty Ltd). You will note from your records that, over the years, our claims for

loss, damage, and other extraordinary matters, have been almost non-existent.

However ... On October 15th, 1981, there occurred a series of happenings of such quaint curiosity I feel we must ask you for a claim form so the details may be filled in for the Insurance Company concerned.

I list in advance, for your information, the happenings of the day, in as close to chronological order as I can manage through the haze of shock and rust, so you may be able to judge for yourself the possible success of our claim. I shall try to keep the story as brief as possible, as, even now, 24 hours after the event, it brings back painful memories.

My wife Daphne and I were invited for a day's outing with business clients and friends, Mr and Mrs Robert Gray, with whom you are acquainted. The outing to be on a cabin cruiser, moored off Cronulla, the cruiser owned by Mr and Mrs Gray. The previous evening, the 14th, Mr Gray had been warmly elected to the exclusive membership of the Royal Port Hacking Yacht Club.

He spent the early part of the morning of the 15th carefully studying the tides, checking the force of the wind and charting the course for the voyage. To indicate to you that the other three members of the group were endeavouring to match Mr Gray's Admiral's Cup-like dedication, I should mention we addressed ourselves to the task of arranging matters such as lobster, prawns, champagne, white wine, chicken and all other such minor affairs.

It was revealed to us by the captain, Mr Gray, that to get to the cabin cruiser it would be necessary to place all four people plus bags and food, etc, in a rowboat, to which we had attached an outdoor motor. I feel now that I should list the happenings as they occurred so you and your insurance companies will have a clear picture of events.

Our captain, with the assistance of several four-letter phrases and Mrs Benaud, eventually managed to push the rowboat four metres, to the water's edge. This was achieved with some difficulty as Mr Benaud was unable to assist. He was wearing a neck brace because of a recent injury and, in any case, was lying on the ground in helpless laughter.

It took the captain only 20 minutes to start the outboard motor, during which time Mrs Gray and Mrs Benaud busied themselves, on Mr Gray's instructions, carrying equipment, food, drink and bags of ice a few hundred yards from house to wharf.

On the captain's orders, Mrs Benaud now positioned herself in the rowboat. Mrs Gray followed and Mr Benaud was instructed: 'For Christ's sake, take the rope off the thing on the wharf.' Mr Benaud was then told to board. He did this, rope in hand, and the captain announced the day's adventure was about to begin. He was exuding an air of quiet confidence.

We will now endeavour to recount what next occurred, though events are somewhat blurred, with the whole sequence seemingly taking a few seconds. The general consensus of thinking is that the captain was facing north and the boat was facing south, though this, even now, is by no means a unanimous opinion. Where there is no argument is that, with everyone seated and relaxed, our captain, as he should have done, gunned the motor. He then suffered what can only be termed a piece of indescribable bad luck.

He turned right, instead of left.

On our left, several hundred metres from the rowboat, was the cabin cruiser. On our right, one metre from the rowboat (39.37 inches on the old scale) was the wharf. When I came up from underneath the rowboat, I had a moment of panic. I could not see any of the others. But I was able to hear them ... quite clearly!

At this stage, I would like to commend Daphne for some version of 'Wife of the Year Award'. When our captain yelled to her that he would come and save her, she shouted, 'Don't worry about me, you pillock. Save Richie. He can't swim.'

This was shown, in fact, to be a slight exaggeration, because, although the tide was going out and although I was weighted down by a Pringle navy blue cashmere sweater, white Gucci shoes and Gucci slacks, I made it back to where the water was only four feet deep. I was helped, I might add, by my neck brace which, amusingly enough, seemed to act as a pair of water wings, keeping my head out of the water, but my body rigidly vertical.

Our band now regrouped in the four feet deep water and guided the rowboat, with the outboard motor dormant but attached, around the left-hand corner of the wharf. The captain was by now fully back in command and offering much helpful advice.

Unfortunately, not all the bags, food, equipment, etc, were recoverable, though we did manage to salvage some items. We would like to pay tribute to our captain's ingenuity. He sent for his daughter, Miss Katherine Ann Gray (13), who was at school at the time, and despite a water temperature of five degrees instructed her in complicated diving techniques, so that many of the important items could be recovered.

The other tribute must be to his knowledge of the lore and history of the sea. When Mrs Benaud, Mrs Gray and Mr Benaud were hurled into the turbulent ocean, the captain somehow managed to be the last to go down with the rowboat.

At the end of the day, Mr Gray was of the opinion that he had solved all the problems and asked if we would like to come back for another try in 24 hours. We said we thought that to do this we would require the permission of our insurance company. Is this correct?

Yours sincerely,
Richie Benaud

As Ian Chappell points out, Richie omitted one detail from his account of proceedings. Katherine Gray on her first dive retrieved a pleasantly cooled bottle of chardonnay that she triumphantly handed to 'Uncle Richie', who promptly threw it back into the water.

'That's rubbish,' he said. 'Go back down, Katherine. There are bottles of Veuve Clicquot on the bottom.'

Richie's sense of perspective clearly was undiminished by the day's events.

– 5 –

WORLD SERIES CRICKET

'This is easily the biggest challenge I've faced in my business life. It is a delightful, delicious, bitter challenge.'

— Richie Benaud, November 1977

DAVID HILL

David Hill was the original executive producer of World Series Cricket, part of Kerry Packer's key WSC 'inner circle' that also included Richie, the entrepreneurial media identities John Cornell and Austin Robertson, and senior Nine Network figures Sam Chisholm and Lynton Taylor. As the founder and head of Nine's Wide World of Sports in Australia, and later with Sky Television in the UK and then Fox Sports in the US, David built an envied reputation as the supreme innovator and storyteller in global sports broadcasting. Rupert Murdoch has described him as 'a dynamic and imaginative leader who changed the experience of nearly all major sports on three continents'.

THE very first time I met Richie Benaud, I lost the power of speech. My mouth opened and closed, but nothing came out. It was like being in the presence of an immortal.

My dad revered Richie Benaud as much as he disliked Bob Menzies.

Richiebenaud, it was always one word, was Australia's handsome, tough, fearless, smart, canny cricket captain — shirt open, bowling sizzling leg-breaks to confused Pommy batsmen, square-cutting to the boundary for the winning runs, diving to take a fingertip catch in the gully.

He stood for honesty, integrity, mateship, ingenuity, toughness — you name it. He exuded confidence, leadership and, at the same time, a wry, self-deprecating sense of humour.

He once said, 'The hallmark of a great captain is the ability to win the toss — at the right time!' He commanded a god-like figure in the Hill house in South Turramurra.

It was September 1977. Sam Chisholm and Kerry Packer had asked me to become the executive producer of the Nine Network's coverage of World Series Cricket. Sam was no fool. He could see the potential for a cataclysmic disaster and clearly he didn't want any of his people being hurled into the outer darkness by an apoplectic Kerry, so I became the television equivalent of cannon fodder.

World Series Cricket was put together seemingly in minutes. The world's top cricketers were hired in secret to play a three-way series, which would be televised by Kerry's Nine Network.

Kerry, with eminent sense, approached Richie Benaud to become his strategic adviser in its creation and also the lead television commentator.

That meant, with Richie, World Series Cricket got his indefatigable wife Daphne — a born diplomat, problem solver, lateral thinker and blessed with a tinkling laugh that smoothed over any potential disasters. There were plenty of those.

All the staff, including Kerry, turned to Richie or to Daphne for advice and often for instruction. I always felt Richie never got the credit he deserved; his mind was in everything and was everywhere. He loved the concept; he loved that cricketers were getting (finally) a fair deal; he loved the fact cricket was front and centre in everyone's mind.

It was an amazing time of undisguised fear and loathing. Everything changed: rules, uniforms, grounds, pitches, balls, competition structure and marketing. And with that came court cases, universal disdain. Former friends were given the cold shoulder. Through everything, all the turmoil, the shouting, the angst, Richie Benaud was, well, Richie Benaud.

So there I am, meeting the Great Man, making like a goldfish. Wearing jeans, T-shirt, woolly hair (it was the 1970s, folks!) — and here was Richie Benaud, Mr Cricket, looking, well, elegant. Hair: immaculate. Blazer: immaculate. Shirt and tie: immaculate. Shoes: immaculate. Slacks: knife crease, immaculate.

The first meeting did not go well.

Kerry wanted me to produce cricket like it had never been seen and his partner in WSC, John Cornell, had some amazing ideas. Richie, who was BBC through and through, was keen, but cautious. And there was me, whose lack of cricket knowledge was profound, but I had worked with, and for, some amazing people in Melbourne, so I did know a bit about television.

So, away we went.

The first season was tough for Richie and me: getting to know each other, working together hand in glove, and Richie spending a lot of time enclosed with Kerry Packer, Lynton Taylor and John Cornell, solving all the enormous logistic, legal and financial problems of WSC. Which, by the way, was far from a smash hit in its first year. I just had to worry about the television coverage, but because that was so entwined with everything else in the project, I'd get roped in as well.

Live television isn't for the faint of heart, and there's no time for pondering.

It's fair to say that Richie and I finished the first season a long way from the state of armed détente with which we started, him as Mr BBC, and me as a rank amateur.

We ended that first season actually liking each other.

The reason was that we had effectively turned cricket coverage on its head and, despite the angry and anguished letters to the editor from retired clergymen and colonels, the punters — especially those under 60 — were really starting to enjoy and engage.

And I had learned a lot about Richie.

First, he was incredibly smart. Second, he loved cricket, cricketers, cricketing lore, and despised (maybe too strong a word) the blazerati he saw impeding the game. He was incredibly driven in writing about and communicating the game. And he was, at heart, incredibly curious.

I suddenly found myself immersed in this cricketing world. The television crew, the commentators and the teams travelled together, and stayed in the same hotels, so it was all cricket, all the time. And when someone would drone on about the game, as we walked away Richie would love quoting words he attributed to WG Grace: 'Those who know nothing else but cricket, know nothing.'

That first season started a 40-year friendship between Richie and me.

He taught me cricket, he taught me patience, he taught me strategy, he taught me diplomacy (well, some), he showed me wisdom, and there hasn't been a day when something he told me hasn't been useful.

Our day would start with a meeting in the commentary box, when I'd make up the commentators' roster. Actually the roster was the first real conflict. I need to explain that. Richie didn't have to say anything to let you know he was seriously pissed off. He would lift his head, turn, look at you, and raise an eyebrow.

Trust me, it doesn't sound like much, but it could be, and was, devastating. Tradition had it that commentators' shifts were 40 minutes long. Start at 11 through to 11.40; 11.40 through to 12.20; then 12.20 through to lunch at 1 — and so on.

And that's the way I'd draw up the roster, until I started noticing that around 25 minutes in, if the game wasn't blazing hot, the commentary became, well, fairly ordinary. Especially in the session between tea and stumps, with a couple of spinners on, it would get positively turgid. Zzzzz. So I shortened the shifts to 30 minutes: 11 to 11.30, 11.30 to 12, and so on. And in keeping with the cricketing world, I used the commentators' initials. So a roster would read FS Trueman and WM Lawry, AW Greig and IM Chappell, and so on.

Richie didn't have a middle initial, so I gave him one: X. So he would appear as RX Benaud, linked with, say, WAL Cozier.

From memory, the X appeared on the first roster with the 30-minute shifts.

Consternation. The lift. The turn. The eyebrow raise.

'What the bloody hell is this? And what's with the X?'

I looked up from where I was working out the opening sequence for when we went on air and said, 'I didn't want people knowing you came from a poor family and couldn't afford a middle name.' Face of stone for three seconds. Roar of laughter.

'RX Benaud at your service, Mr Hill.'

Not a word about the shift change, until we were walking out at the end of the day and he didn't look around, just said, 'Worked quite well, the 30-minute shifts.' And that was that.

He was a dream to work with.

Best cricket commentator ever, and possibly even better in front of a live camera.

The first year of WSC we had two directors: John Crilly — a Perth boy and mate of John Cornell and 'Ocker' Robertson — and Brian C. Morelli from Sydney. Both, by the way, world class. John decided to head back to the quokkas after the first season, so then 'BC' (as he was universally known) took over.

Our coverage developed with the three of us sitting at the end of the day's production, always with a chilled adult beverage, doing a post-mortem of sorts but most of the time playing 'what if?'

Why don't we try this?

How about boring out a stump and sticking a radio mike in it? Holy shit. Can we? Why not? What about using a computer to score? How about putting the score in the corner when the batsmen are running to show the score ticking up? Why don't we do a box with the bowler and the batsman's head?

Hey, let's give it a shot. If it doesn't work, we'll ditch it.

The three of us developed a shorthand, which meant we could do very complicated production sequences with limited resources, in limited time, because we knew what the others were thinking.

Getting 'Greigy' (AW Greig, former England captain) to do the pitch reports was a bit of an effort because he didn't want to do them in the beginning. I convinced him that he'd become a star (which he did) and because I always felt putting the viewer into the state of mind that they were at the ground was vitally important. It all became part of the legend of Channel Nine's cricket coverage, like the hats, which were introduced when a friend of my wife died of skin cancer. They were worn as a warning to the children of Australia. Ironic, isn't it, that Rich came down with skin cancer because he never wore a cap when he was playing.

So Richie would be sitting in the corner of the commentary box long before we went on air, hammering away first at a portable typewriter, and then the early word processors, which became the first primitive laptops. He was inordinately proud of his technical prowess and would proudly show off his latest piece of technical equipment that would enable him to write his columns for papers around the world. With his numerous daily deadlines, especially during an Ashes series, he had got himself a watch with an alarm. I know, primitive, but back then — WOW! So this alarm would go off and Richie would dive into action.

With his on-camera work, as with everything else, he was the ultimate professional. Nothing on teleprompt, no scripts, all in his head. I'd figure out a running order, tell BC, pass the sheet to Rich. He'd grab scorecards from statistician Irving Rosenwater (that's a story in itself), sit in front of the camera, and just do it better than anyone.

And he always kept his cool.

One day, Richie had just started on air, and suddenly the backing with the Nine Wide World of Sports logo toppled forward, whacking him in the back of his head. Crash!

He didn't miss a beat. He leaned backwards and, by tensing his neck, pushed the backing upright. While all this was going on, BC was rolling in the fall of wickets and Richie was describing exactly what had happened on the field, and then the alarm went off — probably signifying a column was due for the *Lower Murrumbidgee Annual,* or perhaps the *Upper Rawalpindi Weekly.*

He didn't miss a beat. Continuing his description of the morning play, he reached over to turn off the watch alarm while continuing his pressure on the errant backing. And through to the commercial break. Just perfect.

He was very proud of his journalistic background, and the skills he learned at the Sydney *Sun* showed through his innumerable newspaper columns and the 14 books he wrote.

I'd started as a copyboy at the *Daily Telegraph,* and had been fortunate enough to work with celebrated police roundsman Ced Culbert as a cadet journalist. Richie and I spent a lot of time talking about the characters, and the crooks, on both sides of the law, that we knew from reporting in that knockabout period of Sydney's history.

It's hard to imagine now, in this age of high-priced sports stars, but back then cricketers, even those as stratospherically famous as Richie Benaud, had to have a job that paid them a living wage, and allowed them time off to represent their state and country.

Cricket players traditionally had been parsimoniously paid, which turned on the cricket authorities when the long-simmering resentment boiled over in the revolt that became World Series Cricket. His innate understanding of the media from those early days as a journo made his move into radio and television seamless.

Always a thinker, Richie had stayed behind in London after the 1956 Ashes tour and went to a three-week commentators' course at the BBC. I guess that move sums up Richie's attitude to life. Plan ahead. It's what made him such a great aggressive captain. Here he is, a young cricketer, 26, on the verge of greatness, and he understands his career is not going to last forever, but his love of the game is such that he wants to spend the rest of his life involved. The way to do it is to become — at some stage in the future — a commentator.

Richie's training there, plus his communications skills, created the legend. We'd often talk about the great sports announcers, and the two we always settled on were both BBC men: Henry Longhurst with golf and Dan Maskell with tennis.

I suspect Richie borrowed 'marvellous', which became his commentary signature, from Maskell, who was renowned, after a 40-stroke rally between Björn Borg and John McEnroe in a Wimbledon final, for uttering that one word. 'Marvellous'.

But the BBC training did create a little niggle in our relationship.

I wanted the commentators to educate as well as inform. I had played cricket growing up (not at all well) and had a vague idea where the various positions were. I had no real idea about the captain's strategy. I wanted the commentators to explain all and everything. I'll give you an example. A player fielding at square-leg suddenly gets moved to fine-leg. I say to the commentator (unnamed) — why did so and so do that? 'Bloody obvious,' comes the reply.

Well, life's not like that, and most people's knowledge is superficial. The more you know about a sport, the more you anticipate and the more you enjoy.

So there was a period where there was some give and take, but we got there in the end. The time there was massive eye-rolling came when I rang my mum (South Turramurra again) and said, 'What do you think?'

'Darling,' she replied, 'I've looked really hard, but for the life of me I can't see any gully in the field, and they keep talking about it.'

So I superimposed the various fielding positions on the screen for a while, but it just got too hard. When that period of the production ended all the guys breathed a sigh of relief.

Richie's understanding of the game was such that he could 'see' what was going to happen and could sense the outcome of a match. The classic was an Australia v New Zealand one-day international, February 1981 at the MCG, with GS Chappell captaining the home side.

With about 15 overs to go, New Zealand batting, Richie walked to my production desk and said: 'I think Greg has got his sums absolutely wrong.'

'Huh?' I replied.

'The way I see it, Trevor [Chappell] will be bowling the final over the way it's going and I don't think Greg's going to realise until too late.'

And that's precisely what happened — and led to Trevor bowling the final ball to Brian McKechnie underarm, to prevent the Kiwi hitting a six off the last ball to tie the match.

Ian Chappell (brother of Greg and Trevor) was on the air and involuntarily came out with: 'Greg, no, you can't do that.' We all watched in horror.

The aftermath is well documented, but the point is that Richie saw something coming well before the rest of us mortals.

He was born in the hard-scrabble town of Penrith. The family ended up at Parramatta, where he went to Parramatta High and started playing first grade with the Cumberland club at 16.

What I couldn't, and still can't, get my head around is how Richard Benaud went from the tough streets of Parramatta to become the elegant Richie Benaud, who could, and did, mix happily and effortlessly with every strata of society, from the British royal family to the bloke who cleaned out the commentary box at the WACA.

Richie's friendships were legendary, a collection of some of the most interesting people I have ever met. It was a privilege to be on the outer circle of Richie's social world.

He and Daphne ran their calendar virtually years ahead, pencilling in dinners, lunches, stays at country homes. Everywhere they went, they were surrounded by a huge wall of old friendships.

I worked closely with Kerry Packer for many years, and Richie was one of the few people whom Kerry deeply respected, admired and had deep affection for.

World Series Cricket was a triumph, and the warring sides made up. I continued working with Richie on Nine's cricket coverage until Kerry sold the network to Alan Bond. I left for London and Rupert Murdoch's exciting dream of starting a satellite television service in Britain called Sky. But by then we had transformed the coverage of cricket, and BC Morelli, Richie and I were justifiably proud of what we'd done, realising of course that without Kerry urging us on to think differently, and to be bold and audacious in the coverage, and always put the viewer first, we would never have achieved what we did.

But that didn't end my friendship with Richie. He and Daphne were always part of my life and my family's life. And that's how I'd like to end this story, because something happened last year that sums him up perfectly.

My ex-wife, Lachie Hill, also became fast friends with Richie and Daphne. They would always attend her Christmas party. Our son Julian met and married a wonderful Mexican lass, Maria de Lourdes Milano Ordonez. She is as beautiful as her name.

Jules brought Lou back to Australia (Jules is working on the 2016 Olympic Games in Rio de Janeiro) and gladly greets Daphne and Rich when they arrive at his mother's party.

He introduces Lou to them.

I'm talking to Jules a couple of days later and he says, 'Guess what happened? Richie sat down with Lou and spent an hour patiently explaining cricket to her. Afterwards, I said to Lou, "Do you realise that you have been taught the game by the world's greatest cricket legend?"'

'Was she appreciative?' I asked.

'Not only was she,' Jules said, 'I think she now gets cricket.'

And that little interchange with my daughter-in-law — to whom cricket was as familiar as the dark side of the moon — sums up the man. His passion for the game, his wonderful heart, his innate humanity, made him sit down in the middle of a swirling Melbourne Christmas party and spend an hour patiently explaining the game that was his life to a total stranger to the game.

Just as a footnote. Through the years I've been lucky enough to have worked with some remarkably gifted on-camera talent and commentators.

John Madden, the American football commentator, explained the job to me this way. 'It's telling people what they're seeing, but not seeing.' Perfect. And Richie Benaud did that for cricket better than anyone has or, I suspect, will.

BRIAN C. MORELLI

Brian Morelli was there at the very beginning of television
in Australia, working as a cameraman for TCN-9 in Sydney
in 1956. By 1977, he was a senior director at Nine when
he was co-opted onto the network's coverage of World
Series Cricket. With David Hill and Richie Benaud, he would
revolutionise the way cricket was broadcast. Today, Hill
describes Brian simply as 'the legendary director'.

I HAD just completed the new season of Channel Nine's 1977
promotional film entitled 'Still the One'. At the time, Nine's CEO
was Sam Chisholm, who in his inimitable way congratulated me on
the job done with a return flight to anywhere in the world I wanted
to go. I chose London. It was suggested that while there I might
like to look at 'some cricket'. At this time, the secrecy surrounding
World Series Cricket was firmly in place so I had no idea why I was
given that suggestion. As a station director, I was required to tackle
anything from ballet to battleships, but I had no clue as to what the
significance of 'some cricket' would eventually mean.

Soon, I would meet David Hill, ex-Melbourne ABC and
Channel Seven, who had just been employed by Channel Nine.
David would be WSC's executive producer. 'Creative' isn't enough
to describe Hilly, as he was known. 'Genius' is probably more
appropriate.

The birth of World Series Cricket brought together David
Hill and Richie Benaud. I really don't know whether we joined
Richie … or Richie joined us. However, the birthright of the baby
'some cricket' couldn't possibly have belonged to two better people
than Hilly and Richie. They would raise it to majestic heights.

In the beginning, from my perspective, a quiet respect existed
between the two of them. Richie, the consummate BBC broadcaster,
golfing enthusiast, reporter and former Australian cricket captain.

Hilly, a producer of sport stories, sports newsreader and an enigma who had not, in my view, been recognised for his true ability. Through the production corridors of Channel Nine, he was a breath of fresh air. Both were writers who possessed a great sense of humour. What they eventually developed with Nine's cricket coverage was achieved with some parry and thrust.

Take an early exchange, when a highlights package had to be compiled after our first game at Melbourne's Waverley Park. A producer would normally write an opening speech for the presenter to read. Hilly duly wrote such a piece and handed it to Richie.

Richie read it slowly, paused, looked up at David and very politely said, 'I can't say that.'

'Why not?' Hilly enquired.

'I wasn't at that game,' said Richie.

David gently took the script from Richie's hands and tore it up.

There were many ways Richie could have answered the 'why not' question; it was the quiet humour in his answer that impressed us. The foundation for a camaraderie and a working relationship that never wavered was established. In the end, David's faith in Richie was such that he was using him in more than just Nine's cricket coverage. In 1985, for example, Richie was co-opted onto Nine's coverage of the 'Australian Skins' event — featuring Jack Nicklaus, Greg Norman, Tom Watson and Seve Ballesteros — which was played at his home course, the Australian.

Hilly set up this huge tent, within which was a massive canvas onto which had been painted all 18 holes. Richie's task was to stand in the appropriate position on the canvas and explain the difficulties the golfers would be facing with particular shots. He did so impeccably.

That Benaud humour was sometimes dry, sometimes forceful, sometimes sublime. In Adelaide, during a game involving the West Indies, Richie was to do a preamble on the condition of the pitch, still covered with canvas tarpaulins as there had been some overnight rain. The day had dawned fine, with a clear sky and typical Adelaide heat building.

On the road, it was not unusual for the travelling television crew and cricket teams to reside in the same hotel and it was the case for this game. West Indies teams, it can be said, always attracted a large following. In his way, Richie summed up the entire situation in a single sentence: the weather during the night, the state of the pitch, the coming heat and the pace of the Windies' bowlers.

'I can tell you there was a lot of sweating under the covers last night.'

During a lull in the same game, on what became a dull pitch, Hilly called for us to show characters in the crowd. I chose hats as the theme. Richie was asked to offer some observations. As the cameras panned around the crowd, he contacted us on the intercom that linked the commentators and the outside broadcast van: 'That fellow in the deerstalker hat, could I see him again? I think I know him.'

At the end of the over, I said, 'Here we go, Rich, roll tape.' A complicated sequence of pictures that included the 'deerstalker man' was then put to air, with that particular bloke holding stage longer than any of the spectators featured. This was done deliberately, to allow Richie to make comment. But there was a deathly silence. Eventually, we returned to the game.

'Thanks BC,' Richie called down the line. 'Never saw him before in my life.'

There was a brevity to Richie's commentary that was sometimes astounding. It was exemplified in an Australia v West Indies one-dayer, played at a time when the Australians, captained by Allan Border during his early tenure in that capacity, were being overpowered by the Windies. In this game, boundaries were scarce and the Aussies were taking chances with their running between the wickets. But perilous attempts at singles resulted in a couple of run-outs. The required run-rate was increasing, the Australian batsmen were under enormous pressure.

There was a change of commentators, and almost immediately a stroke was played into a gap in the offside field … there was a series of exchanges between the batsmen … 'Yes!', 'No!' and the odd 'Maybe?' … and, finally, off they went. Then there was a screeching halt by one, a screeching acceleration by the other, as the Windies fieldsman closed on the ball. All of this was caught dramatically by the cameras.

In a situation such as this, a commentator might become breathless as he seeks to describe everything that is happening. But there was no vocal accompaniment to this excitement … until Richie chipped in just as the fieldsman reached the ball, before he grasped it to throw to the bowler's end.

'Oh no, not again.'

It was brilliant commentary. A range of emotions — tension, expectation, achievement and doubt — all experienced in milliseconds of time, were captured in those four words. The ball smashed into the 'furniture'. Another run-out.

One day, Richie asked me via the intercom if we could retrieve footage from soon after a particular batsman had come to the crease. He asked to see the fifth ball delivered to the player in question, from the fourth over of the day. Confirmation of it being ready was followed by a second request, 'Could you get the sixth ball of the 12th over?' Then Richie asked for the two items to be played together. 'Editing done, Richie, ready to go,' I said.

I heard nothing more, until a number of overs later when he asked if the footage of the two deliveries was still available. It was. A couple of balls later, the batsman was dismissed and Richie immediately asked for the two earlier deliveries to be played, followed by the dismissal. His commentary ran along the following lines: 'This is the fifth ball he faced in the fourth over ... this is the final delivery of the 12th over ... and this [as viewers see the replay of the dismissal] is the third time he made the same mistake today.'

Richie could read a game as no other. His timing on other matters was equally impeccable. I remember many times when a story surfaced around a Saturday or a Sunday game and the press, radio and TV journalists ran riot with opinions. Richie, a columnist himself, wouldn't rush to offer an opinion. He would wait until after all the shouting and the tumult died down and perhaps even a week later would offer a measured view. I have no doubt that most times the public would remember Richie's verdict ahead of the myriad earlier versions. During my years covering the game there were so many times when incidents arose, dismissals were challenged or ethics came under the spotlight, and afterwards cricketers and cricket officials would ask, 'What did Richie say?'

One such instance concerned the MCG's old Southern Stand. There was a time when, to maximise seating capacity, the ground authorities told us our cameras had to be located at the back of the grandstands. They didn't want paying spectators having their view impeded by television equipment. 'Your cameras have zoom lenses,' they told us, 'so it doesn't matter where they're placed.' The Southern Stand, built in the 1930s, had a semi-circle of posts from ground to roof. During a Test match, Richie was describing the significance of how a captain had set his field and requested we pan across all the fieldsmen, from one side of the ground to the other. When the cameraman had finished his job, Richie declared: 'I'm sorry, but one fieldsman I wanted to show you is behind that post.'

As soon as he could, Richie contacted me on the intercom to ask, 'Why was the camera behind the post?'

I explained our orders from the ground authorities. This was happening only a couple of seasons after the truce had been negotiated between World Series Cricket and the Australian Cricket Board. The board's head office was in Melbourne and its ancestral home was the MCG, so we were treading lightly.

'Really?' asked Richie. 'Can you give me the picture again?'

This time, as the camera struck the same hurdle, he fired the full broadside. 'The reason I can't show you the fieldsman I want to show,' he said sternly, 'is because the authorities have told us to put our cameras behind the posts. Extraordinary.'

When we arrived the next morning, the cameras had been repositioned. Overnight, our outside broadcast engineers had been advised they could bring their cameras forward so their view would not be impeded by the posts.

No other commentator of my experience could have achieved the same result.

CLIVE LLOYD

Clive Lloyd was a powerful batsman who scored 7,515 runs in 110 Tests. Under his captaincy the West Indies became the most successful side in world cricket, at one stage boasting a run of 27 Tests without defeat. Players such as Viv Richards, Gordon Greenidge, Michael Holding, Joel Garner and Malcolm Marshall made them nigh on unbeatable ... to say nothing of Lloyd himself. He was a key figure at the start of World Series Cricket.

WHEN World Series Cricket began, the perception was that the top cricketers around the world were climbing over each other to be involved. It is true that we were all unhappy that the great commercial success that cricket was having at the time was not reflected in the money we were paid. We felt hard done by. But when the decision had to be made — should we go with an untried concept? — there was a lot of pressure.

The cricket establishment did not let go easily and we all had to weigh up whether it was worth the risk that our international careers might end, especially if Kerry Packer's dream did not work. But when it came to the crunch there was one element of the new cricket venture that made the difference.

The fact Richie Benaud was heavily involved in World Series Cricket was the clincher. His very presence encouraged a lot of people to join; he was a figure respected by all the players. We knew that if Richie was involved, he would have considered every detail of the new concept. His getting on board was a vote of confidence in it, and that spread to all of us as we took the plunge.

Richie knew how important the whole thing was, firstly as a means of getting a fair day's pay for elite cricketers, but also as a means of shaking up a game that was in need of shaking up. I recall the great tennis player Arthur Ashe saying to a few players at the Centenary Test in Melbourne in 1977 that, with so many people flocking to the game, we all must have been making a fortune. In fact, we were making a comparative pittance. We all owe Richie a debt, because he had something to say about that.

People trusted Richie. We knew there was nobody who knew more about the game than he did. Many young men coming into the game about that time tried to emulate him … tried to carry themselves as Richie and Frank Worrell did. Richie was an excellent soul, very even-handed and considered, and he had so many friends in so many countries. When all is said and done, this is the camaraderie of cricket, and how it should be.

I saw quite a bit of Richie after my playing days ended. Whenever we were in Sydney we would have a meal at Coogee with Rich and Daphne. When we were there for the 2015 World Cup, Richie was too ill, so it was just Daphne who came out with us. It was a great disappointment not to have been able to have dinner with him one last time. He was the epitome of what a sportsman should be.

JOHN CURTAIN

John Curtain was team manager at the North Melbourne
football club in the 1970s when AFL legend Ron Barassi was
coach. He was also heavily involved in the establishment
of World Series Cricket and has been a continuing Swans
devotee, serving for a time as the club's interim CEO. John
got to know the Benauds on both sides of the world and
revelled in their company.

WHEN World Series Cricket was being born in 1977, I had the
grand title of 'General Manager, Administration'. I worked off
seven sheets of paper, which at that time was about all there was
to the whole concept. In those circumstances, you tend to find the
best people to help and I worked seven days a week for about seven
months with Richie Benaud, backed by the not inconsiderable
support of Richie's wife Daphne.

I remain to this day absolutely convinced that WSC — and with
it what has become the modern game — would not have happened
had Richie not been there. He did so much of the early planning,
including the playing conditions and the scheduling. Grounds had
to be found. I organised logistics … everything was by the seat of
our pants, and had Richie and Daphne not been there I doubt that it
would have come together at all.

Daphne was the details person, and as a team they were
outstanding. I don't think Richie ever had a title … he was just
Richie … but he gave so much more to the success of WSC than
merely his pre-eminence as a commentator.

Back in the 1960s, I was mates with a lot of Richie's mates:
Bob Cowper, Bob Gray and Ian McDonald for starters. Cowper, of
course, was an Australian Test cricketer. McDonald was a Melbourne
journo who finished up team manager of the Australian cricket team
for many years. I first got to know Richie through them. Cowper

and Gray shared a London flat and I often stayed weekends. In 1964, there were plenty of high times and Richie, on tour as a journalist with the Australian team, was a regular visitor.

Many people have their recollections of Richie the cricketer and Richie the commentator, but I have so many memories of Richie the man. Some thought him aloof. I actually thought that impression came from the fact that he was a shy person, never really comfortable about being the centre of attention. One of his more impressive qualities that few people ever saw was his acknowledgment of the role his parents played in his life. Many stories have been told about Keith Miller being Richie's hero and I am sure there was an influence there. But Richie's real hero was his father, Lou. I heard him tell stories of Lou so often, always with obvious and deep affection. Lou influenced his cricket and his life and Richie never hid his gratitude.

On the subject of Miller, I remember too how sorely tested was Richie's loyalty to his old skipper when Miller had an interest in a horse that was racing at Sandown. Scobie Breasley was the jockey and Miller's horse was outright favourite at 6–4 on in a four-horse race. We all jumped on it gleefully, including Richie, despite the fact he was a very modest punter, and despite the short price. The horse came fourth — dead last — and Miller's name was mud, at least for a while.

Richie's relationship with Bob Gray, especially in the days when they were competitors in the Sydney afternoon papers, was something to see. They were great mates, even though Bob's rough edges sometimes seemed out of sync with Richie's bent for the immaculate. For a number of years Richie and Daphne had a flat in Pont Street, Belgravia, in London, which they seriously remodelled.

The flat was gleaming when Bob came to visit, a most welcome guest. Everything was new, including the carpets. As Gray entered with great flourish, the inescapable realisation hit everybody that on the way in his shoes had collected a load that a dog had inconveniently dropped in the street outside the Benauds' front door. Much fumigation and carpet scrubbing followed and Bob was a perfect target for Richie's subtle chiding.

That flat was a magnet for Richie's mates in various states of sobriety. Two of them were Jim Kernahan and Ross Jones, who were regulars on excursions that Ian Wooldridge and about 20 other blokes set up to run with the bulls at Pamplona. Most didn't run ... just drank ... and despite the fact that Wooldridge, one of the great sportswriters, and Richie were great mates, Richie was appalled by the whole thing. He couldn't imagine why grown men would run 900 metres down an alley with bulls trying to do them damage. He certainly never went.

On one occasion, Jim and Ross arrived back from Spain early one morning after a Pamplona adventure and decided to call on Richie for a bit of a hair of the dog. They arrived at the flat about 7am, demanding a Bloody Mary, many of which it seemed they had only recently stopped devouring. Richie invited them in, studied their status, gave them the Bloody Marys they were seeking and then politely invited them to 'piss off'. We all knew we'd always be welcomed at Pont Street.

Richie's steadfastness was among his more endearing characteristics. The Sunbeam Alpine he drove for years was one example. So was his food preference. His favourite restaurant in Beaulieu was the African Queen, and it was a lovely place.

I was privileged to dine there with the Benauds on a few occasions and Richie would order the same dish every time: curried mussels. I tried them and they were very good, but I doubt that Richie ever tried anything else. He liked what he liked and that was that.

There were many occasions when Richie was supremely generous with his time. I was involved in the early days of the Sydney Swans, and we instituted from the start a chairman's lunch before each game. Early on, I asked Richie and Daphne if they would like to come, and I took a punt on asking Richie if he would mind being interviewed by the sportswriter Mike Coward as the entertainment centrepiece of the day. I was nervous about asking him, despite the fact I knew him really well, but he was gracious in most things he did and agreeing to do this was no exception. He must have filled this role for 15 years or so; he always came to the first lunch of the season and his stories were always rich and funny, and highly entertaining. There were many tales of his forebears, going back to the first Benauds in Australia, and there was also a fascinating poignancy to his talks.

In similar vein, Ian McDonald started a lunch club in Melbourne called the 'Vingt Cinq Club' in the early '60s. They began with just 25 members and launched with a grand final lunch, in many ways the forerunner to the traditional grand final breakfasts of today. In later years, a lunch was staged to celebrate an anniversary of the Tied Test and Ian Meckiff asked me if I would try to get Richie down as guest speaker. I thought it was a long shot, but he agreed in a flash, would accept nothing for it, and turned on a marvellous occasion in which he was joined by Meckiff, Lindsay Kline and Colin McDonald, who had all played in that famous game.

When I lived in Melbourne I used to look forward to the Benauds' arrival for the Boxing Day Test. My wife Karen and I would have them to dinner each year on the second day of the Test, along with Mark Taylor, Ian Chappell and Mike Coward, and they were always wonderful occasions, filled with many laughs. Richie and Daphne, on the evidence of a rough night about 30 years before, always drank plenty of water with their wine, but I never could get it right — sparkling or still? In the end, they gave up on me and started bringing their own water.

Among the various distractions that made those nights so special was one evening not so long ago when Ian Chappell was focused on a Big Bash Twenty20 game involving the Melbourne Stars. 'Would we mind putting on the TV?' he asked. Richie launched into predictable derision, lecturing Ian in that singular tongue-in-cheek style of his about the inappropriateness of demanding the television when he was having a nice dinner in a host's home.

'But I have to watch some of it,' Ian insisted.

'Why?' demanded Richie.

'Because I'm the Stars' chairman of selectors,' Ian responded, somewhat sheepishly it must be said.

Richie sat with his back to the TV for the rest of the evening and made Ian squirm at every opportunity.

I had lunch with Rich and Daphne at the 18-footers club at Rushcutters Bay about ten days before Richie went into hospital for the last time. Bob Cowper and his wife Dale were there too, and though Richie was physically much diminished ... thin and gaunt ... his mind was as razor sharp as ever. He talked of Lou and of great days, of good people and of fun times, and we had a wonderful day. Richie left us with the uplifting feeling that, although it was clearly drawing to a close, he had lived a wonderful life. For the rest of us, it was a privilege to have shared just a little of it.

FUTURE GENERATIONS

'Australian skippers since Benaud's day have taken him
as their *beau idéal*.'

— **Frank Tyson**

DOUG WALTERS

Doug Walters was a cricket prodigy who made the NSW
team at 17 and the Australian team at 19, after leaving his
birthplace, Dungog, in the Hunter Valley, at 16 to play grade
cricket in Sydney. As his career blossomed, Doug fell under
Richie's wing in a variety of ways.

RICHIE Benaud was a captain out of the ordinary at every level
of cricket, whether it was a low-key club game on a suburban
oval or a Test match. I remember one club game especially,
a one-dayer against Northern District at the old Cumberland Oval,
long before covers were ever invented for grade-cricket wickets. It had
rained all week and the pitch was diabolical.

In grade cricket, Richie was not the most punctual of captains.
Most of the time, someone else had to toss for him. But this day he
turned up in time for the toss and it was an important one for us —
especially the batsmen and more especially the openers, because no
one wants to bat on a waterlogged pitch.

There was great anxiety as Richie came back to the room to
announce that he had won the toss.

Once he had told us there was much hollerin' and hootin'.
'You bloody beauty,' we all cheered, assuming that Rich had put
Northern District in. The impossibilities of batting in the mud
would be their problem and not ours.

'We're batting,' Richie said dryly.

I'm sure his sense of humour was such that he took great delight
in our discomfort. The reaction was swift and ungenerous. 'You

bloody idiot!' (and worse) was the chorus that went up. Richie just smiled. Then he explained.

'It's so wet out there the ball will skid,' he said. 'But after lunch it will pop and it will be a lot harder to bat then.'

Out we went to bat first. All out for 47. Back in the room, all the cussing and cursing started again. The 'idiot' theme got plenty more air. When we walked out for the Northern District innings, Richie took me to the strip and started carving a cross in it. He wore boots with incredibly long spikes whenever the ground looked like being a bit damp, and by the time he had carved a cross in the pitch, the marks were about an inch deep.

'You and I are bowling, and I just want you to hit that cross,' he said. I got five wickets for 20 runs. Rich bowled medium-pace and off-spinners and took 5–21. Northern District were all out for 43. Having been so ready to scoff at him after the toss, we were all very sheepish. He came back to the room with the gloating grin of a Cheshire cat.

It was classic Richie. A decision based on long experience, innate wisdom, great knowledge and the boldness to take a chance. He had an enormous confidence to back himself and his men, and all the players in the teams he captained knew it. His confidence and self-faith were contagious, and failure never held much fear for any of us.

When I left Dungog and came to Sydney to play, I chose Cumberland as my club because Richie was still there. Jack Chegwyn, a NSW selector of the time who used to take invitation teams to the bush, had recommended me after a game at nearby Maitland where I scored 50 and took a few wickets against one of his XIs.

I was 16, and coming to the big city was no small thing. My father died soon after I moved to Sydney and Richie became like a second father to me. He was about 15 years older than me, but the gap in worldly wisdom was wider than that.

I stayed with Harold Goodwin, a stalwart Cumberland player, and his family, and everybody was very protective of me, especially Richie. It was a huge thrill to play with him, first in grade cricket and then for a few Sheffield Shield games when I started as a teenager and he was about to retire from the first-class scene. I did play a lot with him for Cumberland, at a time when Shield and Test players often were seen on club grounds.

One instruction Richie gave me right at the start was priceless: 'Don't sign anything until you've shown it to me first.' And that was pretty much the way it was. He was fantastic as a sort of manager before there were managers, and he didn't have to do it. He was the NSW and Australian captain at the time, and looking after a country kid new to the big city wasn't part of his brief. He just did it because that's the sort of person he was.

Richie continued to support me in very tangible ways after he had retired from cricket. When I made the Test side in 1965–66 and scored hundreds against England in each of my first two Tests, I was suddenly confronted with commercial realities that I had never really thought about. I was offered contracts that seemed pretty attractive, and Richie stepped in and did all my negotiating. He dealt with the Slazengers and the Dunlops of the world, and by the time he had finished I was suddenly the highest-paid Australian cricketer since Bradman. The result was a £1,000 bat contract which, to a 20-year-old from Dungog, was mind-boggling money at the time.

Richie helped me out like that for a couple of years as my career settled. I could have used him at the end of it, though. When I retired in 1981 my contracts for everything — bats, boots, gloves and pads — added up to an inglorious $500.

I did have a brief commentating career with Channel Nine in the mid-1980s. On one occasion, I was on with Richie when Bob 'Dutchy' Holland was bowling against the West Indies. Dutchy had found himself on a turning Sydney pitch and the ball was spinning at right angles. When one ball spun about three feet I turned to Richie and said something like, 'Gee, Richie, I bet you would love to be bowling on this sort of wicket.'

It seemed to me to be a reasonable thing to say. Richie's head turned away. Silence. I assumed Richie had not heard me. The next ball turned even further. I repeated the question. Again, silence. I asked the technical guy if there was something wrong with Richie's earpiece. He shrugged.

At the end of the over, Richie turned to me and said quietly, 'I don't answer hypothetical questions.'

Lesson learned.

I did not see a lot of Richie in more recent years, save for the annual Parramatta cricket club lunches which he always somehow managed to attend. I would have a few beers with him and chat about all sorts of things. I remember at one of them he was telling me that he had added length to his golf game.

'The old Simmons woods have gone,' he declared after I enquired about his golf. 'I have metal woods now, and I hit the ball 50 yards longer.' Those old clubs were something else, minuscule against the metal heads of modern clubs. But he liked them, and he stuck with them for decades. It was the same with his car. From just about the day I joined Cumberland more than 50 years ago, he was driving the Sunbeam Alpine that he drove to the end, and is now in his Coogee garage, somewhat bent. He was not one for change, at least not for change's sake.

Richie was a stayer, always there, always loyal, and brilliant at what he did. It was a lucky day for me when I joined his team and became his friend.

JOHN GLEESON

John Gleeson was Australian cricket's compelling 'mystery bowler' of the 1960s and early 1970s. He appeared in 29 Tests (1967–1972) and 116 first-class games (1966–1975), and toured England, New Zealand, India and South Africa with Australian teams. Except for the days when cricket took him to Sydney and beyond, he has lived in Tamworth in the New England region of northern NSW since 1958. 'I reckon I'm a local now,' he says with a chuckle. It was in Gunnedah, a little further west out along the Oxley Highway, that Gleeson first encountered Richie Benaud.

BACK in 1965, when I was invited to play for a NSW North-Western side in Gunnedah against a touring team that Jack Chegwyn, a wonderful contributor to NSW cricket, had brought up from Sydney, I decided there was only one bloke in the opposition line-up I wanted to impress: Richie Benaud. I had a plan worked out: when Benaud came out to bat I would bowl two orthodox off-spinners and then my 'leggie' that looked like an off break. But the strategy came unstuck when I caught and bowled Barry Rothwell off the second-last ball of an over. Benaud was the new batsman, but I had only one ball remaining in the over.

Unbeknown to me, Benaud and Chegwyn had been down behind the sightscreen while I was bowling, watching through binoculars. Maybe he reckoned he had me worked out when he got to the wicket.

Meanwhile, I was thinking, *If he gets out and I haven't bowled to him, I've missed my chance.* So I decided to throw caution to the wind and bowl the leggie first up. It pitched where I wanted it and he tried to turn it down the legside. But it went the other way and his eyes opened wide.

It would be the only ball I ever bowled to him in a cricket match.

At the end of the game, Richie came over to me and asked, 'Have you thought about playing in Sydney?'

I told him that I wasn't fussed at all about playing in the city. I'd played for Country against City at the SCG — which was something I had wanted to do — and I'd pretty much gone around the world with the Emus (a unique touring club made up of cricketers from country NSW). 'That'll just about do me,' I said.

'I'll just say this to you,' Richie replied. 'In ten years' time you'll ask yourself the question: "I wonder what would have happened if I *had* gone to Sydney?" And you'll never be able to answer that question. How about if I see what's doing and give you a ring during the week?'

'Righto,' I told him.

On Monday afternoon, he rang and said I was playing first grade for Balmain against North Sydney on the following Saturday. If it hadn't been for Richie, if he hadn't done what he did that day, I would never have come to Sydney. I have him to thank for all that followed.

About 18 months after that game against Jack Chegwyn's team I got to bowl to Richie during a practice session at the SCG. This time, I decided I'd bowl him the orthodox 'offie' first up.

I think he was concentrating on a lot of things ... where my bowling hand was ... my approach to the wicket ... and, anyhow,

I hit his off stump. He underarmed the ball back to me with the words, 'I was still in Gunnedah.'

I kept in contact with Richie and Daphne in the years that followed and quite often stayed with them when I was passing through Sydney. We became quite friendly and there were good nights, sometimes as many as ten or more people around the dinner table.

One such night, I looked at him and said, 'By God, you sound like Billy Birmingham!' I don't know where that came from — it certainly wasn't premeditated. Billy, of course, had sold a million records as 'The 12th Man', impersonating all the Channel Nine commentators. You should have seen the look on Richie's face! I changed the subject very quickly and was thinking, *Struth! What did I say that for?* His bottom lip came out, I can tell you.

I've had a fortunate life, all of it to do with cricket. Some great tours and great times. I particularly remember the Emus' world tour of 1961. And I will always remember Richie Benaud, such a good friend, who changed my life with what he said to me after a single ball I bowled in Gunnedah half a century ago.

BRIAN TABER

Brian Taber, 'Tabsy' to his many mates, played 16 Tests between 1966 and 1970 and toured England twice, in 1968 and 1972. Born in Wagga Wagga and an agile, natural wicketkeeper, he made his cricketing progress via Wollongong: from his club, Balgownie, he headed north to join the Gordon club in the Sydney grade competition ... and onwards, all the way to the top. In 1971, he was appointed national coach by the Australian Board of Control for International Cricket (now Cricket Australia), the post being sponsored by the Rothmans National Sports Foundation. He'd continue in that position for more than a decade.

RICHIE was a man of generous spirit. My view is that the countless unknown 'small' things he did quietly in the interests of cricket in the years I knew him add up to being almost as important as his famous contributions at the game's highest level.

I remember a long weekend in the early 1970s at Dubbo, in the central west of NSW, after I was appointed as national coach and Richie had come on board as a consultant. We had worked together by then over a fairly intensive period to produce a coaching manual, which would be the basis of our 'Coach the Coaches' programme. There was a nice ritual to the making of that manual. In the early stages, I'd go over to Richie's place at Coogee some mornings and we'd work together, preparing the material. Then he'd leave me for a short while and would go to his office, and I'd hear the telex clicking away as he dispatched his newspaper stories to England. At lunchtime Daphne would bring out a cold can of Foster's for me, they'd have a glass of wine, and we'd have lunch together. Daphne would then type up the morning's work and gradually, through this process, we constructed that first coaching manual.

Richie was a tremendous help and guide, not just with this manual but also with the constructing of exams for would-be coaches at different levels. When all was ready, we set up a trial Level 1 coaching course to be staged over three nights at Dubbo.

One member of the class was an Indigenous man, who was said to be a very good player and was the father of a promising cricketer. Keen to work with the young players in the town, he showed real enthusiasm in all that came up during the classes. So there was general surprise when he didn't turn up for the final night, until someone quietly made the point that the scheduled written exam was a likely explanation — the fact being that this fellow couldn't write.

I will always remember what followed — how Richie went out of his way to make contact with the missing student and then proceeded, in his typically excellent manner, to make everything right. Richie gave him the exam via a long telephone conversation, question by question. The bloke was spot on in his answers ... and earned his Level 1 certificate.

Richie was always happy to help. On several occasions, I asked him would he have a look at a young player I had identified as having some potential. In his busy life, he never said no. Instead, he'd leaf through his diary and set a date. There was one strict stipulation: no press. Richie insisted that such 'auditions' be done quietly. He didn't want any kudos and he didn't want to put pressure on the young bloke involved. Such private events happened at various venues. On one occasion, Peter Leroy, curator at the SCG, specially marked up a pitch on that most famous ground. Another time, in Adelaide, the 'class' for a left-armer with a good wrong 'un was conducted on the day of a Test match — on a concrete pitch in a South Terrace park at the crack of dawn.

I'd generally keep wicket behind one stump, while Richie watched the budding spinner bowl an over or two. And then he would have a long talk to him about the art of spin bowling, leaving the boy with thoughts on the things he should be working on.

I remember a Country Carnival held at the SCG, where the boys from the bush would sleep at the ground over the two weeks, ready for their days full of cricket. The carnival culminated with games against Sydney's Combined Green Shield teams on the SCG No. 1 and No. 2. Richie was one of a number of former and current stars who came down to help. I particularly recall him stressing to a group of young bowlers the importance of imprinting on their minds the spot on the wicket where they planned to land the ball. He placed a handkerchief on the pitch and then donned a blindfold, saying, 'You've got to practise so much you can do this …'

And then he bowled a delivery that landed spot on, right on the handkerchief.

He was ten years in the consultancy role at Rothmans and in that time I learned a whole lot from him. I wish I'd known some of that stuff when I was playing.

I first met Richie in 1955, when he came to Wollongong with one of Jack Chegwyn's teams. My brother Ross and I were chosen to play in a Wollongong team against them. My memory is a bit faded, but I suspect Cheggy's team was full of stars. I recall Jim de Courcy, who toured England in 1953, was there, as was Ron Kissell, who played Shield cricket for NSW, and Sid Carroll, who would be the major influence in my joining Gordon. Richie certainly was. A memory from the match is of him blasting a hook shot out of the ground and smashing the windscreen of a parked car, which belonged to one of the players. I was 15 and it was an amazing experience to be on the same field as Test and state players.

Years later, I would have my own near-accident with Richie, early one morning at the Australian Golf Club. When we were working on the coaching manual, I'd now and then get a call from Richie suggesting a (very) early hit of golf before we started work. We'd be on the first tee around 6am and, with the help of a cart to get us around, we'd be back at Coogee to begin the working day by nine. On this day, Richie hit his tee shot on the 16th, and then jumped in the cart and moved it forward a little. I mishit my drive off the heel of the club, and it flew at a zillion miles an hour into one of the markers on the ladies' tee, from where it ricocheted straight into the cart, with Richie in the driver's seat. Freakishly, the ball hit the steering wheel but somehow missed him completely. A fraction higher or lower and there could have been a headline!

Richie loved his golf. At one point, he had a favoured Ben Hogan putter that he put out on the balcony at Coogee so the sea air would get to it, and add some rust and character. He certainly had character himself.

I found, whether playing with or against Richie, there was always so much respect for him. The Richie I knew was a man of strength and principle. I recall as clearly as if it was yesterday a lunch I attended with him and Bob Radford, secretary of the NSW Cricket Association, at the Tattersalls Club in Sydney. Not long before, Richie had handed back his life membership of the NSW Cricket Association in protest at the association's actions during the 1969–70 season, after they suspended his brother John, then the NSW captain, for wearing low-cut, lightweight, ripple-heeled boots that they had deemed unsafe and unsound. Only boots with full spikes would be permitted, declared the hierarchy. John's ban was eventually repealed after a month of ridicule. The crazy thing was that, at the time of the dispute, Dougie Walters, John Gleeson and I, all NSW players, were wearing the new boots on the Australian team's 1969–70 tour of India and South Africa.

The lunch at Tatts turned out to be about Richie's resignation. Bob gradually eased towards the subject. Finally, the moment arrived and Bob pleaded with Richie to reconsider his decision.

'No way,' said Richie.

The Association subsequently had a couple more tries on the issue, but each time it was, 'No way.' That was Richie Benaud — rock-solid to the core.

BARRY KNIGHT

Barry Knight played 29 Tests for England as a batsman and fast-medium bowler, and made two Ashes tours to Australia — under Ted Dexter in 1962–63 and Mike Smith in 1965–66. He later emigrated to Australia, played club cricket in Melbourne and extensively in Sydney, and was a coaching pioneer. He established an indoor coaching school in Sydney that over the course of nearly five decades set a lot of teenagers on the way to celebrated Test careers.

IT was extraordinary, bizarre even, the way I got hold of Bill Lawry's baggy green cap. It was at the end of the first Ashes Test in Brisbane in late 1962. I had been picked in England's team after getting a handy 60–odd in the MCC match against a Combined XI in Perth. The Brisbane Test was a bit of an arm wrestle. By the last afternoon England were six wickets down and Richie had nine men around the bat looking for the winning wickets. Fred Titmus and I had to pat away a couple of overs to seal the draw.

I suppose I blocked ten or so deliveries in those final pressured minutes, and I was feeling pretty relieved when I got into the dressing-room and collapsed on the bench, glad we'd saved it. Not ten minutes later, Richie had dropped on to the seat beside me. The rapport between teams after the game was a little more sociable in those days.

We chatted away about the game, about how I liked Australia, about nothing in particular and everything in general. Then out of the blue he said to me casually, 'Have you got an Australian cap?'

'Well,' I said, 'no, I don't have an Australian cap.'

At that moment, Bill Lawry was standing nearby, chatting to Freddie Trueman. Richie reached up, pulled the baggy green cap from Bill's head and gave it to me. I didn't quite know what to say or do, but Bill didn't seem to mind, so I kept it. Still have it. I think the Australians got a few caps in those days, but it was still a pretty strange and very generous thing to do. As I'd come to learn, this was the way it was with Richie.

I didn't play any more Ashes Tests on that tour and I didn't really get to talk to Richie again until about 1970, after I had moved to Australia. I played club cricket for Carlton in Melbourne and then for Balmain and Mosman in Sydney. In Sydney particularly, in the days before daylight saving, I quickly realised that club cricketers didn't get a lot of practice, because by the time they left work and headed off for a net the light was already fading and time was short.

This meant there was virtually no coaching for players in Sydney. Especially the up-and-coming ones. I had worked at Alf Gover's cricket school in London, where good players practised indoors, and also at a coaching school Trevor Bailey had set up, and it seemed to me a similar sort of thing could work in Sydney. So I rang up Richie to see what he thought.

He agreed there were plenty of good young players in Sydney who could benefit from such a project. Some former Test cricketers weren't so sure. I remember Jimmy Burke claiming Australians played naturally and that coaching would spoil the game. Others agreed with him. They didn't want to be like England, I think was the consensus. Richie didn't think like that. He could see the value of proper technique and didn't think that necessarily meant abandoning natural talent.

I obtained a lease on two floors of a building in the city. Richie was writing for *The Sun* in those days and he gave my new cricket school some good publicity, as did his friend and fellow journalist Phil Tresidder, whom Richie brought along to our opening. Richie also got some Test players along, then Phil booked two nets for a few hours every week for the Randwick club. Before long, we had a good thing going.

Richie also suggested one other thing that was quite revolutionary at the time, but a big step forward in the science of sports coaching. He rang me up and suggested I come with him to meet Forbes Carlile, the renowned swim coach who at the time had the world champion, Shane Gould, in his squad. We had lunch and Forbes explained what he was doing with the new concept of video recording, taking underwater shots and the rest so that he could analyse swim strokes.

Richie made the point that it could work with cricket. He organised a video camera for me and soon we were recording players while they were in the nets and then showing them what they were doing and how they could do it better. I kept that coaching school going for 47 years. Of all the young players aged between 11 and 15 whom we coached, 28 went on to become Test cricketers, men like Allan Border, Adam Gilchrist and the Waugh twins among them. They can all thank Richie for the foresight he had.

Richie led the field in other ways when it came to structured cricket coaching in Australia. He was involved early with the Rothmans National Sports Foundation, supporting Brian Taber in the construction of a coaching manual and helping to gather the best of minds to formulate coaching policies and techniques. I remember one seminar over about three days in Sydney, when he chaired a group that included Australian players like Bill Lawry, Jack Potter and Norm O'Neill, and the Australian-born former Leicestershire left-arm spinner Jack Walsh. Ideas sprang from everywhere. Fitness was raised as a field to improve, although I recall Norm wondering how carrying someone on your shoulders up a hill could improve your cover drive.

Richie advised me on all sorts of things, such as when I thought about trying to do some coaching in India with videos over the internet. All right in principle, he would say, but will it work? Always down-to-earth, he would go through the pros and cons. Every new idea I had, I ran past him. Daphne, too, was helpful. When I toured Australia in 1965–66, she was with the party as secretary to team manager Billy Griffith. On the way home, I asked her guidance on buying some jewellery for my wife and she took me to a place in Hong Kong where she said the actor Stewart Granger had bought pearls for his wife, Jean Simmons. Immaculate advice, as it turned out.

For many years, Daphne and Richie would invite my wife Annette and I to dinner at Coogee during the Sydney Test. Bill Lawry would always be there and Tony Cozier, the gifted West Indian writer and broadcaster, was often there as well. I claimed Richie as a friend, although we were never in each other's pockets. He was like that, I think, with many people.

Before he got into television in a big way, Richie was like many ex-cricketers from what was essentially an amateur era, trying to find his place in life after cricket. He set up a catering business for a while, but a partner let him down. Thank goodness he did not stay in that trade too long. Had he remained a caterer, the sporting world would have been a far poorer place.

GREG CHAPPELL

Greg Chappell, second of the famous cricketing brothers, was an artistic batsman who scored a century on his Test debut at the WACA Ground in Perth in 1970–71. This was the first of his 87 Tests for Australia, in which he scored 7,110 runs and captained the Australian Test team either side of World Series Cricket, between 1975 and 1983. Greg worked for a time as a commentator in the Channel Nine commentary team and has had a long involvement in coaching. As Australian captain, he was the architect of the underarm bowling affair in an ODI against New Zealand in 1981, making him the target of Richie's most strident criticism.

RICHIE BENAUD epitomised the words of Mark Twain: 'The fear of death follows from the fear of life. A man who lives fully is prepared to die at any time.'

Richie led a full and creative life in which fear may have played a very minuscule, inconsequential part. As a player, he prepared well and played with abandon. His captaincy was bold and adventurous. As a broadcaster, he was peerless.

I feel like I have known Richie all my life.

When my brothers and I were young, our father imbued a love of the game in us and encouraged us to learn from the best. I can remember as a ten-year-old going to the Adelaide Oval to watch a Sheffield Shield match between South Australia and NSW.

NSW were led by Richie Benaud and contained six of the then Australian team. Dad had suggested that Richie, Alan Davidson, Neil Harvey and Norm O'Neill were the players to watch. I followed their every move on and off the playing field. From memory, Richie scored some runs in the first innings and took wickets in the second to bowl NSW to victory. My other hero, Neil Harvey, scored a scintillating 84 in the first innings.

Even to a ten-year-old, Benaud had an air about him. He was cool and aloof, but when I approached him cautiously to collect my first ever autograph, he couldn't have been kinder and warmer. I was a fan from that day and followed his career closely, even modelling myself on him by becoming a leg-spin bowling all-rounder! My leg-spin didn't survive the journey, as I never overcame growing six inches in one summer holiday period as a teenager. But, luckily, my batting allowed me to follow his footsteps into Test cricket.

My next interaction with Richie came 11 years later, following my maiden Test innings in the first ever Test match in Perth. Richie was now a commentator and was working at that game. Following my successful debut, I was interviewed by Richie at the end of the day's play. At the conclusion of the interview, we walked together back across the WACA and Richie offered me a piece of advice: 'Whatever you do, don't ever stop playing your shots.'

This was intended to be encouragement to a young player, but I misinterpreted the advice and tried to play shots from the start of my innings for the next few Tests and failed to make an impact. Once I learned that I had to be selective about which deliveries I attacked, my career gained the benefit of his wisdom.

During the second season of World Series Cricket, in 1978–79, I went through a lean period against the formidable West Indies pace attack. So I sought out Richie for some advice.

My method to that point had always been to expect the full ball and respond to whatever came along, but, because the West Indian bowlers were pitching so few balls up, I decided to get on the back foot early to get ready for the short balls. Suddenly, I found that I was getting out to full balls and struggling to make the most of the few bad balls that I received. Richie reflected on my problem for a few moments and then suggested that I go back to doing what had allowed me to be successful to that point. As usual, he was spot on and my form and fluency came rushing back.

One of Richie's great traits was his positivity about the game and towards the generations of players who followed him. He never lived in the past and was effusive about one-day cricket when it came in and T20 cricket in more recent times.

He was always supportive of me … other than the infamous day at the MCG when I ordered my younger brother to bowl underarm against New Zealand. His summation of the day was scathing.

I was stung by his criticism, because it came from my boyhood hero. He was, of course, entitled to his opinion and, without any knowledge of some of the things going on in the background, he was entirely correct to be affronted by what I did. I made a mistake for which I have expressed my remorse. It is a decision that I wish I had never made.

We never discussed the incident. I didn't feel the need to and I had no doubt that Richie believed he had said what he felt and moved on. Our relationship was largely unaffected in the aftermath. He continued to be unfailingly generous and gracious in his assessment of me and my career.

Though hurt at the time, I have never held his comments against him. He was not only professional but extremely supportive when we worked together in the Channel Nine commentary box. The Nine commentary team became iconic in the years when Richie led the band of Test-match captains, all of whom held him in the highest esteem.

Amazingly, it was Billy Birmingham, the 12th Man, with his parodies of the commentary team, who took them to an even wider audience. Birmingham really 'caught' the personalities of Benaud, Lawry and Greig — and indeed the commentary box — in a way that endeared them universally. It seemed everyone was practising Richie's 'What a catch!', Bill's 'He's got 'im!' and Greigy's comments about the 'cor pork' and the 'putch report'.

Some of us in the commentary box, too, would practise our Birmingham Benaud-isms, but not when Richie was around! Bill Lawry is the only one I saw who did it to Richie's face and that happened when they were on-air together during a domestic one-day game in Hobart in the 1990s.

South Australia were playing Tasmania and reached a score of 2–222, which Bill mischievously read as 'chew for chew hundred and chwenty chew', including the pouting bottom lip. Bill thought it was so hilarious that he put the microphone in his lap and collapsed in paroxysms of laughter.

Richie probably saw the funny side of it, but he wasn't going to give Bill the pleasure by joining in the mirth, so he put his microphone in his lap and stared down his nose at Bill and silently dared him to go on.

Each time Bill picked up the microphone he collapsed into laughter and couldn't speak. Richie wouldn't commentate either, so two overs went by without a word while Bill composed himself. Once again, Richie showed his dry wit and sense of timing as he had the last laugh, letting Bill stew in the juice of his own making.

Richie led a very full and interesting life, with cricket as the backdrop for most of it. He enriched the game with his love and his knowledge and graced it by never looking backwards and lamenting the past or the changes. He always looked for the positives in the game, and in those who played it. He will be sorely missed and the game will be much poorer without him.

MIKE WHITNEY

A lively left-arm paceman and crowd favourite, Mike Whitney played 12 Tests and 38 one-day internationals for Australia between 1981 and 1993. Whitney emerged as a character of the game with his energetic and spirited approach. He was famously conscripted to make his Test debut while playing league and county cricket in England in 1981. At the end of his cricket career he headed on to a diverse working life, anchored by his role as host of the TV show *Sydney Weekender*, which was first broadcast by Channel Seven in 1994 and is still going strong.

IT was through the great cricket, rugby and golf writer Phil Tresidder, that I first encountered Richie Benaud, during the season of 1977–78. Tres invited 'Mr Benaud' — that's certainly what I called him then — down to a Randwick club practice at Coogee Oval one evening. I was in my second year of fourth grade and things were going well after a good debut season. Phil had told Richie about a couple of 'up-and-comers' and this 'tearaway left-armer, a surfie from Maroubra with an afro hairstyle' whom he should come down and take a look at.

The nets in those days were at the sou'-eastern end of the ground and the moment Richie arrived the intensity of the whole practice session went up by about 30 per cent. Phil brought the Great Man over and I was able to say hello and shake hands with him. Returning to the nets, I proceeded to tear in, bowling as fast as Wes Hall, and in the process hit a couple of our blokes. After a while, Tres called me over again. 'Richie's got something to say to you,' he said. Richie looked at me.

'I'd like to see you pitch a few more up,' was all he said.

Moving on to 1991, I'm with the Australian team in the West Indies and we're getting ready to play in the first Test. Rich is banging away on an old typewriter beside the swimming pool at our hotel. I went up to him and introduced myself.

'How're you going?' he asked.

'I wonder if we could have a bit of a talk about my bowling,' I asked.

And so we sat there for half an hour, talking about reverse swing and bowling on Caribbean pitches, all kinds of stuff. When the conversation finally ended, I thanked him and he looked at me in his way and said, 'It's just nice to see you pitching a few more up these days.'

It was a line delivered with all the typical Benaud dryness. I was stunned. He had remembered Coogee Oval all those years before. I don't know whether he ever realised how funny he could be. I walked away and burst out laughing. It was the way he delivered his message. Again!

Tres once told me a story that captures a little of the dryness of Richie's wit and delivery. He was playing with Richie and another close golfing mate at the Australian. On a par three, Richie landed his tee shot nicely on the green, as did Tres. The third bloke was in the bunker, from where he promptly holed it for a two. Richie and Phil putted out for pars and not a word was said until arrival at the next tee, when Richie looked at the birdie bloke and just said: 'Prick!'

There is another story that is my all-time favourite about Richie, whether true or not. It was during a Test at Lord's after the BBC had lost the cricket rights and Richie went across to Channel 4. It was all happening that morning: as part of their innovative new coverage, Channel 4 had hired a blimp to provide some overhead shots and these were now being beamed out with Richie providing the commentary. 'There is the Thames,' he said, 'Westminster Abbey … the Houses of Parliament.' Then the camera focused on the London Eye, the great new attraction of the city. 'And over there,' Richie declared, 'is the London Wheel.'

As the story goes, Mike Atherton was up the back of the box that day, thinking of the millions of pounds the city of London had spent on the Eye. At an appropriate moment, Athers walked over and tapped Richie on the shoulder.

'Rich, it's the London EYE … not the London WHEEL.'

Richie didn't miss a beat. He half-turned as he answered: 'Not any more, it's not.'

True or not, it's a classic Richie story and part of his legend.

STEVE WAUGH

Steve Waugh made his Test debut as a 20-year-old on Boxing Day, 1985. His first three-and-a-half years as an international cricketer were difficult; he failed to score a Test century but did have some productive days in ODI cricket, most notably at the 1987 World Cup. After being dropped from the Test XI in 1991, he came back two years later to establish himself as one of the game's greatest players, finishing his career in 2004 as the most-capped Australian player and with the best win-loss record among all regular Test captains.

IT just came in the post, out of the blue. It would have been 1987, maybe 1988, not long after the World Cup we won in India and Pakistan in late '87. Simon O'Donnell and I had been mucking around in the nets, trying out various slower balls, but when we began deceiving a few blokes we realised we had a secret weapon that gave us a distinct edge. Simon had plenty of success with a ball he bowled out of the side of his hand, a sort of exaggerated leg-cutter, while mine came out of the back of the hand, with my wrist pointing the opposite way to a conventional delivery at the moment of release. After we claimed the cup as 16–1 outsiders, people knew we were on to something special.

Inside the envelope was a letter, from Richie Benaud. I must confess I was stunned when I saw who it was from. I felt like I had known Richie for just about my whole life, through his TV commentary and what I had read about his playing and captaincy career, but I'm fairly sure I had never had a long conversation with him to that point in my life. We'd regularly see the great Alan Davidson at junior matches and then senior rep games, and he was always supportive of the team after each match no matter the result. I'd bumped into Neil Harvey at various exhibition games and he was helpful and friendly. But while I was in awe of those blokes, Richie was somehow a rung higher. There was Bradman, then Benaud. And he was writing to me.

Richie wrote how he had been impressed by my slower ball and how I had the courage to try something different. It was a trait, he wrote, that he admired. He encouraged me to explore other variations to extend my repertoire. Attached to that letter was a photocopied article from an American sports magazine that he thought would be of interest to me. It showed different grips used by US baseball pitchers — for an assortment of pitches such as curve balls, change-ups, cutters, sliders, splitters and so on. Maybe one or more of these grips might inspire another new delivery.

The information was interesting. The fact Richie Benaud had taken the time to do the research, write a few comments, get my address and send the letter … that blew me away.

As it turned out, while I read his letter and the article closely, and I tried a variety of experiments in the nets, it didn't lead me to discover another effective delivery. But I still believe what Richie did for me played an important part in my development as a cricketer and as a person. Here was the best cricket brain in the business encouraging me to think outside the square, that all the answers might not be found in conventional coaching manuals, that it was okay to look beyond cricket in my quest to be a better cricketer.

It was also a huge encouragement for me, aged 22 and struggling to find my feet in Test cricket, to have a man of Richie's calibre noticing what I was doing on the field, seeing some potential in me, wanting to help. That was a real boost to my confidence.

I never became an intimate friend of Richie's, but — except for the guys who moved to the commentary box — I don't think many of my cricket generation did. It wasn't his way to get too close to the players he was commentating on, and I respected him for that. By keeping that distance, he was never in a position where his views might have been compromised by a friendship. I was a bit the same as a player. I didn't want to get too friendly with the members of the media, for fear that would change their expectations of what I could and couldn't do to help them.

In my view, what set Richie apart as a commentator was his fairness. He was authoritative and unbiased, and he came across as open and honest, which meant that players and fans alike respected him. If he criticised, he was constructive — it was never just for the sake of it.

Whenever I ran into him and Daphne, and found myself in conversation with them, I always found the subject and the way they approached it to be very interesting. The best chats were rarely about cricket. They were what I would describe as 'worldly' people, able to talk with authority and passion about a wide range of subjects. I'm not sure Richie was a man to tell too many long stories, but he had an amazing ability to get to the nub of a conversation, to sum things up in a few words. He had an almost mesmerising effect on people. When he spoke, people listened.

In 1998–99, I missed a number of one-dayers because of a torn hamstring, and was consequently invited into the Nine box to call a bit of the action. As is the way, I was thrown in at the deep end — no rehearsal, no training, fend for yourself, good luck. At this stage of my life, I hadn't ruled out maybe one day doing some commentary, so I was eager to pick up some pearls of wisdom from the experts. When I had the chance, I peppered Richie with questions: 'How do you do the live cross to the studio without an autocue? ... How do you close the coverage? … How do you remember what you're going to say? … Do you have advice?'

He paused …

'Well, Steve,' he finally said. 'Just don't make any mistakes.'

That was all he said.

At first I thought he was taking the mickey out of me. But then I realised his message was this: *It's not easy. Don't complicate things unnecessarily. Keep it simple.*

I know now that this advice works well with a lot of things, not just crossing to the six o'clock news. It was typical Richie.

SHANE WARNE

When Shane Warne emerged on the world cricket stage in the early 1990s, he was soon regarded as 'the best Australian spinner since Richie Benaud'. In fact, Shane went on to a career of unprecedented achievement, finishing with more than 1,000 international wickets (708 in 145 Tests; 293 in 194 ODIs). Best of all, he revived the art of leg-spin bowling. In the years since his retirement as a player after Australia's 5–0 Ashes clean sweep in 2006–07, he has established himself as a popular and perceptive TV commentator in England and Australia.

I WAS an 18-year-old cricketer at Lord's trying to ply his trade when I first met Richie, and it wasn't long before we got onto the topic of spin bowling. His passion for this subject was apparent from the very beginning. I count myself very lucky that as time went by I was able to call Richie Benaud, and Daphne, true friends. Over dinner now and then through the years, Richie and I would inevitably talk about spin bowling — grabbing bread rolls or whatever was in the vicinity that might be useful to demonstrate grips, how to bowl flippers and all of that.

Of spin bowling, he had a favoured phrase: 'Give it a rip!'

To me, he was the Marlon Brando of cricket: the Godfather. He was also a wonderful guy. It seems that everyone talks about Sir Donald Bradman being the biggest figure, the most influential person in Australian cricket. But, for me, it's Richie who will be remembered as the most influential individual of all, considering everything he contributed to the game over so many years. His achievements were across the board — on the playing field, then through the revolution of World Series Cricket as a broadcaster and on to become, in my view, the greatest of all sportscasters. He was the master of the one-liner and the pregnant pause. His silences were as famous as his brief declarations, which could be as simple as 'practise' when he was giving advice to a young cricketer trying to become a better one.

And he seemed always to be right on the money. From the first time I met Richie, my opinion of him was always one of absolute admiration.

The 'Gatting ball' from the first Ashes Test of 1993 changed my life. As soon as play ended that day, it was back to the hotel waiting for the highlights. (Maybe I had a pizza in between!) To watch it back then was fantastic. To have Richie call the moment, as he did, took it to another level.

He set the scene with characteristic simplicity: 'The first ball in Test cricket in England for Shane Warne.' Then the ball took Mike Gatting's off bail. 'He's done it!' Richie called. 'Gatting has absolutely no idea what has happened to it ...'

One of the greatest things about Richie was the generous way he passed on the knowledge — his knowledge — of leg-spin bowling. And he handed it on for such a long period of time, and not just to Aussies, but worldwide. He loved cricket, the game itself, but he especially loved leg-spin bowling.

I'll always consider myself lucky that he passed on so much of his wisdom and information to me. In turn, I'm trying to pass that on to as many young leg-spinners as I can, wherever they happen to be.

Richie Benaud was one of a kind. In the minds and memories of those who saw him play and those who came to know him, and for all of us who appreciate his standing in the game, he will never be replaced.

SIMON KATICH

Simon Katich played 56 Test matches for Australia, the first of them at Headingley, Leeds, in 2001. Katich has never forgotten the words offered then, nor the understated support that followed him through his career.

EVERY Australian player who is presented with his first baggy green cap is filled with pride when that moment comes before his debut Test match. For me, it was more than that, because Richie Benaud was involved. I remember being blown away when I was told such a revered figure was doing the presentation. To say the moment was special is a grand understatement.

The words that Richie offered as he handed me the cap have stayed with me always, proof enough I think of the wisdom, the balanced perspective and plain common sense he maintained throughout his time in cricket.

'There are many more important things in life than a baggy green cap,' he said. 'But to an Australian cricketer it is the ultimate achievement. Every time you wear it, wear it with pride … and enjoy yourself.'

I felt a certain affinity with Richie after that. I would often bump into him at functions and the like, and he always had a kind word. I made my Test debut some 50 years after he started, yet all the players of my generation had an enormous respect for him … for his achievements as a cricketer and Australian captain, and also for the balance of his television commentary.

It was in his nature to be positive. He was never negative. If he criticised he did so in a constructive way, even a nice way, and though the message was always clear it was done in such a manner that offence was never taken. We always found him fair, and it was impossible not to respect his judgment. Impressively, too, he was a humble man. He never imposed himself or his opinions on the generations of cricketers who followed him. And he never forgot his roots. I remember an evening when I was invited to speak at the Parramatta club dinner. Richie was there, honouring the club that gave him his introduction to cricket, and mixing with the young players.

The young men lapped it up. There was no generation gap here. Richie fitted in as he might have done more than half a century before, when he was one of them. It was the nature of the man.

MICHAEL CLARKE

Michael Clarke retired from international cricket after the Ashes tour of 2015. He had been in the Australian team for more than a decade, and captain since 2011. Michael amassed 8,643 runs in 115 Tests, including 28 centuries, and his 31 Test wickets included one haul of 6-9 against India. He made a century on his Test debut, was part of two 5-0 Ashes series wins (as a player in 2006-07 and captain in 2013-14) and two World Cup triumphs (in 2007 and as captain in 2015), and scored 329 not out against India in 2011-12, the first triple century ever scored in a Test at the SCG.

AS with most cricketers of my generation, I grew up with three distinctive voices always in my head. The television was our link with the big time, and Richie Benaud, Tony Greig and Bill Lawry somehow made it all come to life. Richie had a style all of his own and the voice seemed to fit it perfectly. He was all dignity and common sense and knowledge.

The first time I met Richie, officially anyway, was at the Allan Border Medal in 2005. I had won it for the first time, and I remember talking to Richie on stage and marvelling at the fact that he sounded in the flesh exactly as he sounded on television. I have no idea why I was surprised. Maybe it was the fact he had been parodied so often, but somehow I had it in my head that the TV voice was just that, and he would probably be different face to face.

I called him Mr Benaud at that first meeting. It just seemed right, given the standing he had in the game and the way I had looked up to him from early childhood. We all idolised him when we were kids, and not only because of his work on television. We had all heard the stories of his deeds as a cricketer.

I had always soaked up as much of the history of the game as I could and wherever I turned there was always an aura about Richie Benaud. I have loved talking cricket with players of past generations and without exception they have always had a special regard for Richie — as a player and a competitor, and as a gentleman of the game.

Through my years in first-class cricket I would see Richie regularly, and he always had time for a chat and to provide some gentle encouragement. He would often tell me to back my gut instinct, to play the game as I felt it.

I came to respect the help that was always available from the Channel Nine 'old guard'. I got to know Tony Greig especially, given he was on the pitch so often before the start of play, and when I had a go at commentary myself, during the Melbourne Test match of 2014–15, it was a real thrill to work with Bill Lawry. Regrettably, I never got to discuss the art of commentary with Richie, but I have spoken to so many who did, and the wisdom he offered was unique.

I would have loved to have seen Richie play. I have read and heard so much about him; he must have been a brilliant player and leader. He has left a wonderful legacy, part of which, I believe, relates to the role he played in the modern resurgence of leg-spin bowling, especially as it was embodied in Shane Warne. I know Warnie took a lot of inspiration from everything Richie achieved, the guidance he offered and the remarkable example he set.

FOR SIR DONALD BRADMAN, ADELAIDE, 25 MARCH 2001

Exactly a month after the death of Australia's Great Cricketer, a public memorial service was held at the Adelaide Oval. Richie delivered the eulogy.

It's not quite perfect outside, I guess. Rain coming down. A bit of a dodgy pitch. Wind blowing. But I reckon he would have handled it with all his consummate skill, no matter what it might provide out there. There is a crowd out there filled with memories. The bowling changes here at the cathedral end have been many and varied. We've now got an ageing leg-spinner and I think The Don might have welcomed that.

He was the most famous of them all at a time when despair ruled Australia because of the Great Depression. Seventy years later, one hundred selectors from around the world nominated the five greatest players of the century. The Don received one hundred votes. Not far away from him was that finest of all-rounders, Garry Sobers, who got 90. But one hundred out of one hundred is pretty good.

When I was six years old, Bradman was captain of Australia in the concrete storeroom at Jugiong where I played Test matches. When I was ten he was still captain on the back verandah at Parramatta where he led and won and was absolutely brilliant in all those Test matches I used to play against England. I wasn't alone, in that thousands and thousands of other youngsters around Australia played their Test matches like that — Bradman and McCabe made all the runs and then O'Reilly and Grimmett bowled out England every time. Wondrous days ...

I was lucky to be around as captain when that extraordinary series of Test matches was played against West Indies in 1960–61. One of the significant happenings in Australian cricket came about at the start of that series when, the night before the first day of the Tied Test, The Don came to me and asked if it would be all right if he came to speak to the team ... The gist of his short talk was that he and Jack Ryder and Dudley Seddon, the other two selectors, would be looking in kindly fashion on those cricketers in Australia who played the game in attractive and attacking fashion and thought of the game rather than themselves. The unspoken words were that anyone not wanting to fit in with those plans shouldn't think about giving up their day job.

The more important tour was the one he undertook in 1948. That was the one where he was captain of the Invincibles, and some of those great cricketers are here tonight. He was always of the opinion that it was close to impossible, because of changes in conditions, to judge which was the best ever cricket team. One thing we can be sure of, though, is that those Invincibles would have given more than a reasonable account of themselves in any contest against any other combination in any era. Three of those — Miller and Morris and Lindwall — were wonderful mentors for me. They did a superb job of trying to get me to think about the game and people and to do the right thing, all in their completely different ways.

Miller underlined for me the fact that it's a good thing never to take oneself too seriously. Back in 1950–51, Freddie Brown had the MCC side out here and NSW was playing South Australia in Adelaide in the Shield game just before the first Test in Brisbane. It was November and as a selector Don was watching the match just 20 yards along to the right where the visitors' dressing-room was and still is. 'Pancho' Ridings gave us a most awful hammering that day, thrashed us everywhere. We were a very weary bunch at the end of the day, resting in the leather chairs and looking over here to the cathedral, not saying much. Except I was chirping away. You've got to bear in mind that I had just turned 20 and I knew most of what there was to be known about cricket, so I chirped. I didn't get much response at first but I chirped again. I said to Miller that because Bradman had retired the moment I came into the game it was one of the sorrows of my life that I had never been able to bowl my leg-spinners to him. It was still very hot, about 85 to 90 degrees at that time of the day, and South Australia had just belted their way to four for 374. 'Nugget' never took his eyes off the cathedral. He didn't turn to me but just looked straight ahead and ruminated for a full two seconds before murmuring: 'We all have one lucky break in our lives, son, and that could have been yours.'

In the images of the family funeral a few weeks ago there were some memorable moments; sad but memorable. I was particularly taken by three things, which to me had a bearing on the fact that he was regarded with affection by old and young.

There were older people standing silently and just looking. There was a youngster, a boy scout, who saluted and held his salute. And then there was what a few people had said to me they thought to be a little irreverent, and that was: 'Aussie, Aussie, Aussie! Oi, oi, oi!' Because he was a sportsman with such vision and because he had a feel for young cricketers — no one ever had a better feel for them; of all the people I have known, he wanted to see youngsters get on — I think he would have liked the blending of the modern with the old in that moment with the funeral procession going past. It all marries into something that he used to talk about: that cricket simply is a reflection of life.

Above all else he was very much an Aussie. He was an Aussie sportsman and a great sportsman, said by his critics never once to have questioned an umpire's decision. He was a sportsman and it wasn't just for a few sessions or a few days, it was for all eras and for all sports followers.

Above all else, he was a sportsman.

– 7 –

A GENEROUS SPIRIT

'We never had a cross word. Richie's word was his bond.'

— James Packer

JOHN FORDHAM

For the last ten years of Richie Benaud's life, John Fordham and The Fordham Company acted as his talent management team. They lined up Richie's last work assignment and despite failing health Richie gave it everything. The result qualifies as an Australian classic.

THE final year of Richie's life was spent recovering from his October 2013 car accident, and fighting cancer. But with marvellous support and encouragement from Daphne, he stoically battled on.

In late 2014, my son and business partner Nick visited Richie and Daphne at their Coogee apartment with a business proposition we felt would interest him.

It was for Richie to become the face of the 2015 Australia Day lamb campaign. The fact that it involved Australia's national day of celebration immediately attracted his interest. The television commercial, in which Richie 'invites' the likes of Captain Cook, Ned Kelly, Burke and Wills and Ita Buttrose to join him for a lamb barbecue on Australia Day involved a demanding single–day shoot running close to ten hours.

A weakened Richie amazed the production team with his professionalism and good humour. Looking back now, it was a herculean effort from the great man considering the state of his health. Then, on Australia Day 2015, true to his word, Richie attended the barbecue at a harbourside home in Sydney's eastern suburbs.

Ned Kelly and Captain Cook turned up as well. A group of Richie Benaud look-alikes who'd been imitating the captain of the Nine Network commentary team for a few years had some private time with him they will long cherish.

Afterwards, as we assisted Richie up steep stairs to his awaiting car, he turned and enquired, 'How did we do?'

The answer was easy. One of your best, Rich!

I was 15 when I first saw Richie Benaud in the flesh. My father took me to the Sydney Test of the 1958–59 Ashes series against Peter May's team ... Richie's first as captain. From the old Sheridan Stand, we watched every ball bowled as Australia worked towards a 4–0 series win.

I met Richie for the first time six years later, when I was a journalist working in the Fairfax interstate bureau in Sydney. Richie had retired from first-class cricket the previous year and was a writer on *The Sun* newspaper, preparing to cover the forthcoming Australian tour of the West Indies under new skipper Bob Simpson.

Seizing an opportunity to shake his hand and request an interview for a preview story on that tour, I strolled across the corridor to Richie's desk to ask if he would help me. As one who always impeccably observed the correct process, he suggested I run the request by his editor Jack Tier, and if he gave me the go-ahead everything would be fine. With Tier's green light, the next day I spent an hour with Richie picking his brain about the West Indies tour.

Fast forward 40 years to 2005 and Richie is sitting in my Sydney office, having agreed to become a client of our talent management agency a few days earlier. That the deal was sealed with a good old-fashioned handshake reminded me we were dealing with a pretty special individual.

At that meeting in our office, I produced the original yellowed copy of the story I'd written in 1965. He immediately sat back and read it from start to finish. Then, in trademark Benaud fashion, he remarked: 'Absolutely, perfectly accurate.'

I can hear him saying those words so clearly as I pen these recollections.

Richie enjoyed an incredible appreciation of other sports, golf and racing holding particular appeal. He studied them closely and established many friendships far away from cricket ovals and the broadcasting box. I learned this first hand in 2009, a few days before the Ashes Test at Lord's.

Richie and Daphne had been invited by the now defunct *News of the World* newspaper to dinner at a twilight race meeting at Windsor to mark his 40 years as a cricket columnist. Ian Chappell, also a client of ours, and I tagged along.

Sitting there that evening with Richie, Chappelli and other good friends, including the great England cricketer Sir Alec Bedser and legendary racecaller Sir Peter O'Sullevan, was a special privilege I will long remember.

Before the first race, a bookmaker who'd been despatched to our private room to take bets approached our table. Without any knowledge of the field for race one, I was about to place a bet when Richie tapped me on the shoulder.

'I would only back that horse if it's your intention to lose your money,' he candidly offered.

'So, what would you do, Rich?' was my response.

'Well, for starters,' he offered with a wry grin, 'you might note that Frankie Dettori only has one ride here tonight, so you might ask yourself why he's come all this way for just one race.'

So my 20 quid went on the Italian's mount and it rocketed home by a couple of lengths. The result gave Richie as much satisfaction as this novice punter.

In Adelaide a few years ago, a day before the Test started, I attended a lunch winemaker Grant Burge hosted for the Nine Network commentators. Benaud, Chappell, Greig, Healy, Taylor, Slater, Nicholas … they were all there. Towards the end of a very long private-room lunch, I attempted to replenish Richie's glass with Burge's mighty Meshach Shiraz and in so doing unfortunately directed a high proportion of the contents onto his beige jacket.

Richie was totally undeterred and continued to explain to Burge his decision to bowl around the wicket to Peter May in a 1961 Ashes Test, the move that sparked a great Australian victory.

Sheepishly, I accompanied Richie back to his hotel and offered to have the coat cleaned before play commenced the next day. Richie graciously declined my offer and retired to his room. The next morning, Richie tapped me on the shoulder and, pointing to the beige jacket he was wearing, said with a smile, 'I want you to know that I have more than one.'[1]

In every way, Richie was a gentleman. He was also a worker, and right to the end. Captain Cook and Ned Kelly will testify to that.

BOB COWPER

Bob Cowper was an accomplished left-handed batsman and right-arm off-break bowler who bookended his 27 Tests with Ashes tours to England, starting and finishing his career at Headingley in 1964 and 1968 respectively. He scored 307 in one Test innings against England in 1965–66 and finished his Test career with a batting average on home soil of more than 75. Bob retired early to launch a highly successful business career, living for many years in Europe, where time spent with Richie and Daphne Benaud was one of life's singular pleasures.

IT was my loss that I did not have the chance to play cricket under Richie Benaud's captaincy. My career in Test cricket started a few months after Richie retired, though I had played a little Shield cricket against him and well knew the fighting qualities with which he imbued his teams.

I did get to know Richie really well later on, when our cricket was behind us. For 30 years, I lived in Europe, in Monte Carlo,

---

1. One day in 1977, Kerry Packer was in his Sydney office watching a WSC match being played in Adelaide, when he had what Richie would describe as a 'light bulb moment'. Mr Packer wanted his No. 1 commentator to stand out from the other men in the box. A light grey sports coat was organised, but the Nine boss wanted it even lighter, for maximum effect. The master tailor, John Cutler, warned against a white jacket, because white can be very harsh on TV. 'I suggested cream and showed Richie several samples in the various ranges of cream in lovely high-quality wools,' Cutler recalled in 2013. 'He chose a very nice one; he had very good taste and was a very stylish man. Once we had the right fit I produced a second coat, both of which were for Richie's sole use.'

just up the road from where Richie and Daphne had a place in Beaulieu, on the southern coast of France. The Benauds spent a lot of time there in the northern summer, while Richie commuted to England for his television commitments, at first with the BBC and later with Channel 4.

Richie loved getting to the south of France, for the anonymity it brought him as much as anything else. Richie essentially was a private person and it was hard for him to escape his own celebrity. Like Sir Donald Bradman before him, he sometimes found his fame just a little suffocating. Sir Donald struggled with it through life and never quite came to grips with it. Richie had a calmness to his personality that meant he coped with it a little more easily.

Yet it was probably worse for Richie than it was for Bradman, given the exposure the television age brought him. When The Don retired from cricket, he could retreat a little. But Richie was on the 'telly' throughout every summer for half a century after he finished as a player, and in England and Australia his was among the most recognisable faces in the land.

It was undoubtedly a pressure for him, to be recognised and confronted wherever he went. So he loved France, where cricket remains a mystery; Richie had no television exposure there and he could move about unnoticed and unchallenged. We played a lot of golf, we dined at wonderful places, we drank lovely wines. It was an escape for Richie from the trappings of his success.

Only once did I ever see him recognised in France. We occasionally went to Paris to tour the galleries and the like, and on one occasion a fellow spotted him with a polite enquiry along the lines of: 'Aren't you Richie Benaud?' The chap was from India, where cricket is an all-consuming passion, and Richie took five or ten minutes to chat with him. This reflected not just Richie's politeness and tolerance, but a shared passion. A sensible conversation about cricket was never a chore for Rich.

I'd first run into Richie when I was playing for Victoria as a very young man. I had perhaps three seasons with Victoria before Richie retired, so I batted against him a few times and I saw first-hand the way he led his teams.

He was a tough cricketer to play against, a real competitor. It was a beautiful thing to learn from him, because he had an attitude that was irrepressible.

He played to win and never seemed to fear failure, as so many great sportsmen do. His influence then, and I suppose still, was profound. Ian Chappell, for instance, did so much for the game through his competitive attitude and the fact he was always striving to win. I'm sure he got a lot of that from Richie. For both men, chasing a result was always more important than protecting yourself.

Richie, however, was very protective of his achievements. I was a left-hand bat and I used to chide him about leg-spinners to left-handers being a waste of time. He didn't argue. But he went in search of evidence, scoured the stats books, and came back to me armed with the evidence of left-handers he had dismissed. He took his cricket pretty seriously, and joking or not, he wasn't going to let such a statement pass unchallenged.

Richie also had a cheeky sense of humour, which like his commentary could provide maximum effect with very few words.

He and Daphne were occasional guests at our holiday home on the south coast of NSW, and sometimes we had a few English friends there as well. It was often noted by our UK guests that while Richie had never lost an Ashes series to England, and he was captain for three of them, he could claim no better than a 50 per cent record in the golfing Ashes we contested at 'Royal' Pambula Merimbula Golf Club.

The Merimbula layout is a typically rural Australian course, with lots of trees and native bush to attract the local fauna. Charlie, a first-time visitor from the UK, was lamenting the fact that he had never seen a kangaroo despite several trips to Australia. I suggested that Pitt Street in Sydney or Collins Street in Melbourne were not necessarily the places to find them, but that is where his business seemed to take him. Richie said nothing.

We introduced Charlie to our course, where our local knowledge was an advantage. Richie expected there would be kangaroos around, and we both knew there was a big one that always seemed to be at the final hole. As we stood on the 18th tee, the match was all square and Richie knew the kangaroo would come into play. At the crucial point, Richie quietly suggested we should be careful. And there he was, the big kangaroo, not far from where Charlie's ball had landed.

There had been an edge to Richie's warning that suggested impending danger. Charlie froze. He was clearly petrified, too frightened to maintain the quality of golf he had produced to that point. We won the hole and Richie was happy to take the spoils of victory.

On another occasion we had a guest, Martin, who was similarly unaccustomed to kangaroos, and was clearly disturbed when we ran into about 50 of them beside one of the fairways. His ball had landed perilously close to them, but Richie helpfully advised that they would not move if he walked towards them repeating the line: 'One, two, kangaroo … one two, kangaroo …'

Richie had a way of getting out those 'twos' and 'roos' with a musical lilt, but our friend was much less melodic. Nevertheless, he waded in, calling out 'One, two, kangaroo' at the animals, over and over. We knew they wouldn't move, but he didn't. It was a bizarre scene. It didn't help us though. Martin hit a pearler and we finished up coming second. Richie loved the golf course. It was a relatively private place for him, away from the celebrity and the inevitable public attention that seemed to follow him around. It was a place, like the south of France, where Richie could be Richie.

CHARMAINE HUTTON

Charmaine Hutton's long association with the Benauds amplified an already distinguished cricket story. Charmaine is the daughter of the late Ben Brocklehurst, who captained Somerset and later became the managing director and proprietor of *The Cricketer* magazine. She married Richard Hutton, who played for Yorkshire and England and is the son of Sir Leonard Hutton, one of England's greatest batsmen and captains. Charmaine and Richard's sons, Ben and Ollie, both played first-class cricket.

I FIRST met Richie and Daphne when — following in Daph's career footsteps into cricket — I was secretary to David Clark, manager of the MCC team that toured Australia in 1970–71.

At the end of that tour, the Benauds asked me to work for them at Coogee, which I regarded as a huge honour. I accepted happily and would go on to enjoy thoroughly the next two years in Australia. I would spend hours listening to Richie's voice on the dictaphone, transcribing material for his many newspaper articles on cricket and golf. One of my regular tasks was to go through the Australian papers to find information that might prove helpful for his stories. I also cut out amusing cartoons that were strategically placed on his desk, generally raising a wry smile or, occasionally, a laugh.

One strong memory of my time with Rich and Daph is of their beautiful but quite fierce grey cat called 'D'Oliveira', who was much adored by Richie. It was characteristic of his generous spirit that in later years Richie always made a point of bowling to our boys in the garden on the occasions when he and Daph visited our home in Kent in England. There were enjoyable and busy times in London, too, where I helped them at John and Gillian Morley's flat in Knightsbridge, their UK base for a number of years.

Gillian (who was known to all as 'Dumpy') and John were the greatest of fun. They were big entertainers and it was through them that Richie and Daph met some of the stars of the Royal Ballet, the start of their long love affair with ballet.

Life at Dumpy and John's in those summers was often one big party for touring teams, but in the background you would inevitably find Richie tapping away on yet another cricket report.

He and Daphne built a wonderful partnership, working hard from the early hours of every day of the week.

JAMES ERSKINE

James Erskine has been a major player on the world sports and entertainment landscape for more than 35 years. Arriving in Australia in 1979, he pioneered sports marketing in the region as managing director of IMG's operations in Australasia. In a fruitful career with IMG and then Sports & Entertainment Ltd, James managed many iconic global figures, including Muhammad Ali, Greg Norman, Tiger Woods, Dame Kiri Te Kanawa, Shane Warne and Sir Michael Parkinson. He remembers with affection and appreciation longstanding links with Richie and Daphne.

I HAD just failed medicine with great success, and was playing too much golf with a professional called John Cook. One night, John invited me to a dinner at Pont Street, SW1, one of London's posher boroughs. It turned out to be the home of Daphne and Richie Benaud. It was the summer of 1975 — the year before Seve Ballesteros exploded onto the golf scene at Royal Birkdale.

I soon joined Mark McCormack's IMG and by 1979 was sent to open an office in Sydney. Daphne and Richie invited me to their Coogee home for dinner on my first night in Oz. The other guest was Austin Robertson, who had the original idea for World Series Cricket. It was a fascinating evening. Listening to Richie, I soon came to realise the esteem in which sport was held down-under.

Richie was thoughtful and precise — not measured, just economical. He understood all the aspects of a sport: the content, the spirit, public expectations, the participants, the responsibilities and also the commercial aspects. His genius was that he could see all the moving parts required for success, but the sport itself always came first, was never compromised.

Richie and Daphne took me under their wing. Spasmodic advice was quietly given and disapproval in the same manner. We would meet — sometimes with the famous, such as Parky, the Shark or Warnie — or have a quiet chat on the practice ground at the Australian Golf Club, where Richie would continue with his methodical routine.

I tried to learn. It was hard to take in his modesty, hard to believe the understated elegance that surrounded everything Richie and Daphne did. Apart from the underarm bowling fiasco, I never heard Richie say an unkind word about anyone; he thought the best of all. The glass was always half full, never half empty.

The partnership with Daphne was something to behold. It was both magical and mystical, as though each knew what the other was going to say before it occurred. They could finish each other's sentences, but never did.

All I know is that I was very fortunate to have been allowed into their sanctum, to get their advice and their help and to be welcomed by them to Australia.

Had Richie been a Pom he would have been Lord Benaud long ago and had a castle bestowed upon him. There won't be another. Thank you for the memories.

ALAN CARDY

Alan Cardy played nine rugby union Tests for Australia between 1966 and 1968. Switching to rugby league — with Eastern Suburbs in 1969 — he suffered a broken leg in a pre-season game, the worst of a series of injuries that cut short his football days. Cardy's subsequent highly successful business career was built in part on a long friendship with his near-neighbours at Coogee: the Benauds.

PHIL TRESIDDER introduced me to Richie around 1965. I met Daphne soon after she and Rich were married in 1967, and the four of us became a group of friends who met regularly to wine and dine. On occasions we would discuss my business and personal problems, and Rich was always supportive and helpful. Indeed, for any confidential business problems that might arise, the first person I would go to was Rich, knowing he would always give me the best possible advice. He was a good person to consult on just about any subject.

For my part, I was able to offer advice to Richie and Daph when they wished to talk about what they were doing in France and London. As with all of us, life wasn't always smooth sailing for Rich.

Our friendship developed to such a stage that by the time I was married, on Rich's birthday in 1986, Daph was 'best man' for me.

We even delayed the start of the wedding because their flight had to turn back to Singapore because of a mechanical fault. They were my constant friends.

JACK NEWTON

A loyal son of Newcastle in NSW, Jack Newton built a highly successful golf career in the 1970s and early 1980s. In 1975, he went within an ace of winning the British Open, pipped by one stroke by the great Tom Watson in an 18-hole play-off. A terrible accident at Sydney Airport in 1983 left him with permanent injuries that ended his golf career, but he re-emerged as an acclaimed radio and television commentator on the game.

BACK in 1970, I played with Ian Chappell in a pro-am that preceded the South Australian Open, which led to us becoming mates. It was through Chappelli that I first met Richie. I was playing in Europe in the early 1970s and doing my best to organise my schedule around the cricket Tests in England, especially when there was an Ashes series in progress. That was a fantastic Australian team — the Chappells, Dennis Lillee, Jeff Thomson, Rod Marsh, Doug Walters and the rest — and good blokes all of them. I used to go into the dressing-room and get treated pretty well.

Richie, with Daphne, was always around the big games and I found him a very interesting man to talk to. I enjoyed his dry wit. A friendship developed and subsequently he used to watch me play quite a lot — over there and back home in Australia.

I said to him one day, 'Richie, why the hell would you watch me with all these good players around?' And he answered, 'I like watching you, Jack. You're more interesting.'

A fair paraphrase of that would be: 'I love watching you get out of trouble!'

We spent some time together on the golf course, too. Richie was fanatical about his golf, and was always talking about how he might improve his game. In the years to come, I'd catch up with him and Daphne on the road at events such as the British Open and the Masters. Generally, there would be a glass or two of wine around. Richie liked his wine.

After I had my accident in 1983, Richie was there with valuable advice that would help shape the years ahead.

'Jack, when you look at what I do, you might be able to work out something similar,' he said.

Richie talked about his own schedule of summers in the different hemispheres — recurring months of TV broadcasting, some journalistic stuff and radio during cricket seasons on both sides of the world, all of them contributing to the 'pot'. His philosophy was essentially the old one of 'small fish are sweet': add 'em all up and you've got a big fish! It was wise counsel. I was able to shape my own life in and around golf in a similar way to how he shaped his life around cricket. Over time I worked as a freelancer for all the TV channels in Australia, until Christopher Skase made me an offer I couldn't refuse when he was in charge of Channel Seven.

When I started commentating on golf, Richie and Daphne invited me over to their place at Coogee for lunch one day and Richie produced something that would prove to be a real help and guide for my new role in the commentary box. He had gone to the trouble of converting EW Swanton's private guide, effectively the 'Ten Commandments of TV Cricket Commentating', to golf parlance for me. He thought I was going well in this new direction in my life and that perhaps these dos and don'ts of sports broadcasting would be useful.

In fact, the wisdom and advice offered proved an enormous help. One of the commandments that resonated strongest with me concerned the inclination of some commentators to make a declaration and then seek support or confirmation from an associate sitting alongside. The firm message from Swanton/Benaud was if it happens you don't agree, don't say anything. It was a policy I adopted whenever I was working with other commentators in the broadcasting box. I was essentially just doing what I was taught by Richie.

He was, of course, a fantastic commentator, with that quirky sense of humour always lurking just beneath the surface. He could string words together, for sure — but he chose them carefully and never 'over-talked' what he was trying to say. In this regard, he was just adhering to a further point made in the commandments: always remember that it is *not* radio. The message is that with TV sending out the pictures of what is happening, using too few words is always better than using too many.

GRAHAM CORNES

Vietnam veteran, footballer, coach, broadcaster and businessman ... Graham Cornes is a legendary figure in Adelaide life. He played 317 games for Glenelg (1967–82), briefly for North Melbourne and 47 games as captain-coach at South Adelaide (1983–84). Graham coached Glenelg for six seasons (1985–90), winning two premierships, enjoyed remarkable success as coach of South Australia, and was the Adelaide Crows foundation coach in the AFL.

WE of the baby boomer generation knew Richie Benaud initially through his exploits as a Test cricketer. Then he was our Test captain and a great captain. Charismatic, handsome, articulate and most importantly competitive, he inspired successive generations of young Australians.

When he retired we got to know him better through television. He was the face of cricket, and while Australian cricket did suffer from the image of the 'ugly Australian' for a time, Richie was always above that. He was cultured, polite and incisive. We absorbed the integrity of the game through his refined, succinct comments. He towered above the rest who presented our cricket, even if they were also legends in their own right.

When the World Series Cricket adventure started, he recruited a South Australian, Graham Ferrett, to help with the organisation and administration. Ferrett, a gregarious and popular figure, had close ties with the Glenelg Football Club, who were a powerhouse of South Australian football in the 1970s and 1980s. A powerhouse except for one small detail. While Glenelg had a great record of reaching grand finals, the club had a shocking record of losing them.

Richie was in Adelaide in September 1982. He agreed to address the club at the post-grand final dinner. Predictably, Glenelg lost, the seventh defeat in eight grand finals dating back to 1969, so there was a very subdued audience in the room when Richie rose to speak.

He made cursory reference to the disappointment that he had just witnessed and then uttered two short sentences that were unforgettable.

'They say that winning isn't everything,' he said slowly and deliberately, this paragon of propriety. 'But it beats the fuck out of coming second.'

He almost spat the words out, then sat down in front of the stunned crowd.

Glenelg won the next two grand finals in which they played.

RON LUXTON

For many years Ron Luxton was the teaching professional at the Australian Golf Club, where Richie Benaud became one of his more dedicated pupils. These days, Ron is the professional at Royal Sydney.

THE last time I saw Richie on the golf course was a few years back at Royal Sydney, where his partner for the day was Brian Johnson, the lead singer with the iconic Australian band AC/DC. It was an unlikely partnership, but an example of just how many friends Richie had in so many areas of life.

I first met Richie some 45 years ago, and from the start he gave me great support. I had been appointed golf coach at the Rothmans

National Sports Foundation, which at that time had been set up to launch coaching programmes in a wide range of sports. Richie was a consultant, I was only 22, and from the start he encouraged me in so many ways.

I saw him regularly through my 15 years with the Foundation, played golf with him occasionally and got to know him for the generous man he was. When I was about 23, I met him in London, and he took me to the Connaught Hotel for lunch. It was a rich experience for a young bloke just starting out, and the beginnings of a long association through golf. I went back there 30 years later, just to relive the experience.

In 1985, I was appointed to be the professional at the Australian Golf Club. It was Richie's club and when he saw in the club newsletter that I had been appointed he rang me from London to offer congratulations. He made me feel he was genuinely pleased I had got the job. When he was at home through Australian summers, Richie was a regular on the practice fairways and a consistent lesson-taker. He had a wonderful attitude and was an easy student. I remember him explaining to me how long it had taken him to perfect the flipper that he used so tellingly in his bowling when he was such a force in the Australian cricket team. He spent two years working on it in practice before he was confident enough to try it in a game.

His golf was much the same. He would practise interminably, out on the practice fairways on his own, working hard on a game that I felt never came naturally or easily to him. He worked meticulously on overcoming all that, and he got down to a single-figure handicap — nine, I think — which put him at A-grade level among club golfers.

He left no stone unturned. I remember after one lesson he walked to the seventh hole and paced out a particular shot that troubled him. It was something the average club golfer would never have worried about, but an example of how hard Richie would work at being better.

You couldn't miss him on the course. When he played golf — which wasn't that often compared to the time he spent practising — it was usually with his great friend Phil Tresidder, who had known him since they played in a Combined High Schools cricket team together. Richie carried his own clubs ... I can't remember him using a buggy … and had a pencil-thin bag that was very old-fashioned. He played for so long with old woods — genuine wooden ones. It was a long time before he was convinced modern technology had made it to golf, and didn't purchase metal woods until one of my assistants, Gary Barter, suggested his clubs be donated as antiques. He was slow to change and liked what he liked; he wasn't a great buyer of gear or golf's trimmings.

When he replaced his irons he gave me his old ones and asked me to give them away. I gave them to a member for his boys, insisting that they send Richie a thank-you letter. They duly sent the letter and sometime later received a beautifully addressed reply from England. They were thrilled that Richie had bothered enquiring about their golf and school.

One of Richie's greatest qualities was that he cared. In 2001, it was time for my contract at the Australian to be renewed, and the negotiations were going more slowly than I would have liked. Richie sensed my concerns and offered to help. Four or five times he invited me to his Coogee home at 7am to work through the club's offer. He had had many similar battles with cricket's Board of Control, he said, and if he could help with words or ideas he would. He worked on my problems for an hour or so each time before he started work himself. He was an amazing help and a rich encouragement. The contract was eventually renewed on acceptable terms.

Richie's individual quirks were part of his persona. I remember him asking for his tee time one day, and as fate would have it the starter told him it was '2.02'. Richie repeated that to all and sundry with the distinctive emphasis he gave to his 'twos', to great mirth all round.

He also loved crème brûlée. My wife Kerry makes a special crème brûlée, many of which were happily supplied to Richie over the years. In his latter days, when he was clearly quite ill, we took over ten or so, which delighted him. It seemed such a small thing for a man who had given so much.

CATHY GAULD

Cathy Gauld has enjoyed an unmatched view of Team
Benaud in action. As the Benauds' personal assistant,
she expertly 'smoothed the path' — mainly from the Chez
Benaud office at Coogee, with its east-facing windows
gazing out over Wedding Cake Island.

THE year of 1998 was a difficult and significant one for me. One
month after my father passed away, I went job-hunting for part-
time PA work. Soon I was working for Richie and Daphne Benaud.
Seventeen years on, I am still here, now working with Daphne. I
couldn't have hoped for a better job.

Daphne and Richie welcomed me as part of their dynamic
'team'. There was always time for a chat. Richie would ask how
my weekends went and took a special interest in my golf. We spent
quite a bit of time discussing putting techniques and I appreciated
other tips he passed on. I remember discussing a matchplay event I
had entered and telling Richie I was feeling nervous.

'Cathy, if you are good enough to be there, you are good
enough to win,' he replied.

Suddenly, any negativity I was feeling was gone and on the day,
I was the winner. He was such an inspiration to me.

Richie and Daphne never big-noted themselves. Sometimes,
they would come to my place for a drink, as on the day his contract
was renewed by Channel Nine. When my neighbour heard the
champagne cork popping, he asked if the contract renewal was the
reason for the celebration.

'Oh no,' I replied. 'Daisy has just turned 21. The celebration is
hers!' Daisy was our Burmese cat, whom Richie and Daphne loved.

Our friendship extended beyond work. On a couple of
occasions, I was invited to spend a week at their home in Beaulieu,
in the south of France, with my family. These experiences were

wonderful, not least the daily walks around Cap Ferrat and the delicious boulangerie treats. Their kindness and generosity of spirit meant so much to me.

I have been so fortunate to have worked in such a warm and happy environment, and to be able to continue assisting Daphne now that Richie is gone.

WARREN SAUNDERS

The years of Warren Saunders' input into the premier sporting clubs of Sydney's St George district span endless winters and summers, with his interest and involvement continuing 70 years after its beginning. The beneficiaries were St George Cricket Club, whose first-grade team he captained to five premierships, and the famed St George rugby league club, where his association began as a ball boy during the war years and where many seasons later his administrative roles were at the highest level. On the field, cricket was his game. He played 35 first-class matches for NSW between 1955 and 1964.

IN 2010, my insurance broking company celebrated the 40th anniversary of an event we conduct each year at Pennant Hills Golf Club. It is a day when we entertain existing and prospective clients and some personnel from within the industry. Richie was always a great supporter of the occasion — even when it was difficult or inconvenient for him to come along he'd still be there, and he didn't mind one bit whom he played with.

'If someone is important to you as a client put me with him,' he'd say.

He fitted in so well and became an integral part of a much-anticipated day. Each year, he'd address the gathering we traditionally held after the last putt was sunk — on the subject of the progress of cricket during the season. And each year it was the same: you could hear a pin drop when Richie was speaking. He had that aura about him; he always commanded total attention.

Richie never wanted anything in return. 'There's no need for any of that,' he'd say.

But in 2010, as we reached our 40-year milestone, we decided we wanted to honour Richie. He had been such a great supporter. When I got him up at that year's function, I said to him, among other things: 'Rich, you're a good giver, but you're not a very good receiver.'

And then I made a presentation to him — a fine whisky decanter — to convey our thanks.

Richie was self-effacing as usual, and protested mildly. 'You've got no need to do that,' he said. 'I don't expect anything. I so much enjoy coming to these days.'

He then offered a few words of appreciation …

'When I get home,' he told the gathering, 'my wife Daphne will ask me, "Did you have a good day?" To which I'll reply, "Yes, I had a lovely day."

'Then she'll ask, "Did you have a hole-in-one?" And I'll tell her, "No."

'And then she'll say, "Did you win anything?" And I'll say, "Well, have a look at this … I have a gift."

'And she'll open it and say … "Not another fucking decanter!"'

It brought the house down! The people who were there still talk about it to this day.

Richie was a pretty good golfer who for a long time played off about ten. My wife, Clare, and I went with Richie and Daph to the Kapalua Resort in Hawaii a couple of times in the 1980s on golf trips, which led to me witnessing a funny moment involving him and Hale Irwin, the three-time US Open champion, who was the touring golf pro at Kapalua at the time …

We chanced to have just finished a round one morning as Irwin was walking out to have a game with his young son. Richie said g'day to him.

Now, someone had obviously told Irwin that Richie had been a sportsman of note, or perhaps he had encountered Richie in days when he was covering some golf, because in a very American way he declared: 'I know you! You're that Bennett … or Burton … or

Bernard guy from Australia.' He got the 'B' right, but that was as close as he came to 'Benaud'.

This could never have happened in Australia, where Richie was as well known as any prime minister or rock star. But I think he quietly enjoyed Irwin's faux pas. He was never one to seek the limelight. I always saw him as self-effacing and quite shy, and there were occasions when I was with him and he was downright reticent — he just didn't want to be the focus of attention. Yet on his home turf Richie always was, and as his life went on he only became more so.

TONY SHEPHERD

Tony Shepherd is chairman of the Sydney Cricket and Sports Ground Trust. Richie made his first-class debut and Test debut at the SCG, and also played his final Test at the iconic venue.

ONE of the more remarkable things about Richie Benaud's lifelong involvement with the Sydney Cricket Ground is that after his playing career finished, he rarely set foot on the field of play. Richie would tell curator Tom Parker and others that the outfield and the pitch were for the cricketers of today, not for him.

He had more claim than most to take to the field whenever he pleased. His preference for the press box, rather than the playing field, tells much about the man.

The occasions when he broke his own enforced absence from the ground were rare — the most memorable being when he joined his fellow Channel Nine commentators to pay tribute to the late Tony Greig. Other than that, Richie restricted himself to the working-press areas of the SCG.

On arrival, he would unfailingly offer a polite welcome at the security gate, always announcing himself rather than expecting to be recognised. Richie would park his Sunbeam Alpine in the outside broadcast compound behind the MA Noble Stand. To reach the lift to the media boxes, there is a short walk alongside one of the main entries to the ground. Richie's appearance always resulted in plenty of cheers from fans queuing to take their seats for a day's play. Autograph requests were myriad, but Richie was always prepared — carrying a pencil case full of varied writing implements to suit whatever it was he was being asked to sign.

Richie made few demands of the SCG staff, who saw him every summer, greeting the regulars by name and happily discussing summers past and present. There was one constant though: Crunchies had to be part of the afternoon chocolate run. Any absence of the honeycomb chocolate bars was met with the same raised eyebrows that had marked Richie's character on the field as Australian Test captain.

As cricket history was made at the SCG, Richie was either on the field taking part, or up in the stands telling the rest of the country about it. He is an SCG life member and is recognised in the Walk of Honour that is a feature of the precinct. His likeness is among the most popular features of the Basil Sellers SCG Sports Sculpture Project and he is one of 15 inaugural inductees in the SCG Media Hall of Honour.

This recognition is sure to continue as the grand old SCG continues its evolution. The SCG was Richie's home ground and it is right that his presence remains permanent.

Richie himself once said:

> Many grounds have their own built-in charm — the tradition of Lord's, the Oval gasometers, the joy and enthusiasm of spectators from Jamaica and Barbados. All are great grounds, but it's nice to be back here [at the SCG], where the light seems a little brighter ... the ground just a little softer ... and the grass just a little greener ... and really feel you're home.

MICHAEL HENNESSY

Sydney-based marathon runner and fitness expert Michael
Hennessy is the founding father of 'The Richies', a colourful,
bewigged, good-humoured group who since 2010 have
dressed up and added an extra quality to day two of the
Sydney Test each year.

BY the 2009–10 Australian season, Richie Benaud was so widely
loved and such a part of the fabric of cricket and summer that I felt
as if we'd almost begun to take him for granted. Then came reports
that he might be retiring from the Channel Nine commentary
team. It was at that point that The Richies concept was born. There
were ten of us involved at the start; we just wanted to show Richie
how much we'd appreciated him and his amazing service to cricket
over the years.

We were soon joined by friends and other cricket fans keen
to show that they felt the same way. In five years, the original ten
swelled to become 300, as we sought to turn the second day of the
SCG Test into 'Richie Day'. I guess the fact our small annual tribute
has developed this far already, with photos and footage of us being
seen around the world, is a testament to the high esteem in which
Richie was and is held.

Initially, we weren't sure how he would take us, dressed up as
we were in cream jackets and silver wigs. But he always gave us a
genial nod and was happy to field any cheeky questions from fellow
commentators during breaks in play when they might quiz him on
what the hell such a large group of grown men were doing dressing
up as him. I especially remember Tony Greig's enjoyment at giving
Richie a bit of a stir whenever the cameras panned to the Richie
bay.

A few of us Richies were involved in a promotion featuring
the man himself on the beach at Bondi in 2012. He was engaging,

happy to give us time for a chat, and had us all mesmerised with the stories he told … of his own development as a leg-spin bowler, the wise advice he had been given by Bill O'Reilly back on the 1953 Ashes tour, and how it all came together on the 1957–58 tour of South Africa. He even gave us a demonstration of how to hold the ball to bowl a flipper. He was in his early 80s by then, maybe moving a little slower, but his mind was still so sharp and so full of fascinating details from his life in cricket

We ran into him again on Australia Day 2015, when a few of us were involved in the filming of a TV commercial for Aussie lamb. It would be one of his last public appearances and he was clearly frail, but even though he had battled through a long morning of interviews and media commitments, he still generously stayed on to give our group the chance to grab a quick word and some photos.

The dry Benaud sense of humour and deprecating style were also on show. 'You guys have more hair than me,' he observed, looking out across our sea of cheap grey wigs. Always, there was the sense of him trying to put us at ease in his company.

NEIL HUTCHINSON

The old garage-workshop where Richie's much-loved Sunbeam Alpine was meticulously looked after for more than 20 years stands about a nine-iron from Chez Benaud at Coogee. Richie's garage of choice was of a similar vintage to himself, dating back into distant mists, perhaps 80 or 90 years. The current proprietors, the Hutchinsons, have been there for almost 35 years, over three generations. Norm Hutchinson, his son Neil, and Neil's son Kim are sporting men, and Richie's kind of people — expert at what they do, hardworking, no-nonsense. He trusted them with the car of his heart, and they worked with care and patience to keep it

going smoothly. This was Richie's second Sunbeam Alpine.
Former teammates remember him in a red version back in
the 1960s.

IT was in the early 1990s that Richie first brought his 1963 Sunbeam Alpine coupé to our little family business, Conella Motors, at Dudley Street, Coogee, where I was working alongside my father Norm. Little did we realise back then that it would become the most identifiable car in the district. It was beige in colour, in tune with the jackets Richie had made famous in his role as a TV commentator.

Richie came to see us on the recommendation of his then secretary, Margaret Roseland, who was one of our customers. He was seeking someone who could provide regular servicing for his car, the type of which was rarely seen on the streets of Sydney. We struck it lucky that day, as we do whenever we get great people like he and Daphne as clients. Richie was lucky, too, in that it happened that Dad had once managed a Rootes Group dealership that specialised in Humber, Hillman and Sunbeam cars. When Richie first brought his car in, Dad would have been one of the few blokes around town who had an expert working knowledge of the Sunbeam Alpine, which is a rather challenging car to maintain. It was also a hard car to drive for anyone who wasn't familiar with it, with a strange clutch that didn't want to be depressed too far. Richie found this out to his distress one night when, arriving in town for a cricket function, he handed the keys to the valet parking attendant. The young fella promptly flattened the clutch to the floor, and it virtually disintegrated.

The car became part of our life at Dudley Street. Summer or winter, whether Richie was in Australia or the northern hemisphere, we'd collect it from his home once a month for a service. Sometimes we'd have to scour the city for a particular part; they were never easy to get, but we had great backup from an old motoring man named Peter Rudland, who was always able to find what we needed. And so we kept it going. For years it was the oldest car we looked after at Conella Motors.

Richie loved that car. Once, when there was a minor mishap negotiating the awkward driveway down to his garage and it was noticeably scratched, he was devastated. The story goes that after each of his trips away he would unload his luggage at home and then head straight to the garage to say 'hello' to his car. On one occasion, someone associated with his television work provided him with a brand-new car. He never drove it; the vehicle was left sitting outside the Benaud home.

I don't think anyone else apart from Richie ever drove the Sunbeam in recent years, except for my son Kim and me. I know that Daphne didn't enjoy getting into it.

It was a real jolt when Richie's friend and clubmate at the Australian, David Cox, rang one morning in late October 2013 with the news that Richie had been involved in an accident in the car and was in hospital. The Sunbeam was placed in a holding yard for some days, then brought to our workshop. It was a sorry sight, a real mess, and there was nothing we could do but organise for it to be towed to the Benauds' home, where we had to jack it up to get it into their garage. The car was so badly damaged we couldn't roll it, or steer it in.

Richie was such a decent guy, an absolute gentleman. With his status, he could have been demanding, but he never was in all the years we did business with him. Every December, from the first year he linked up with us, he'd arrive down with a Christmas hamper. When he was sick, Daphne turned up with a hamper.

My lasting memory of Richie will be that of him at our garage in the afternoon, chatting with such ease and friendliness to other customers. He was the great cricketer and commentator, but on these occasions he was just a friendly, genial, genuine bloke who had popped in — as they had — to pick up a car.

– 8 –

SEASONS IN THE SUN

'Benaud was always a meticulous man with a great love of the fine things in life.'

— **Alan McGilvray**

VICKI JONES

Vicki Jones was at the coalface in the struggling early days
of World Series Cricket, co-opted to do what she could to
'spread the word'. History judges today how an exciting,
if bumpy beginning turned into a revolutionary sporting
success story. For Vicki, the opportunity that came her way
led to a mighty bonus: a long, enjoyable and much-valued
friendship with Richie and Daphne Benaud.

I WAS the young public relations director for Channel Nine when
I first met Richie in those early, heady days of the 1970s — when
World Series Cricket was not going too well at all, to say the least!
Executives were scrambling for new promotional ideas and heads were
rolling.

I was summoned to Kerry Packer's office one day to join a
meeting of Channel Nine executives who were trying to come up
with ideas and solutions to better promote their breakaway games. It
was a baptism of fire for me, because I had absolutely no idea about
cricket, but after a tumultuous two-hour meeting, I found myself
taking on the PR job for WSC, while continuing with my regular
job promoting all of Nine's on-air programmes.

In part because of my lack of knowledge of the finer points of
cricket, I focused promotion on the broader media, steering clear
of the sports pages. The sporting media were initially hostile, so
I decided to treat my new-found 'stars' — Richie, Tony, Bill and
Ian — like 'TV personalities', wheeling them out to the latest movie
premiere or arranging photo shoots with visiting celebrities. I will

always fondly remember our time with the visiting rock star and cricket lover Elton John.

As WSC evolved into a ratings tour de force for Nine, Richie's fame and his fan club grew exponentially. His informative commentary, timing and dry wit made him a favourite with diehard cricket fans and newcomers alike. A public relations dream in his cream jacket, Richie's commentary became the soundtrack of our summers. Elegantly attired and ever-punctual, Richie was a joy to work with. He was a stickler for detail, well prepared for any media interview.

The elegance of Richie Benaud continued throughout his life. In the rough-and-tumble world of commercial television and sport, Richie's impeccable manners and welcoming smile remain a stand-out for me. He loved a glass of chardonnay and had a particular way of holding the stem of the glass, twirling it between thumb and forefinger. And he was a great listener. Whether he was at a crowded cocktail party or at the dinner table, he would listen intently, twirling his glass, never interrupting … waiting until his dining companion had finished his or her story before commenting.

In the years that followed I spent so many fun times with Richie and Daphne, here in Australia, and in London and Europe.

Through mutual English friends, Libby Reeves-Purdie and John Chalk, we were invited to Royal Ascot races each year. Richie was resplendent in grey morning suit and top hat; no cream jacket here! And Daphne with her glorious English complexion and fetching hat … they made such an elegant couple. Together with his great friend, the famous English sportswriter Ian Wooldridge, and Ian's wife Sarah, we spent many a happy hour at Ascot, studying the form and placing our bets with the bookies, usually assisted by a glass of champagne or chardonnay, of course! Richie was a very well informed and quite successful punter — nothing too large but successful nonetheless.

I was always astounded at Richie's star quality in England and Europe. I guess when you know someone like Richie for a long time, you tend to forget how famous they are — and that they are part of so many people's daily lives. Even though there were many notable stars in the marquee at Royal Ascot — among them the likes of Sir David Frost, Nigel Havers and Joan Collins, plus large numbers of lords and ladies, knights and dames, barons and baronesses — Richie always attracted attention. He was ever-gracious in granting photo requests from fans and stopped regularly to sign autographs on his way to the Royal Enclosure with Daphne.

At the beginning of July each year, Richie and Daphne hosted Nine's hospitality marquee at Wimbledon. I was fortunate enough to be sent to London to assist them in ensuring that our important clients and major international stars were entertained royally at the tennis. On many occasions, I observed a big international star or corporate heavyweight quite overwhelmed by the fact they were being greeted by the great Richie Benaud! The marquee was a wonderful forum for networking and many lucrative deals were concluded by network executives over lunch there.

Following Wimbledon, we often met up with mutual friends holidaying on the Amalfi Coast in Italy or in the south of France. There were many occasions when touring Australian cricket fans couldn't believe their luck at spotting Richie and Daphne having lunch in one of the small local restaurants. Most approached the table respectfully to request an autograph or a photo. It never seemed to bother Richie that they had interrupted his lunch; inevitably, he took time out to chat.

I remember a day in Positano when a group of gorgeous bikini-clad Aussie girls in their twenties recognised Richie and draped themselves around him for a souvenir photo. Richie, tanned and relaxed, was beaming throughout, clearly chuffed by the attention of this bevy of beauties. The girls got their photo and immediately texted it back home with the caption: 'You're not going to believe who we met in Italy!!!'

Even on holiday in these exotic locations, Richie always took his work commitments very seriously. On many an evening, after having spent the day enjoying lunch and the sun, Richie would slip quietly away to write a piece for one of the many publications to which he contributed. His work followed him everywhere, and he loved it.

It was a tradition of Christmas mornings that I would receive a call from Richie and Daphne to wish me the compliments of the season. They knew exactly where I would be — most often in my car driving to the west of Sydney to visit my mum and dad. Rich and Daph would be making the same trip: travelling west to see Richie's mum.

I grew up in Sydney's western suburbs and attended Parramatta High School. When I was there — and I'm sure in the years before and after — every student was aware that the school's two most famous ex-pupils were the actor Rod Taylor and Richie Benaud. Little did I know back in those schooldays that I would become a friend of Richie and his gorgeous wife.

It was a great pleasure to have had him as a part of my life. I will miss his Christmas morning phone calls, although I suspect Daphne will keep up the tradition.

The Benauds are like that.

RENTON LAIDLAW

Renton Laidlaw is a highly respected golf writer and broadcaster who has been honoured with lifetime achievement awards in Britain and America. The first Open Championship Renton saw as a reporter was at Muirfield in 1959; in 2013, he was recognised as the first non-American to cover 40 Masters tournaments. His commentary is familiar to viewers of golf on television all over the world, not least because of his work with the BBC, ITV, Sky TV and in recent years as the 'voice of the European Tour' for Golf Channel.

RICHIE BENAUD had many golf partners and I was fortunate to be one of them. The games we played around the world were always enjoyable but had to be taken seriously because that was Richie's way.

We reigned unbeaten for more than four years, thanks mainly to amateur golfer Richie's determination and innate professionalism — a feature of everything he did. He was always well prepared. He always thought long and hard about the shot he was about to play. Nothing was rushed. He played his golf the way he lived, in a measured, organised and sensible manner.

At the MCG in 1981, Dennis Lillee became the leading Australian wicket-taker in Test cricket when he dismissed Indian opener Chetan Chauhan, passing Richie's previous mark of 248 wickets. The two great bowlers met later in the home dressing-room, with the old record-holder congratulating the new champion.

Above left: Richie with Peter May after Australia's stunning victory in the first Test at the Gabba, 1958–59. **Above right:** John Woodcock, cricket correspondent for *The Times*, took this photo of Richie with Len Hutton in 1963, prior to the annual encounter between a Woodcock XI and the village of Longparish.

Brian Taber, Richie, Lancashire off-spinner Jack Simmons and Australian leg-spinner Kerry O'Keeffe in 1974, discussing the recently released National Cricket Coaching Plan.

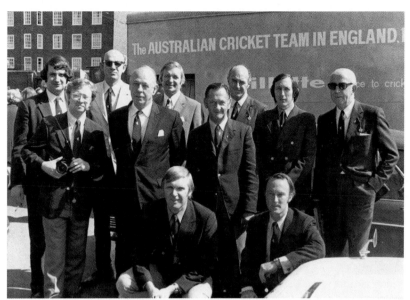

The Australian press in England, 1972. **Standing (from left):** Mike Coward (AAP), Russell McPhedran (*Sydney Morning Herald*), Dick Tucker (*Daily Mirror*), Jack Fingleton (freelance), Richie Benaud (BBC, et al), Percy Beames (*The Age*), Phil Tresidder (*Daily Telegraph*), Graham Eccles (Melbourne *Herald*), Alan McGilvray (ABC). **Front:** Norm Tasker (*The Sun*), Phil Wilkins (*Sydney Morning Herald*).

A BBC team from the early '80s. **Back:** Ted Dexter, Richie Benaud, Michael Fordham (scorer). **Front:** Jim Laker, David Kenning (producer), Peter West, Tom Graveney.

Team manager Richie Benaud and captain Greg Chappell talk to the media at Sydney airport prior to the International Wanderers' tour of South Africa in 1976. When asked why he took on this role, Richie explained that he had heard conflicting reports about whether racial barriers were being removed in South African cricket. 'I decided to have a look for myself and make up my own mind,' he said.

Richie and Daphne with the champion stallion Without Fear at the famous Lindsay Park stud in South Australia.

Some greats of Australian cricket climbed the SCG Hill for the launch of Brian Booth's autobiography, *Booth to Bat*, in 1983. **From left:** Arthur Morris, Richie Benaud, Keith Miller, Brian Booth, Bob Simpson and Neil Harvey.

John and Richie Benaud with Doug Walters at a Parramatta Cricket Club function in 2007.

Right: Richie on the day he took delivery of his freshly restored 1963 Sunbeam Alpine.

Below: John Benaud's son Jamie hops behind the wheel of his uncle's prized car in the early 1980s.

Richie with some of his fellow participants in the BBC's 1979 *International Pro-Celebrity Golf* series. **From left:** Sean Connery, Richie, Seve Ballesteros, Christopher Lee, Henry Cooper, Lee Trevino, Peter Falk and Bruce Forsyth.

Right: Richie on the golf course with tennis champion Ivan Lendl.

Below: On the first tee at the Bob Hope British Classic pro-am in 1980. Richie's playing partners at the RAC course at Epsom, Surrey, were (from left) Scotland's Sandy Lyle, Jim Davis (a star of the hit TV show *Dallas*) and Zimbabwe's Mark McNulty.

Richie with Ian Chappell at the back of the Nine commentary box at the WACA Ground in Perth, February 1991.

Channel Nine's leading commentators in 1998–99, with some of the stars of the Australian team who joined them in the box during the summer. **Back (from left):** Simon O'Donnell, Ian Botham, Tony Greig, Bill Lawry, Ian Healy, Michael Slater. **Front:** Shane Warne, Ian Chappell, Richie Benaud, Mark Taylor, Steve Waugh.

Ironically, one of sport's greatest captains insisted that I should captain our golf partnership. Maybe he thought I was captaincy material or maybe — more than likely — he wanted to be relieved of making all the decisions. Cricket was his business; golf was his recreation, something to enjoy.

Mind you, I found it tough trying to emulate the master! On one occasion when playing in Kenya at the beautiful Karen Country Club, where there was a sign saying that golfers were permitted to take cover if a lion emerged from the scrub, I hit the green at one of the short holes — I cannot remember which one — and Richie hit into the trees, found the ball and played out short of the putting surface.

He walked over and went to pick the ball up, indicating he was out of it. Sternly, I ordered him to leave it where it was. He rocked back on his heels. I explained I might three-putt — a not unusual occurrence as I did not have my favourite Maxwell hickory shafted putter with me — and he might chip in and win the hole.

For a moment I worried about what I had done. Few people dared to speak to Richie in that manner, or indeed needed to, but there was no cause for my anxiety. I made the three, we won the hole and we moved to the next tee. Richie never ever raised the matter and we went on to win the match and enjoy a jar or two in the delightful clubhouse.

I was fortunate to have Richie as a partner because he hated to lose. On another occasion we were playing a two-day double-header over the Old Course at St Andrews and the beautifully manicured Muirfield course, home of the Honourable Company of Edinburgh Golfers. The opposition was provided by a top executive from Rupert Murdoch's empire and the late Tom Ramsey, who at the time was golf correspondent for *The Australian*. It was a tight match. After nine at St Andrews, the game was all square. Richie and I were one-up after 17 only for the redoubtable Ramsey to hole a far-from-easy putt across the green at the 18th to even the match.

After the first nine at Muirfield, it remained all square and it was still that way playing the last — in this instance the par-five 9th because the club's secretary had informed us that the course was very busy, which meant we had started at the 10th. The rough was up for the soon-to-be-held Open Championship and a tough westerly breeze was against us, and I hit into a particularly thick patch at our final hole. I could only hack out and was still short of the green in three. Richie hit a majestic drive and second shot which left him with just a gentle wedge to the green. We could sense victory … and as usual Richie was poised to guarantee our success.

Only this time the unbelievable happened. Richie had cross-checked the yardage several times, thrown up grass to gauge the strength and direction of the wind again, and carefully — ever so carefully — selected the club that he felt would ensure our success. He was looking for the ball to nestle close to the hole for a winning birdie four, but in an untypical, never-to-be-explained moment of heartbreaking drama he hooked his shot violently, 30 yards off line. The ball hit the boundary wall. Had it bounced to the right, it would have ended by the pin but instead it shot left and finished out of bounds. My first thought was he must have had a bad lie. The ensuing silence was deafening. I am sure the disappointment he felt was similar to being bowled out in a Test when one short of a century.

Yet minutes later, after our opponents had won the hole to beat us, Richie, always the proper gentleman, was showing us just how gracious to be in defeat. Mind you, over lunch he was still working out why that approach to the last — the worst shot he hit in two days of intense competition — had gone so wrong.

Having been brought up in Scotland, where cricket — because so many games are rained off — has limited appeal and despite being taught French by RHE Chisholm, opening bat for Scotland, my knowledge of the game is limited. Of course, I knew Richie by reputation and it was my good luck that after I moved to London we became good friends.

Indeed, my first full-length interview for BBC Radio's *Sport on 2*, which I anchored for more than two-and-a-half years, was with Richie. I trotted along to his home in Pont Street, Belgravia, with my trusty Uher recorder. Surprisingly nervous in the presence of undoubted sporting royalty, I recorded the interview in his little office under the stairs, simply a table in a corridor. It could not have gone better. In a gesture that I found out was typical, he corrected me gently when I got a fact wrong and we were able to re-record that bit.

Sometimes meeting for the first time a personality whom you have admired can be a big disappointment, but this was not the case with Richie. He was amiable, understanding, generous with his comments and put me at my ease. The result was an excellent interview. He also helped my colleague, Ryder Cup golfer Ken Brown, when he was starting his commentating career by pointing out when and — more importantly — when not to speak. He also explained that he wore his hair long over his ears to hide his earpiece.

Little did I think then what the future would bring. Richie and I would meet up many times at the parties of mutual friends, and we would often have dinner in the south of France, where his apartment at Beaulieu was just 15 minutes from where I lived at Villefranche-sur-Mer.

It was at Beaulieu during the European summers in between Test matches that he did much of his writing and where his wife Daphne seemed forever to be diligently correcting proofs. Richie and Daphne were a team. They powerwalked around the village. Richie knew, because he had carefully paced it out, how many steps it was from his home to the coffee shop, to the newsagents and even to the railway station. He was the most organised man I have ever known. He knew what he would be doing on any day for months in advance and you were lucky if you caught him when he had a 'free window'. He was always in demand.

Richie, who so loved his visits to France, was patron of the French Cricket Association. He was a welcome visitor at most of the top restaurants on the Riviera, including his particular favourites: the African Queen, Les Vents d'Anges and La Mère Germaine. He remains the only person I have known who has asked the waiter in a Sydney restaurant what waters were available.

I count myself fortunate to have known Richie not only as a top-class cricketer but more importantly as a generous friend with a puckish sense of humour. In Britain, Peter O'Sullevan in racing, Bill McLaren in rugby, Dan Maskell in tennis and Henry Longhurst in golf were unforgettable commentating geniuses, respected by all. So, too, was Richie Benaud — the much-loved, always authoritative, entertaining and irreplaceable voice of cricket. What he achieved for the game could well be summed up by one of the phrases he regularly used … and I can hear him saying now …

'Pretty good effort there.'

BASIL SELLERS

Irene and Alf Sellers and their sons, Basil and Rex, came
to Australia from India in the late 1940s, to forge an
extraordinary success story. They landed in Adelaide, from
where Rex, a leg-spinner, earned a place in Australia's Ashes
touring team of 1964. Basil became a giant of the Australian
business world, a renowned philanthropist, and a keen and
generous backer of sport. He has financed sports sculpture
projects at the SCG and the Adelaide Oval. His support for
the Sydney Swans has helped that AFL club become a model
for other sporting organisations, while his long-running
cricket scholarship programme has benefited many fine
young players who have gone on to represent Australia.

IN 1988, a Test match between Australia and England was played
at the SCG to celebrate Australia's bicentenary. As part of the
celebrations, a Captains' Dinner was staged at the Regent Hotel.
I was the benefactor of that dinner and it was a fabulous night.
The next day, I was invited to Channel Nine at Willoughby to be
interviewed by Richie Benaud about my background, my love of
cricket and how I came to be involved with the dinner.

As you can imagine I was extremely nervous. I was in awe of
this great cricketer and broadcaster, and very humbled that he was
talking with me.

Of course, I remembered him as one of the finest Test players
of my youth; his retirement in 1964 opened up the opportunity for
my brother Rex to be picked for that year's Ashes tour. I might have
met him briefly at functions before 1988, but this was certainly the
first time that I could remember being involved in a one-on-one
conversation with him.

I had never done an interview like this before. What I will never
forget is the way Richie calmed my nerves through his manner and

his professionalism. He eased me into the interview, he had done his research and he was genuinely interested in my story. I went into that studio with no preconceived idea about what I wanted to say, but came out having expressed my belief that whatever you do in life, you must always be prepared to 'give it a go'. This is a mantra of mine. Richie recalled examples where I'd had a go and achieved some success, and talked me through them. The result was a much more satisfying interview experience than I had expected. My respect for Richie was immense.

Five years later, I was lucky enough to purchase a villa, 'Cuccia Noya', at Saint-Jean, a coastal village on Cap Ferrat, in south-eastern France. My intention was to spend some months each year in this beautiful part of the world. Soon, I learned that during northern hemisphere summers Richie and Daphne lived nearby — they had recently bought an apartment in Beaulieu, which is the next village on the peninsula, perhaps a 30-minute walk away.

The first time my wife Clare and I visited our new 'neighbours', we worked out they could see Cuccia Noya from their terrace. Richie promised to raise a glass to us from time to time. We became firm friends.

Over the next 20 years, we had some wonderful days and nights. Richie was always so comfortable at Beaulieu, out of the limelight, he and Daphne doing their thing. He wrote his books there: Richie writing, Daphne editing. They got on so well, two peas in a pod. When we saw one, we saw the other. Their favourite restaurant was the African Queen, where we had many great meals together. In late July 2013, Clare and I caught up with them there. Richie was wearing shorts, and he was nice and relaxed. 'We'll have dinner again in Australia,' he said as we parted. Sadly, we never did.

The Richie I came to know was never bombastic. The word that comes to mind when I think of him is 'immaculate': he was always well dressed, had superb manners and never got flustered.

One day in Sydney, we had arranged to go to lunch with some friends. I remember Bob Cowper was one person who joined us — he had arrived at our home and we were waiting for Richie and Daphne and another couple before we headed across to the restaurant. Bob must have been early, because Richie was never late. Suddenly, it got a bit dark, as a storm approached. There was some lightning and thunder, and then the lights flickered and went out. It was a blackout. And still no Richie.

Soon, it was raining and raining hard. Then it occurred to me: *If the power is out, the electronic doorbell won't be working.* I ran outside and there they were — huddled under what little protection they could find near my high front gate, and Richie jumping up and down, his head bobbing in and out of view, as he tried to catch someone's attention.

I pressed the button to let them in, but of course that needed electricity, too. All I could offer was a feeble, 'Sorry about this. I'll run and get the key.'

The key was in a drawer that, for security's sake, was locked. Just enter the security code and it's open. But, of course, that needed power, too. By now I was scurrying around madly, and I could still see Richie's head bobbing up occasionally as the rain got even harder. For a moment I wasn't sure what to do; I was locked in my own house. Then a friend from America who was staying at our house emerged to ask what all the fuss was about. I thought she had gone out. She had the spare key. Only then could I let my wet and shivering friends into the house.

Richie was entitled to be upset and angry and frustrated. I certainly was. But he was none of those things. He handled it all with the same aplomb he used to show in the commentary box if something went awry. Despite the stress the weather and I had put him through, he was still Richie. We had a terrific lunch.

During the 2007–08 Australian summer, I hosted a cocktail party in Adelaide, at which Barrie Robran was a special guest. Barrie is a hero of mine — in my view (and in the view of plenty of others), the greatest footballer South Australia has ever produced.

He was also a cricketer of some ability, good enough to play Sheffield Shield cricket in the early 1970s.

Barrie played his club football for the SANFL team I supported, the North Adelaide Roosters, who wear red and white, the same colours as the Sydney Swans. At the time of this cocktail party, Barrie had recently celebrated his 60th birthday, and his wife Taimi had told me that his all-time idol was Richie Benaud.

'If you could get something from Richie as a present,' she said, 'it would make his night.' She was thinking I might be able to organise an autographed bat, a book or a photo.

As soon as I knew Barrie was coming to my small function, I rang Richie and asked if he could come, too. I explained that Barrie was a close friend and that I'd like Richie to meet him. He agreed.

Barrie was already there when Richie arrived. I took Richie over and said, 'Barrie, this is Richie Benaud.'

The reaction was priceless. Barrie's jaw dropped. He actually started crying, an extraordinary reaction coming from such a brilliant, brave footballer, a man accustomed to meeting celebrities and sports stars of all eras. 'One of the best moments of my life' is how he later described meeting Richie to me.

For me, what was most magnificent was this: once I'd introduced them, I stood back a couple of metres and just let these two great men chat. Initially Richie did most of the talking, asking Barrie about all the wonderful things he had done in football, talking of specific matches and achievements. Then he asked about Barrie's cricket career, about playing with Les Favell and the Chappells and the like. Once again, Richie had done his homework.

Little wonder then that I was keen to have Richie as the first of the sculptures that are now a feature of the SCG precinct. The choice of subjects was a joint decision between me and then SCG Trust chairman, Rodney Cavalier. Once we agreed we wanted four distinct periods recognised (pre-World War I; between the wars; 1946–1970; and the 'modern era') it took about five minutes of conversation to decide who the four would be: Fred Spofforth, Stan McCabe, Richie and Steve Waugh. Because Richie meant so much to so many people, as a cricketer, captain and commentator, we felt he was a natural choice to lead things off.

Next, we had to decide how we wanted the sculptor, Terrance Plowright, to interpret Richie. Interestingly, when Rodney put this question to Richie, he replied: 'It is best to leave such matters to the artist. Point out the error of his ways very, very gently, if necessary.' I actually suggested to Terrance that we have a Janus-type figure: on one side, there would be Richie as a cricketer; on the other, Richie, the broadcaster, perhaps with a microphone. That was quickly dismissed as being too complicated.

We settled on Richie as a cricketer. One thing that took a while to resolve was getting his shirt right. He was renowned for playing with his chest uncovered, with some of his shirt buttons undone … but how many? This took much longer to get right than we had imagined. Secondly, we wanted to capture Richie the leg-spinner *and* Richie the captain, a figure of authority. How could we emphasise this?

One day in France, I was discussing with Richie the problems we were having and I asked, 'How did you change the field when you were bowling?'

'Often,' he said, 'I'd look around and I might just twitch my eyebrow.'

'Richie,' I said, 'we can't twitch eyebrows on a sculpture.'

He smiled knowingly. His dry humour had got me again.

'Sometimes, at the end of my run, I'd just go like that,' he offered. As he said this, he waved his hand slightly, fingers bent a little, the palm of his hand facing upwards, as if he was motioning for the fieldsman at mid-wicket to come closer, or for the man at cover to move around more towards cover point.

I said, 'Stop, stop, that's it!'

That is the gesture Terrance so brilliantly captures in the sculpture. Richie has the ball in one hand, ready to bowl; the other hand is asking for a small but important alteration to the field.

Richie had said that he didn't want to see the sculpture before it was unveiled. Daphne didn't want to see it, either. This meant that the 15 minutes before NSW governor Marie Bashir performed the unveiling on day three of the 2007–08 Test against India were among the most nerve-racking of my life. I felt as if all the responsibility for getting it right was on my shoulders, though in truth, of course, Rodney and Terrance shared the load. Adding to the tension, the governor had trouble removing the cloth that had been keeping the identity secret. Rodney had to step up to help her. Finally, it was there for all to see.

Richie was required to make a speech. He walked over to the bronzed sculpture, looked up and down at it, taking his time, and then he told us all that he approved. Daphne was happy. Richie was never a man to show much emotion, but when I spoke to him a few minutes later I could sense he was chuffed.

The relief I felt is beyond description.

CLARE OLDRIDGE

Clare Oldridge's association with Richie began in 1961, when she was ten. She first met him at her home, during the annual party her parents — Brian (the great BBC commentator) and Pauline Johnston — hosted on the Friday of the Lord's Test.

I BEGAN working for Richie and Daphne in London in 1989. Three years later, they decided to sell their London flat and buy an apartment in Beaulieu-sur-Mer, a few miles from Nice, having fallen in love with the area while on a short holiday. Quite by chance I spoke French fluently, which proved to be a huge asset in the circumstances.

Richie was very interested in researching his family history — his paternal family sailed from La Rochelle, a coastal city in south-west France, to Sydney in 1838 — and he had already made a visit to the tiny hamlet of Benaud, near Clermont-Ferrand. In order to learn more about his ancestors he asked me to contact the local mayor, through whom I was able to trace more documents and who, in turn, invited Richie to lunch. It turned out that the mayor shared Richie's love of wine and, according to the mayor's secretary, despite neither speaking the other's language, the lunch went on late into the afternoon. At one point, the mayor invited Richie to inspect his precious wine cellar. The mayor's secretary told me that she had never, in all her long association with him, known him to share this with anyone!

Having only learnt basic French at school, Richie threw himself into all things French. He and Daphne enrolled themselves at the Institut de Français in Villefranche for an intensive one month's tuition. Thereafter, Richie would take his audiotapes with him everywhere, listening intently on long-haul flights and even on the beach to the conjugation of verbs and grammar lessons. He was never able to speak with a good accent, but he made every effort to converse with the locals and managed to make himself understood. One of my more arduous tasks was translating the rules of cricket — as taken from the well-known tea towel — into French for their local taxi driver. Trying to make a Frenchman understand 'Each man that's in the side that's in goes out, and when he's out, he comes in and the next man goes in until he's out' is not easy!

I got to know Richie and Daphne well when I went to live in Australia for three years from 1972. From that point on, Richie always showed an immense interest in my life and that of my family. When my two sons, Nicholas and Rupert, were young he gave up his valuable time and coached them in the nets at Lord's. In later years, he gave my daughter Sophie an important lesson on how to open a bottle of champagne while we gathered at the annual picnic on the Coronation Garden during the Friday of the Lord's Test. This picnic became a fixture on the calendar for many decades, as several of us contributed food and drink and various friends sought us out in the melee of picnickers on the lawn. However, after the commentary box moved from the Warner Stand to the media centre on the far side of Lord's, Richie's hoped-for time with us became shorter and shorter, as he was constantly stopped en route by ardent fans.

When I moved to South London with my three children after my divorce in 2000, Richie was so concerned about our safety he insisted that I install bars on my windows and put locks on the windows and doors, at his expense. He and Daphne also ensured that the children could each buy something they really wanted for their new rooms to make the move a little easier for them. He would always ask me what the family was doing and was always there with advice. My children, in turn, treasured their link with him. If any of them were in Australia, he would invite them for drinks or dinner. He would visit my son Nicholas, who has lived in Melbourne since 2009.

When I was in Sydney in February 2014, Nicholas came up with his girlfriend Lisa and baby Charlotte, and Richie made his first public outing since his car accident in the previous October. Despite undergoing debilitating radiotherapy and chemotherapy treatment and obviously being not at all well, he and Daphne joined us for a drink. It was an enormous effort on his part. He knew how much it meant to them and to me, and we were all very touched. Sadly, I never saw him again.

DAVID COX

As with many others, David Cox's first connection with Richie came through the Sydney sportswriter Phil Tresidder. All three were members of the Australian Golf Club in Sydney. Following his retirement from a successful real-estate business, David and his wife Helen several times experienced the Benauds' 'Mediterranean life' in Beaulieu.

ONLY once did I decisively beat Richie Benaud to the draw. It happened at a favourite hotel and restaurant, La Colombe d'Or (The Golden Dove), which is situated on the edge of the French village of Saint-Paul-de-Vence, not far inland from Beaulieu.

Richie was ferociously hard to stop when it came to settling a bill, as I found out at the very first luncheon Helen and I had with Daphne and him at a beautiful poolside restaurant at Cap Ferrat. That day, on the presentation of what would have been a huge bill, I demanded to pay a hefty share. 'I don't let Australians pay!' declared Richie, leaving no room for debate. He proved equally hard to catch whenever we socialised in times ahead. He was the most generous bloke I ever met.

The 'victory' at Saint-Paul-de-Vence was manufactured only via a careful pre-emptive strike by Helen. She made it unobtrusively to the counter very early, a winning move, though one followed by Richie's inevitable protests at what we had managed. Richie had picked the wines and blued most about not being allowed at least to pay for those. And when it came to wine, he knew what to order. On summer days in France, he especially liked rosé and it was a great enjoyment of my life — and remains a wonderful memory — to have sat there on occasions and talked cricket and golf and other things with him, while sipping some Benaud-selected French rosé.

We became friends comparatively late, largely through his lifelong friendship with Phil Tresidder, who was also a very special mate of mine. Phil died suddenly in 2003 at a time when I had been going through some health problems, and Richie and Daphne stepped into the gap.

The accident he had in his Sunbeam Alpine — a car that was nearly as famous as he was — came in late 2013, the day after a dinner a few of us had at Catalina restaurant in Sydney's Rose Bay. Next day, Richie was at the Australian to hit some practice balls. He was a touch unsteady when he carried his clubs up to the car park afterwards, and fell and hit his head on a concrete kerb. My brother John was in the locker room, and when Richie came in he noticed that there was blood on his head. Richie assured John he was 'okay', rinsed the blood and headed off for the drive home. On the way he hit a nature strip and a fence, and ended up in Prince of Wales Hospital with some severe injuries.

John regrets that he didn't insist on driving Richie home that day, but I've reassured him: 'It's pretty hard to insist with someone like Richie.'

Richie was a bloody great bloke, and also a man of character and firm opinions. He was *always* going to drive himself home.

LIBBY REEVES-PURDIE

Libby Reeves-Purdie's association with Richie and Daphne proved to be an unforgettable spin-off from her days working as a valued overseas associate of Kerry Packer. There were wonderful trips, and wonderful food chased down by fine wines ...

MY connection with Richie and Daphne started in the 1980s when I was a vice-president of Channel Nine Australia, based in Los Angeles. Nine was broadcasting Wimbledon and signed up for a hospitality marquee that became my responsibility. Without a UK office, we based the operation at the Benauds' London residence and

I would arrive each year for the tournament. Richie and Daphne helped to host the marquee and for several years we laughed our way through days of rain, sun, too few tickets and too many guests — some glorious, some demanding. A special friendship was born.

Richie Benaud was an awe-inspiring sportsman, commentator and all-round hero. But how many knew that beneath that cool and clinical exterior beat the heart of a passionate foodie and sous-chef extraordinaire?

Over many shared holidays, we witnessed Richie slice and dice his way through Europe. His precision with bat, ball and words was rivalled only by his knife skills. With a holiday glass of something cold and crisp by his side, we have watched him expertly bone a Dover sole, perfectly cube meat for cassoulet and finely slice a tomato. In fact, at breakfast one morning in Gascony, we once saw him slice a tomato with such finesse and concentration we gave him a huge round of applause.

Cricket's gain was surely brain surgery's loss. Without the wine, of course!

So many wonderful feasts have been shared around tables with Richie and Daphne: creamy risottos on sunny beaches in Positano; loup de mer under the ancient figs on the terrace at La Colombe d'Or; moules aux curry at the African Queen in Beaulieu; flying fish cutters between matches in Barbados; baby lobsters at Ascot; corned beef hash with poached eggs in London; truffled mashed potatoes in Sydney.

Every dish will remind us of him.

Most of all, our abiding memory will always be of crème brûlée, his favourite and one of the last things we shared on our final outing to Lucio's in Paddington shortly before he died. Someone once said, 'All sorrows are less with bread.' Perhaps so, but sadly for us now, all sorrows will be greater with crème brûlée.

JACK BANNISTER

Jack Bannister was a right-arm fast-medium bowler for Warwickshire in English county cricket, taking 1,198 first-class wickets at 21.91 in a career that spanned the years 1950 to 1969. At the end of his playing days, Bannister worked as a bookmaker in Wolverhampton before moving into the cricket media, where he became a familiar voice on BBC-TV's coverage. Jack and Richie became great friends, bound together in their shared interest in cricket, golf and the turf. He continues to commentate on cricket for talkSPORT radio in the UK.

WHEN the young Australian batsman Phillip Hughes tragically died in November 2014, my dear friend Richie Benaud was asked to provide the voiceover for a short tribute video. As always, it was pitch perfect.

Afterwards, his fellow commentator Bill Lawry asked about Richie's own condition — he had been receiving treatment for skin cancer — and queried whether a refusal to wear a sun hat during his playing career, which Richie blamed for the illness, was due to a commercial deal with Brylcreem.

In true Richie fashion, he paused and considered the response. 'I'm not going to tell you whether I had a contract or not, Bill,' he replied with a glint in his eye. 'Nor am I going to tell you how much the fee was.'

That was the humour of the man — always slightly off-key and understated.

As a commentator, you arrive early before the start of play and often finish past seven in the evening. That was a long time for seven or eight people to share a small space and often tempers would fray, fall-outs would occur. But never involving Richie. He was always the coolest of the lot.

After every stint on air he would simply retire to a small table in the corner of the room to watch the play, quietly reading the newspaper or studying the *Racing Post*. He always brought sandwiches to the ground and was so meticulous when it came to organising his day.

Richie became my best friend in life. We first met when I was playing club cricket in Johannesburg during the 1957–58 season and the Australians were touring. He took more than 100 first-class wickets on that trip, a feat I do not believe has been achieved since. I then played against him for Warwickshire in the early 1960s before I joined him on the BBC television team in 1987 following a spell with the radio team.

That was where I really got to know him. We discovered early on in our time working together that we shared two passions away from cricket: golf and horse racing. We would play a round of golf before every Test at Trent Bridge, Headingley and Edgbaston, and Richie, who had a single-figure handicap, won more often than not.

His love for horse racing was infectious. And from 1987 to only three weeks before his passing we had a personal nap competition. Every Saturday for 28 years, we would talk on the telephone and swap the names of our horses, totalling up the wins from April to September in England and October to April in Australia, with the winner buying a slap-up meal for the other. I would study the form day and night and still the bugger would win.

On one of the last times I called, his wife Daphne told me he was back in hospital receiving treatment. I, of course, said to put off the nap competition but he insisted it went ahead and told me his horses. But on the final Saturday she said he was coming home and there would be no more treatment; it would be a matter of days.

Daphne was his rock. They met through the cricket writer Jim Swanton — she was his secretary — and in 1967 Jim told her to make an honest man of him. They bought a house in the south of France due to Richie's Huguenot heritage and during the English summer they would commute from there to the Test matches.

His other big passion was his car, a 1963 Sunbeam Alpine. When he crashed it in October 2013 he was more concerned about it than his own health. He had a great sense of humour but would never set out to take the mickey. That did not stop him making gentle, witty points about people or situations, though. In short, Richie Benaud was a true gentleman.

SARAH WOOLDRIDGE

The story of the friendship of Sarah Wooldridge and her husband Ian Wooldridge, the peerless sportswriter, with Daphne and Richie Benaud reaches across half a century. Sport at its highest levels — and especially cricket — was at its heart, but equally so the enjoyment of life itself through many golden summers.

ON the day the world changed, September 11, 2001, Richie Benaud was taking a siesta in the warm sunshine of a beautiful beach at Positano, Italy. A group of us had just enjoyed a delicious and very jolly lunch at Da Adolfo, a restaurant on the beach.

It was the first day of a holiday break in Positano for the Benauds, after Richie's long summer of broadcasting in England, and for the Wooldridges, after Ian had written about many of the major sporting events of the previous months, including the just completed Ashes series. After lunch, Richie had headed off alone, to sunbathe. Before long the restaurant owner came rushing out with the news: 'Something is going on in New York!' We headed into this man's kitchen — where he had an old black-and-white TV — and it was there that we watched BBC World's coverage of the unfolding tragedy. Almost immediately, the second plane crashed into the South Tower. Ian's nephew, Mike Wooldridge, was involved in the BBC's coverage, another reason why this day stays indelibly in my memory. Initially, we thought it best to let Richie rest, but soon we realised it was such an appalling, momentous event that we had to rouse him. I shall never forget that day.

Positano holidays were usually great fun, though it was scary going on the boats with Richie and 'Woollers', as neither of them could swim. But the only way to reach the lovely little seafood restaurants along the coast was via wooden boats. So we went.

By then, I had known the Benauds for many years. I had first met Richie in 1964, when I had begun working in London for Mark McCormack at IMG. Richie was a friend of George Blumberg, who was an IMG director, renowned in the world of golf as the generous benefactor who put Gary Player, one of McCormack's highest-profile clients, on the road to stardom. However, I didn't really get to know Richie and Daphne well until 1980, when I married Ian. Over the following years, I spent wonderful times with them in Australia, France, India, Italy, the West Indies and, of course, London.

Ian adored and admired Richie; they were the very best of friends. The pair of them used to enjoy gin and tonics together discussing the world of sport. They were a joy to listen to. Ian particularly enjoyed discussing Richie's career after he retired as a player, when he was a journalist and broadcaster, and especially when he was involved in the launch of World Series Cricket. Ian broke the Kerry Packer/WSC story exclusively in the *Daily Mail*, but he would never tell me how he secured the information ... even after many whiskies! I don't think it was from Richie, but we will never know for sure.

Richie always called Ian by his surname and Ian did the same whenever he greeted Richie. It was 'Benaud' and 'Wooldridge'. They had first met when Richie was captain of Australia and Ian was the cricket correspondent of the *Daily Mail*. They got on immediately.

Towards the end of Ian's life, when he was very frail, he insisted on flying out to Sydney for his annual visit to Australia. Emirates kindly helped us with the long flight in first-class comfort. It was Christmas time. Ian was on a lot of medication and I had placed all the relevant pills to be taken during the flight in an envelope. But when we arrived in Dubai I realised I had posted them at Heathrow Airport with a bunch of last-minute Christmas cards! Ian drank Bloody Marys for the entire flight and when we finally landed in Sydney I was so relieved. We headed immediately to have lunch with the Benauds and other friends, and I recall how impressed and amused Richie was by Ian's courage and determination. It was a very special lunch.

They were tough and generous men. For the 1996 World Cup, I was hired — via IMG for the Board of Control for Cricket in India (BCCI) — to arrange the official hospitality at all the key matches around the country. It turned out to be a most challenging project.

The first game I was assigned to was a big one: India v Australia in Mumbai. Some bright spark at IMG had guaranteed via our sales brochure that celebrities would be attending lunch in the hospitality village, but at the last minute I discovered that nothing had been organised. We were really stuck, but dear Richie agreed to walk out of the ground to visit our official, non-air-conditioned tented village and shake hands with and chat to lots of clients. It was so kind of him and so typical.

It was an arduous tournament. I recall that Richie had a terrible time on a train travelling from Delhi to Jaipur, where Australia played the West Indies. The air-conditioning in his carriage was on full, and he caught a chest cold and lost his voice. At other times, we wrapped ourselves up in newspapers to try to keep warm on the trains during that World Cup. But he soldiered on.

On Woollers' death in 2007, Richie was a commanding figure at the Memorial Service, which was attended by 1,000 people at the Guard's Chapel, near Buckingham Palace. He delivered the most magnificent address, taking so much care with some wonderful Wooldridge stories. I had asked Richie if he could introduce a special musical item — *Waltzing Matilda*, sung by the Australian opera singer, Dean Robinson — and he was brilliant, ending his address very slowly and gently, leading into the music. It was such a special moment for me and I knew that Ian (up there) would have been so thrilled. He just loved Australians and Australia.

The Benauds continued to invite me to France for holidays and I was so lucky to spend many happy hours with Richie and Daphne, drinking chablis on their wonderful terrace at Beaulieu. We'd discuss sport, IMG, food and a great deal more. Richie was always very interested in how IMG was going, in part, I'm sure, because they had helped Mark McCormack set up the company's Sydney office many years ago. For lunch, I used to buy cooked chickens on the spit and Richie would carve them precisely and beautifully, to accompany his superbly sliced ripe tomatoes, plus mozzarella with chopped basil and plenty of black pepper.

For Richie, the black pepper was a crucial ingredient. On his travels, he invariably carried a favourite pepper grinder.

Everything was delicious and perfect. That's how I will remember him.

TONY LEWIS

A Welshman to his bootstraps, Tony Lewis played cricket for Glamorgan and captained England on his Test debut, leading the MCC to India and Pakistan in 1972. He also won a Cambridge Blue for rugby, and played senior rugby for Neath and Gloucester. He was a brilliant writer on cricket and rugby, and worked with Richie Benaud on the BBC television coverage of cricket for more than a decade.

I FIRST met Richie early in the Australians' 1961 tour of England, when he led his side in a three-day match against Cambridge University. He appeared to glide onto the Fenner's ground, stardust sparkling from the crown we undergraduates imagined he was wearing following the Gabba Tied Test.

We had the chance to talk about hopes and fears at the Black Velvet drinks party on the lawns of Queens' College — champagne and Guinness — but scarcely got a word in past Dai Davies, the old Glamorgan cricketer who had umpired Australia in Tests on eight occasions.

Spin on to 1968. Richie, although retired from big-time cricket, agreed to lead a short Commonwealth XI tour of Pakistan. It was here that I first experienced and admired the Benaud leadership as a member of his team, which extended beyond the boundary. I see him sitting opposite the hotel manager who was trying to rip us off in multi-rupees after a five-day stay.

The mathematics were too tough for our tour manager, Alex Bannister of the *Daily Mail* in London, but I watched our captain

RICHIE

remove his jacket, take out his pen and proceed to scrutinise each
sheet of paper of the final account made out for 14 cricketers.
Richie, without help from anyone else, stood up after more than an
hour, shook hands with the hotel manager, slipped on his jacket, and
announced that he was very grateful for the help he had been given
in spotting the back office slip-up and that a 50 per cent reduction
would be fine.

Famously, he recommended being ahead of the game. 'Think
two overs ahead and be lucky.' That was certainly the strength of
his leadership at Old Trafford back in 1961, when he came on to
bowl wrist-spin from around the wicket at England's best, and
demolished them.

The Benaud style on the field was a considerable education to
the Commonwealth boys. In the second four-day match at Lahore,
he decided that the Pakistan Universities opening batsman, Aftab
Gul, was simply incapable of playing even the simplest of strokes to
the offside; everything, even the defensive blocks, went to leg.

In the second innings, satisfied with his research, he alarmed
his team by placing every Commonwealth fielder on the legside and
advised his bowlers to bowl straight. Aftab was rendered strokeless
and runless and retired hurt.

But the captain would also draw attention to his own lack of
foresight. There was the journey of the team across the Thal Desert
down to Karachi, winding along a narrow, twisting road over
burned-out terrain and a million miles of sandy dust.

The 'first-class luxury coach — air-conditioned' was a tricky
beast to handle. To begin with, it was air-conditioned only because
it had no doors. The luxury was elusive and comfort doubtful.
When the driver slammed the giant gearstick into fourth, it
rattled, screeched and shot down to first again. A boy, aged about
15, was hired to wait for the crunch and to stretch forward to grab
the gearstick and hold on like hell. His shoulders shook violently
all the way across 80 miles of desert!

Well into our second hour, the driver shouted 'wagon is
coming'. True, there was a dark speck on the horizon. We had been
told that the strip of hard road was not wide enough for two drivers
to pass each other without both vehicles having their outside wheels
on sand off the highway. I was sitting immediately behind Richie
almost at the back of the bus on the right offside.

The speck grew larger over ten minutes, at which point our driver was face to face with a giant transcontinental wagon. He refused to give way. The wagon claimed right of way on account of size and the inevitable game of chicken ended with the scrunch of serious contact. Our windows were smashed on the offside; glass flew inwards. The driver stopped. Cricketers shouted and jostled to the front exit, all intent on making panicked examinations of the bus.

It was at this moment in life that Richie and I discovered that we shared a similar temperament. We did not do panic. He stood up, kept on reading his paperback, grabbed his suit-holder from the rack and moved across the aisle of the bus without a single word. I did similar, but I could see he was annoyed with himself. How could he have failed to foresee a possible game of transcontinental chicken in the subcontinent? The bottom lip curled.

In 1980, I entered Richie Benaud's BBC television commentary box on a permanent basis. I left in 1998 when I became the president of the Marylebone Cricket Club in the days when the club did not wish to have a president who earned his living from the game.

Together thereafter we found golf to play, cool drinks to sip, cruises to Test series, Italian vineyards to explore, a couple of Bob Hope Classic golf charity tournaments and visits to Beaulieu-sur-Mer.

On a couple of sunny Septembers, Mr and Mrs Lewis with Mr and Mrs Benaud took coffee and cognac on the pavement cafe opposite their Beaulieu apartment. The English cricket season was over again. Not that the computers of Rich and Daph would close down.

We were off to visit the home of our mutual friends, Graham and Angela Chidgey, Graham deeply involved in the wine trade, but also a scorer of a first-class century as an amateur batsman playing for the Free Foresters, and Angela an internationally known artist.

We relaxed daily in the shades of the olive groves on the slopes of their old granary in the village of Cetinale, opposite the 17th-century villa belonging to the Lambton family. We took important tasting experiences in the vintages of Chassagne-Montrachet, Puligny-Montrachet and Meursault, plus all the Italian wines that Graham was himself discovering. Richie and I walked for an hour each morning and I guess Daphne, also a walker, could not have been far away. The note in my diary confirms that the stopwatch was out to keep our speed at 4.3 miles per hour.

Hardly a word of cricket was ever spoken.

BOB HAWKE

Bob Hawke, prime minister of Australia from 1983 to 1991 and a noted cricket aficionado, pays tribute.

OTHERS will provide the statistical evidence to support the fact that Richie Benaud was one of the most effective all-rounders ever to represent Australia. No statistics however can explain the flair and intelligence that made him one of the best captains to lead our country.

But of course beyond these great achievements on the field I, like millions of others, am always going to remember Richie for his post-playing career as arguably the best television commentator and analyst the game has seen.

He combined unrivalled knowledge with a sharp analytical mind and also a generosity of spirit that made him unique.

Thank you Richie Benaud for all that you did throughout such a distinguished and honourable career, for the tradition of our great game.

THE CALM VOICE OF REASON

In the balmy days of late summer and early autumn 2015, Steve Crawley, head of sport at Channel Nine, calmly steered an endeavour that ensured Richie Benaud would be remembered by the television station he had graced for almost 40 years. As Richie's health faded, Nine's CEO David Gyngell quietly reminded his team of their duty to farewell Richie in the best possible way — as he deserved, with real class.

The ongoing contact between Nine and Daphne through Richie's final days was respectful, caring and regular. 'We knew from a week out that things weren't good,' Crawley explains. The door had been kept ajar for the great commentator at Nine ever since his motoring accident in October 2013. Richie's distinctive voice was occasionally still heard, such as when Phillip Hughes died in late November 2014, then when the 2014–15 cricketing summer began and finally — in what is now seen as his farewell piece — in an introduction to Nine's coverage of the Boxing Day Test, when he talked of Coogee, his beloved Sydney home.

Without fuss, Nine began recording some reflections on Richie, the man and his life from some of those who had known him, worked with him, played with or against him, socialised with him, admired him. The project stretched across the globe, from Australia to England via the West Indies, taking in an eclectic bunch of friends and admirers. These included renowned English broadcaster, journalist and author Sir Michael Parkinson, the great fast bowler Dennis Lillee, and businessman James Packer, who was nine years old when his father Kerry launched World Series Cricket. There were exceptional cricketers-turned-commentators such as Sir Ian Botham, David Gower, Michael Holding, Michael Slater and Ian Smith. There were the high-profile media figures, Ray Hadley and Eddie McGuire, whose influence as commentators goes well beyond sport, and a number of Nine's best sports presenters and callers, including James Brayshaw, Phil Gould and Ken Sutcliffe. And there were, inevitably, many who have contributed so willingly to these pages.

'So many people were close to Richie,' says Crawley. He remembers the process as a 'difficult assignment', one built on pending and inherent sadness.

When the sombre news came, on the dawning of Thursday, April 10, 2015, that Richie had died in his sleep during the night, Nine went into overdrive. On the Saturday night, a programme went to air — *Richie Benaud: A Marvellous Life* — that was at various moments brilliant, touching, funny, sad and revealing.

Here are some excerpts from that programme, offered generously by Nine for use in this book ...

Sir Ian Botham
A player when I was a youngster, he was a great leader of teams and men. I got to know Richie much better when he was a commentator. He was a fascinating man. I did interviews with him, shared some glasses of red wine with him in various parts of the world. An amazing guy.

James Brayshaw
The first time I ever worked with him was at a domestic one-dayer in Adelaide. It was terrific when I went on with him and I thought, *I know my place. I won't speak until he speaks*. Well, he didn't say a word for an entire over. In the ad break the producer got into my ear and asked me, 'Whose name is first on the roster?' And it was 'JB', *then* 'RB'.

'That means you're on lead, mate. Start talking!'

The sweat was dripping off me and I turned to Richie, who was looking straight ahead. 'I'm so sorry, Richie,' I said. 'I didn't realise I was supposed to lead.'

And he said: 'That's all right, young man. I just thought you were easing into it.'

Phil Gould
He was just like part of the family. Every year at this time of the year he'd come around with his descriptions of the cricket. Richie was one of the sounds of summer.

David Gower
The Benaud voice was outstanding ... unique. Everyone picked up on the way he said his 'twos'. If anyone does a Richie Benaud impression you can guarantee straightaway they're going to go: *It's chew for chwenty-chew*. But obviously he was much more than

just a voice. There was the way he looked down the camera, very directly at you, in effect, to address *you* on the game of cricket.

Ray Hadley

Wit and entertainment … he did it in a way that no one had done before or probably will do into the future. I remember sitting next to him at a function and we talked about what he did and what I did, and he reminded me that all of us commentators are guests in someone's lounge room and we should always maintain dignity. He did that right through his career.

Michael Holding

When I was playing I never paid too much attention to what journalists wrote or what commentators said, but when Richie was on television you would *always* want to hear what he had to say. When I started in commentary and got the opportunity to work with Richie Benaud, it was a great feeling.

Dennis Lillee

On the day in Melbourne in 1981, during the third Test against India when I broke his Test wicket-taking record, Richie was upstairs in the commentary box. When the wicket fell — Chetan Chauhan, caught by Bruce Yardley — I turned and gave the thumbs up to the box. Then I saw Rich out the front of the box, waving, and I waved back.

Later, Richie came into the dressing-room with a beautiful bottle of champagne. 'Enjoy that,' he said. It was a lovely gesture. I thanked him and got out a few words along the lines of, 'I don't think I'll have it right now, but I'll have it after the game!' I recall Richie then made some comment about there being enough problems already with the variable bounce out there. We shook hands. 'Anyhow, a great performance,' he said. And he was gone. It was typical Richie, thoughtful, succinct and to the point.

There was a sense of awe in any meeting with him. We remained friends after my cricketing days were over and I would ring him now and then just to see how he was going.

Eddie McGuire

He was a force of nature. He was a cricketer, the Australian captain, a journalist, an author, a broadcaster, a father, a husband, a great friend, a leader, a pillar of society. He did all those things and did them with elan and dash. He had his own way of dressing ... the Richie Benaud coat. He did ads before other sportsmen even knew what they were. He was that far ahead of everybody in just about every facet of life. When you looked at him, analysed him and scratched beneath the surface, you realised how smart he was.

James Packer

There's a story I remember my dad telling me. He was chuffed that he'd been able to sign up so many players without the news of World Series Cricket leaking to the media. He'd bring Tony Greig and Ian Chappell and other members of the Australian team into the office and say, 'What I'm going to speak to you about is confidential. And you mustn't talk to *anyone* about it.' And they agreed. Dad was a great salesman and by the end of these meetings he'd got their signatures.

Then he told me of the day that Rich came into the office. My father said to Richie, 'What I'm about to talk to you about, you must not tell anyone else. Can I have your word on that?'

And Richie said, 'No.'

Dad was a bit surprised. 'What do you mean?' he asked.

And Richie replied, 'Well, I have to speak to Daphne about it.'

There was a pause. Then Dad said, 'Okay, okay, I can accept that.'

They kept going with the meeting and talked about Richie joining World Series Cricket. From all accounts from my dad, the meeting went very, very well. At the end of it, Dad said to Richie, 'Do we have a deal?'

And Richie said, 'I'm not sure.'

Dad said, 'What do you mean?'

And Richie said, 'I've got to speak to Daphne.'

Next morning, Richie rang back. 'You've got a deal,' he said.

Sir Michael Parkinson

Richie managed to commentate all his life without resorting to cliché, but more than that he was the calm voice of reason, sitting there and analysing exactly what was happening when others were getting hysterical. That's what I want from a commentator.

Michael Slater

He was as revered in England as he was in Australia. At the Oval in 2005, I was in the commentary box when he was saying his farewell [from the Channel 4 coverage]. England were winning that famous series and everyone in the box was emotional ...

At the end of the game, the England crowd — a packed house — was going ballistic because England had won. And Richie had to walk across the hallowed turf for the presentation.

When the crowd spotted Richie coming out onto the oval, they all stopped their chanting for England and they all started ... 'Richie! Richie!' ... right the way across. It's a memory I will never forget.

Ian Smith

He was a fantastic bloke and with his skills and his presence, and what he brought to cricket will never be replaced. He was an absolute icon and an absolute genius. I am privileged to say I was a friend and a colleague.

Ken Sutcliffe

He was a great commentator, but he was also a terrific listener. What I admired about Richie as much as anything else was that he was always relevant; he never lived in the past. He embraced the future, he embraced technology, the new ways of doing things and he encouraged new commentators. Richie never imposed his view on you until you sought it. Then he would provide an honest and considered opinion — one with which you may or may not have agreed.

Something I liked about him was that he never got lost in nationalistic fervour when he commentated. He loved Australia to do well, but more than that he wanted *cricket* to do well. Richie to me is no greater in death than he was in life: a giant.

– 9 –
A MARVELLOUS INNINGS

'Richie was a truly remarkable man with his own place in the history of broadcasting. His standards never changed at all throughout the years.'

— Sir Michael Parkinson

IAN CHAPPELL

When the great Australian captains of living memory are recalled, Ian Chappell sits with Sir Donald Bradman and Richie Benaud as the very best. They were players and leaders to shape and reshape the game. Richie was still playing when Ian started out. He mirrored many of the Benaud traits, including aggressive and positive captaincy, and down-to-earth public relations. They were key figures together in the revolution that began with World Series Cricket, and for more than three decades they worked together as members of a pioneering Channel Nine commentary team. Ian Chappell will tell anyone who cares to listen that being around Richie Benaud enriched his life.

'AFTER you, Ian.' They were the first words spoken to me by Richie Benaud. It was 1962 and South Australia had just enjoyed a rare victory over a star-studded NSW line-up. Richie, as the not-out batsman, magnanimously stood back, allowing Les Favell to lead his team off the Adelaide Oval and soak up the enthusiastic applause. I was on the field as 12th man and wasn't about to leave ahead of the Australian captain — a man whose leadership style I'd admired from afar. But he insisted.

That story is indicative of Richie. He was a thorough gentleman and meticulous in his preparation. I was staggered he knew my name.

He was also a generous man. Not long after the Adelaide Oval experience, a Gray-Nicolls bat arrived in the post while I was playing in the Lancashire League. It was from Richie, and so began a relationship that only ended after 52 rewarding years with his passing.

I say rewarding — that was from my perspective, but I'm not sure what Benords received in return. Often, when I spoke to him or called, he had a helpful suggestion, which emanated from a mind that was regularly in lateral-thinking mode.

When I was a young man, he told me, 'Ian, cricket's a simple game. The simpler you keep it the better off you'll be.'

Not long after I'd taken over the Australian captaincy, I called to explain how a mate had told me, 'You've got the field in the wrong place for Garry Sobers.'

Richie laughed. 'There's no right place for the field when Sobers is going,' he explained. 'All I'd say is you're wasting a fieldsman by putting someone in the gully. He hits the ball in the air in that direction, but it's six inches off the ground and going like a bullet. No one can catch it.'

When I retired and turned my hand to writing and television, he organised for me to commentate for the BBC during the 1977 Ashes series. He also suggested — Richie rarely advised — that I become a member of the Australian Journalists' Association so no one in the industry would object to me writing columns.

Generally, Richie's response to any situation was measured, subtle and quite often humorous. His good friend Phil Tresidder regularly visited Richie and Daphne's unit for New Year's drinks. In December 1999, Phil selected his 'team of the century' for the *Inside Edge* cricket magazine. Unable to restrict himself to purely one team, Phil picked a second XI to 'placate those cricketing buffs who still find their heroes missing'. In two Australian teams of the century, Phil hadn't found a place for Greg Chappell.

Normally, for obvious reasons, I avoid passing comment on my brother's prowess, but I couldn't let that one pass through to the keeper. In the following issue of the magazine, I wrote in my 'Stumps' column: 'Call it nepotism or accuse me of bias, but I think Phil Tresidder's second *Inside Edge* team of the century lacked credibility. If there was room in that XI for Steve Waugh and Allan Border, then there had to be a spot for Greg Chappell.'

My comment obviously stung Phil and he was keen to discuss it when he arrived at Richie's place. Only seconds into his first drink Phil said, 'Richie, I think Ian's a bit upset with me.'

A sip of white wine and then Richie responded, 'With good reason, Phil.'

Becoming very defensive about his selections, Phil spluttered, 'Well, you can't pick everyone.'

Richie took another sip. 'No, you can't, Phil,' he said. 'But at least you can pick the good bastards.'

ENGLISH commentator David Lloyd stumbled upon the doyen status Richie had achieved at the SCG in 2006–07. 'Bumble' had finished his day's commentary with the Sky network and decided to try for an early getaway ahead of the capacity crowd.

He headed for where his car and all the other commentators' cars were parked against the Showground wall in the lane between the Football Stadium and the Cricket Ground. Just short of his destination, he encountered a gaggle of security guards who appeared to be readying themselves for action.

'What's goin' on 'ere then, pal?' Lloyd enquired of one of the security men.

'We're preparing for the prime minister's departure,' came the reply.

Pointing in the direction of his vehicle, Lloyd asked: 'Can I quickly get to my car and take off?'

He was given permission as long as he was quick about it.

As Bumble reached his car he turned to see what was happening behind him. He noticed a florid-faced, middle-aged Australian who appeared to have had a very good day at the cricket. Just as Lloyd was about to clamber into his car, he heard the gentleman ask the security guards, who had now linked arms to clear a path for the PM, 'What's happenin' here, mate?'

A security guard politely informed the gentleman they were waiting on the PM. His reply was short and to the point: 'Fuck the prime minister — I'm here to see Richie.' His comment was a rather succinct appraisal of the average Australian's preference for sport over politics.

ONE of my favourite Richie stories concerns his old mate, Bob Gray. Richie and Bob were friends for a long time, all the way back to the 1960s when Bob was the cricket correspondent for the Sydney *Daily Mirror* and Richie wrote for *The Sun*. Despite the fact that it was often open warfare between these two afternoon papers, Benaud and Gray didn't let the rivalry spill over into their friendship.

It was a relationship built along similar lines to many of the rivalries between interstate cricket teams. On the field it was intense; off the field it was friendly. Friendly to the point where Benaud and Gray could often be found playing golf together on tour.

They were a marvellous contrast on the golf course: the dapper Benaud, immaculately attired, while Gray was an extrovert dresser who mixed gaudy colours that rarely matched. If you ignored skill, Gray resembled the outlandish American professional Doug Sanders, who was described as 'the peacock of the fairways'.

The pair were covering Australia's 1966–67 tour of South Africa. It was an off day on the schedule and they decided to have an afternoon game of golf at the Wanderers club in Johannesburg.

The day before, Gray had been shopping in the city and returned to the Langham Hotel all excited. 'Look at these marvellous blue shoes,' he implored Richie. 'They're the only pair like it in the world. I'm going to wear them at golf tomorrow.'

'How do you know,' asked Richie, 'that they're the only pair like it in the world?'

'The shop assistant told me,' beamed Gray.

Given Bob's penchant for putting everything on the 'world stage' — something was either the best in the world, or the worst in the world — the claim did sound as though it contained a modicum of Gray hyperbole.

Always ready for a challenge, Richie didn't waste his morning hitting golf balls or practising his putting. He went shopping. He scoured Johannesburg's shops until he found a pair of blue shoes, exactly like those Gray had bought the previous day.

There was only one pair left in the shop and they were size nine, not exactly ideal for a typically large-footed African caddie, but Richie bought them nonetheless.

On arrival at the Wanderers course, Richie sent Bob on ahead: 'You clear things with the secretary, while I engage a couple of caddies.'

As Gray disappeared inside the clubhouse, Richie reached the caddie master's hut and asked for 'two caddies, one with size-nine feet'. He then added, 'I want the caddie with the size-nine feet to wear these blue shoes for the whole round and afterwards he can keep them.'

The caddie master was a bit perplexed. Firstly, it would be difficult, almost impossible, to find one with such small feet and secondly, African caddies hate wearing shoes. Looking a little bewildered, the caddie master trudged off to try to fulfil this near-impossible request. Eventually, he returned with a young man in tow. He was introduced to Richie as Baruti and being on the small side there was a chance his feet would fit the blue shoes.

Richie explained to Baruti that he would be caddying for his friend and he had to stand very close to him wearing the blue shoes. 'My friend,' explained Richie, 'is very short-sighted and a bit hard of hearing, so you will need to stay very close.'

Richie wasn't exaggerating about Gray being short-sighted, as we'd found out when he played golf with wicketkeeper Brian Taber earlier in the tour.

Gray was renowned for being a steady player who didn't hit his drives far but kept them on the fairway with his gentle fade. Gray teed off first and hit his driver. 'Where did that go?' he quickly asked Tabsy.

Tabsy stood by the edge of the tee shaking his head, 'You've hooked it,' he mumbled quietly. 'I think it's out of bounds.'

'But I never hook,' exploded Gray. 'I'm the best fader in the world.'

With Tabsy still shaking his head, Gray took another ball from its wrapping and hit a provisional drive. 'Where did that one go?' asked an anxious Gray.

'Oh, mate, you've over-compensated,' a serious-looking Taber replied. 'That one is out of bounds to the right.'

'Jaysus,' mumbled Gray, 'I've got to be the worst driver in the world.'

With that he took another ball from his caddie and proceeded to hit a third drive.

'Where did that one go?' he enquired again.

'That one will be all right,' explained Tabsy. 'About 150 metres and near the middle of the fairway.'

The pair strode off the tee and marched down the fairway to where the caddies were waiting with the bags. 'You're a bit short off the tee today, Tabsy,' observed Gray as he spied two balls in the middle of the fairway.

When he noticed a third ball in the group, he turned to Tabsy: 'Whose ball is that one?' On closer inspection he realised all three balls belonged to him. His three drives had come to rest in a circle no bigger than your average dartboard and that was why Taber was doubled over laughing.

Considering the state of Gray's eyesight, it wasn't surprising then that despite Baruti's close attendance, the Australian didn't notice the caddie's blue shoes until they were standing on the sixth tee.

There was a hold-up ahead and while Richie was discussing the racing form for the day, Gray happened to look down. 'Where did you get those bloody shoes?' he screamed at Baruti, who looked, at least in the footwear department, like his identical twin.

The poor caddie didn't know where to look, let alone what to say, and just shrugged. He did, however, happen to take a peek at Richie.

'Benaud,' growled Gray, 'is this your doing?'

'Well Bob,' replied Richie, 'I really didn't want you completing the tour not knowing you'd been had by the salesman.'

FOR a man who lived up to his 'keep the game simple' advice on the cricket field, Richie had a propensity for complicating golf. I remember when he proudly announced he'd bought an odometer so he could measure courses and distances. I was quick to remind him that his good friend and five-time British Open champion Peter Thomson always said, 'It's a hand and eye game.'

However, Richie did live up to his 'keep it simple' advice as a television commentator and presenter. 'Don't say anything unless you can add to the pictures' was his mantra. He also had that marvellous ability to make it look like everything was progressing without a wrinkle, when in reality all hell was breaking loose in the studio.

It was illuminating to hear people's comments on Richie Benaud. Occasionally they would say: 'I love Richie's commentary but it's a pity he hasn't got a sense of humour.'

I felt like replying, 'So you watch television but you don't listen to it.'

His was a droll sense of humour and at times it could border on wicked. Michael Slater once described a batsman as 'having snuck a ball to the boundary', and immediately had reservations about his English.

Turning to Richie, he enquired, 'Is there such a word as "snuck", Rich?'

Following the trademark Benaud pause, Richie raised the microphone and purred: 'Michael, there are a number of "uck" words in the English language, but "sn" isn't one of them.'

On another occasion, Richie and I were discussing the supposed unwritten rule concerning fast bowlers not bouncing fellow speedsters, when I turned to him and brought up an incident where Ray Lindwall hit Englishman Frank 'Typhoon' Tyson in the head at the SCG in 1954–55.

Tyson had taken a pounding in the first Test of that series at the Gabba, as Australia thrashed England. However, the roles were quickly reversed when Tyson took ten wickets after being hit in the head by Lindwall. In conclusion, I said: 'But you were playing in that game at the SCG, Richie. What happened?'

He slowly picked up the microphone and said of Lindwall bouncing Tyson: 'It was a mistake.' Then he gently rested it back on his knee. I was still laughing when, uncharacteristically, he raised his microphone again.

'I'll rephrase that,' he said. 'It was a very big mistake.'

Richie made very few mistakes in his life and he certainly didn't with his choice of life partner. If anything, wife Daphne is even more organised than he was, and apart from cricket they also had a shared love of ballet and cats, both the animals and the musical.

At his 2007 induction into the Australian Cricket Hall of Fame, Richie finished his speech with a number of thank yous and concluded with: 'And Daphne, who is much loved.'

The same could be said of Richie Benaud. He was much loved and will be widely and sorely missed.

MICHAEL ATHERTON

Mike Atherton worked with Richie Benaud in the Channel 4 commentary box, learning a new trade from the master. Mike had captained England in 54 of his 115 Tests. Since 2002, he has carved for himself an outstanding career as a commentator and as cricket correspondent for *The Times*.

'WATCH Richie.'

Like most sportsmen starting out on a second career in broadcasting, I did so without formal training. So, like any sensible novice, I sought advice. Gary Franses was the producer of Channel 4's cricket coverage in 2002 and that was the advice he gave me.

'Watch Richie.'

So I did. One of my early broadcasts was from Lord's and, before the start of play, the cameras were to alight on each of the commentators in various parts of the ground, from where they were to analyse a particular aspect of the day's play. We were to come to Richie last of all, up in his eyrie in the commentary box, and he was to be the scene-setter for the day — the last voice to be heard before live play.

I had finished my bit down below and hurried up to the commentary box to listen to the great man do his bit — to watch and learn as instructed. I stood behind the camera at the back of the box and waited. Richie's turn came; on the director's cue, he turned to the camera, with that one-eye-half-closed look, and began to speak. Maybe he thought he had a lapel microphone attached to his (beige/cream/off-white/bone) jacket. He did not. Richie spoke, but the viewers heard nothing.

Franses stood behind the camera, frantically waving and pointing to the hand-held microphone on the desk and instructing Richie to pick it up. Without moving his stare from the camera, Richie felt around blindly on the desk, picked up what he thought was the microphone, lifted it to his mouth, and began talking into his glasses. He didn't miss a beat and later laughed the mistake off and was happy to be the butt of everyone's humour. Therein, I suppose, lies Richie's first Law of Broadcasting: 'It's live telly; mistakes happen.' It's also sport on telly and not the most important thing in the world, so don't get too hung up about it and don't imagine yourself to be more important than you really are. You are only a television commentator.

That links in to his second Law — these laws by the way were not written on stone (or tablet these days, I guess) but rather as I imagined them to be, having worked with and watched him for four years and listened to his advice — which is, as he said to me once, 'Remember, above all, that you are a guest in someone's living room, often for six hours a day, so try not to irritate them.'

Not irritating the viewer may sound like a limited ambition for a commentator but — as countless viewers of live sport would attest, no doubt — it is not as straightforward as it sounds, especially in cricket where a game might progress for five days, six hours a day. Ideally, you don't want the viewer switching off, or over, or turning the sound down. So remember, above all, that he or she is there to watch the action and the cricketers and not listen to you. Don't impose yourself too heavy-handedly between the viewer and the action. You are a conduit — no more, no less.

If you can succeed in that, Richie may allow you to progress to his third Law which is: 'If you can add to the picture, do so.' Aside from not irritating the viewer into switching off, you are there to add some insight and to inform, based on your knowledge and experience. That insight may be in the form of an anecdote or technical or tactical or human observation, and may be more suitable when the action is slow rather than dramatic, according to your discretion. But anyone can read the score and tell the viewer what has just happened. It's not radio.

Richie's third Law links into his fourth: 'Michael, always engage brain before speaking.' I can't remember what particular bit of commentary of mine prompted that from Richie, but it is good advice nonetheless. Radio demands immediacy, since, obviously, people cannot see what is happening. Television occasionally — not always, but occasionally — allows for a momentary distance from the action, just enough time for the brain to function. Use it.

Richie's fifth Law — 'Nobody ever complained about silence' — is an old-fashioned notion these days, as increasingly television companies move to three commentators in action rather than two, and so there is a battle for air-time. It also might not apply to an Indian audience who, I am told, enjoy a full-on visual and audio experience — one reason perhaps why Bill Lawry, say, was always more popular on the subcontinent than Richie. Richie was always immensely popular in England where, I think, audiences enjoyed his understated style, pauses and silences.

And finally: 'Never use the term "we" when talking about a team.' Neutrality and fairness are non-negotiable for two very good reasons: first, you are an observer, not a cheerleader; second, although there will be a home audience, within that there may be many people cheering for the other team. You need to be fair to both sides. Most broadcasts these days go around the world in any case, so you are speaking to cricket-lovers of all nationalities.

Richie understood television. He played in an era before television gripped cricket, became a key mover in the Packer revolution, and knew how television could help to sell and grow the game.

He was not averse to a little understated showmanship: the beige jackets that came to define him; the sayings — 'morning, everyone' — that did the same. He worked the camera beautifully. The best commentators provoke imitation and Richie had thousands of those. Who, among us, has not said some phrase or other in Benaud-speak?

He saw television commentary as a craft, and one to try to excel at. So, in meetings before the start of a Test series, he was meticulous about the pronunciation of names, especially so if, for example, Sri Lanka were touring. And I have lost count of the number of times he said to me: 'It's a pitch, Michael, not a wicket. The three bits of wood are wickets.' Or, 'Please don't start interview questions with "must".' ('You must be pleased with, etc, etc,' being a statement and not a question.) Small things, but important nonetheless.

Richie never morphed into an old-school bore. He rarely talked about his playing days or his considerable achievements as a player.

He never began a commentary stint or a sentence with, 'In my day...'; he admired the modern player; he loved Twenty20 and all the technological advances, especially his beloved 'Snicko'. He wore his playing achievements lightly. He recognised that times change and comparisons are pointless. Because of that, the modern players loved him.

He was loved. For longer than people care to remember he was the voice of the English summer, just as he was in Australia. Thinking now, I can hear him, at the culmination of the greatest Test match I have seen, at Edgbaston in 2005, exactly the right man for the moment, as he followed the pictures with succinct but dramatic precision: 'Jones! Bowden! Kasprowicz the man to go and Harmison has done it! Despair on the faces of the batsmen and joy for every England player on the field!' Benaud's Laws distilled.

BILLY BIRMINGHAM

As 'The 12th Man', Billy Birmingham has introduced cricket to a whole new audience over the past 30 years, through his mimicry of Richie and the other members of Channel Nine's commentary team. The 12th Man phenomenon began in 1984, with the release of the *It's Just Not Cricket* maxi-single. Three years later, Billy released his first full album, *Wired World of Sports*. Over the next 25 years, he made six more 12th Man albums and two singles, all of which went to No. 1 on the national ARIA charts. On Richie's passing in April 2015, Fox Sports in Australia invited Billy to pay tribute ...

IT was always my hope that Richie would get a standing ovation at every Test ground in Australia whenever he announced his intention to hang up the 50 Shades of Beige jacket once and for all. But unfortunately that bloody Sunbeam Alpine got in the way!

It's hard to put into words the way I've been feeling since I heard Richie 'From The Body Of The Same Name' Benaud has passed away. Very sad. Quite nauseous, actually. Struggling to find the right words. Disoriented.

What is the appropriate response to the passing of a man who has been such an integral part of your life, your career, your identity for more than 30 years? How are you supposed to feel when the bloke with whom millions associate you has delivered his last *chew for chwenty-chew*? I know I won't be alone in feeling this way. Richie has occupied a special place in our homes and our hearts for decades. The world changed so much over that time. Richie didn't seem to. The hair was always cut halfway over his ears and fastidiously swept across from one side. The cream, bone, white, off-white, ivory and beige wardrobe was unchanging. The 'Welcome back to the MCG' intro was almost reassuring in its familiarity.

And the calls of 'Marvellous!' and 'Shuuuper effort, that!' and 'What a catch! What. A. Catch!' were the soundtrack to summer for generations of Australians.

Richie certainly had some reservations about my 12th Man stuff over the years. My colourful use of language didn't sit too well with a man who always tried to exude an image as white as his jacket. That said, as an old media man from way back, he couldn't fail to see how the 12th Man albums were transforming him into a cult hero and Nine's cricket coverage into one of the most iconic broadcasts in Australian TV history.

I was nervous about the first album. It didn't have my name on it, because I naively thought that if I left it as 'The 12th Man', Richie wouldn't know where it came from.

Then I got a call out of the blue from a Melbourne disc jockey called Kevin Hillier. He said he knew it was me on the record, he'd sent Richie a copy to listen to over the weekend, and he was interviewing him the following Monday.

I'd hoped the record would have a bit more time to get some airplay and sell a few copies, just in case an injunction was slapped on me. But the horse had bolted. So I listened to Richie's interview on Melbourne radio station 3XY.

It went something along the lines of: 'My wife and I have been listening to it all weekend in the flat. We've just packed it in our bags before we head to England. We're looking forward to playing it over there. I'm sure everyone will be rolling around with laughter.'

I was absolutely thrilled.

In the early days, I would send Richie a copy of each album upon release, figuring that attack was the best form of defence. He would write me letters in response — on that beautifully embossed 'Benaud & Associates' letterhead of his — critiquing my work like it was a bloody Broadway stage production.

Here's what he wrote to me after *Wired World of Sports* was released:

> Dear Billy,
>
> Thanks for the cassette and record of your latest creation.
>
> Plus mark: excellent entertainment as always. Minus mark: the same as last time. A bit too long, too much swearing for the sake of it and Chappelli's voice still not right.
>
> But in a word: brilliant.
>
> Kind regards and good luck,
>
> richie

And this is what he wrote after *The 12th Man Again!* was released:

> Dear Billy,
>
> Thanks for the LP, tape and CD of the '12th Man Again'.
>
> The usual critique follows, the fee for which will be $A87,000. [To this day, I have no idea what this meant or where the amount came from.]
>
> There are some wonderfully funny and brilliant sequences again and the production is excellent.
>
> Demerit marks: too much swearing just for the sake of swearing. In this, I'm right on the side of your daughter with her published remark about Daddy using the F-word … and possibly your mum as well! [I used to record at home and my daughter heard me swearing and reported it to Mum. Mum then had to explain that it was part of Daddy's work.]
>
> Some of the voices don't seem quite right, particularly Chappelli's again. It seems I have a voice that is easy to copy. But in general terms, other than Greigy, they don't seem quite as spot on this time.
>
> I see you've hit Number 1 again. Perhaps I should reconsider my retirement!

In a word, as the tautology kings would say, wonderfully amusing.

Cheers and salaams,

richie

I found it interesting that he always signed in fountain pen and spelled his name in all lower-case letters. But what a fabulous piece of correspondence for me to receive from the great man.

For a bloke who spent so much of his life in the media, he remained a private man. Richie wasn't a fan of people fussing over his work or accomplishments. I remember getting a call from *60 Minutes* once asking whether I'd be part of a story they were wanting to do on Richie. 'Sure,' I said. No sooner had I hung up than the producer was back on the blower to tell me Richie had no interest at all in the idea of being on *60 Minutes*. The flagship programme on his own network!

I must admit that I was quite shocked to see how his health had deteriorated when we shot his brilliant Australia Day 'lamb' commercial together at the start of the summer.

The first thing I noticed was that his always impeccably coiffed hair had succumbed to the ravages of chemotherapy. Then, when I put my arm around him and felt just how much he had wasted away, I was profoundly shocked and saddened. The recovery from the accident in the Sunbeam had clearly taken it out of him, but he was now facing an even bigger battle as his years of playing cricket hatless had resulted in skin cancer.

There was something in his eyes, too. If you asked him how he was, the reply was always along the lines of, 'Pleased to report I'm on the mend.' But you knew that was stoicism, not reality. I was bloody amazed that he even had the strength to show up at all.

How thrilled I was to have been able to catch up with the great man one more time and to be a small part of his fabulous TV ad. I took the piss out of him for more than 30 years and now here I was working with him on what turned out to be his last major project.

How marvellous!

It's hard to imagine there is another Australian out there as universally loved as Richie. It was a kind of affection that isn't conditional on cricketing skills or commentary work. People just adored the man.

That's why everyone gives their mate a knowing nudge when the scoreboard ticks over to 2–22, why entire sections of the crowd don silver wigs and beige jackets at the Sydney Test each year, why reciting Richie's commentary gems has become a national pastime.

Rest in peace, Richie.

Incomparable, irreplaceable, the one and only (it always seemed to me he didn't like the word 'doyen').

Billy Birmingham,
April 10, 2015

IAN HEALY

Ian Healy made his Test debut against Pakistan in September 1988. Ten years later, Healy broke Rod Marsh's then world Test record for most wicketkeeping dismissals. Through that decade, 'Heals' became the major on-field voice and a driving force for the Australian team. On his retirement in 1999, he had completed 395 Test, 233 ODI and 767 first-class dismissals. His subsequent move from the playing field to the commentary box was seamless and successful.

RICHIE was a private colleague in the commentary box, continually tapping away on the laptop at his own table, churning out his numerous articles for the wider cricket world — and often managing at the same time to compete fiercely with his good mate Jack Bannister in their ongoing tipping battle at the races. Despite the distractions, at all times he would somehow be keeping an ear on the progress of the game in the middle that he was about to commentate on.

There was a day, however, when a couple of us thought we had caught him napping in the commentary box. He might even have been asleep, we thought, with his head down and an ear resting on the keyboard. Richie was motionless for what seemed a number of minutes. Finally, we were glimpsing a chink in the pro's ability to fit it all in! Our disappointment was immense as he rose from the table, wide-awake. Turned out he had been listening to a horse race!

The Richie humour was always as dry as dust. He was always gently testing the reactions of people; most would not get it the first time. His wry smile wouldn't surface until the penny dropped with the helpless victim ... who by then might be two rows or two tables away.

In Richie's world, socialising was for night-time. I remember well an occasion when I asked him out to dinner during a match in Perth in the early 1990s. Would he like to come out and have a bite to eat and meet a couple of the 'youngies': our spinners, Shane Warne and Tim May?

'Yes, I would,' he said.

It was characteristic Richie that arrangements for such an event had to go through the necessary protocol — in this case, through our coach, Bob Simpson, and then via a handwritten note confirming arrangements for the dinner.

The dinner took place and was fantastic. We talked about everything we possibly could. At one stage, I posed the question: 'Did you drink much in your playing days?'

He broke into a story from the 1953 Ashes tour ...

Well, I didn't drink at all before then. I was the youngster on that tour and had made three and nought in the first Test at Trent Bridge. The night before the rest day, the Nottingham lace factory put on a party for the touring team and I was sitting in the corner — exactly as a youngster who had made three and nought should — when Mr Hassett [skipper Lindsay Hassett] asked me, 'What is your drink?'

'I don't drink, Mr Hassett,' I told him.

'Try this, Benaud,' he said, reaching for a glass.

'Ah, that's terribly strong!' I said, after taking a sip.

'Well, try this one, Benaud,' he said, grabbing a drink out of someone else's hand.

'Ah, that's better,' was my verdict.

'Benaud,' he declared, 'your drink is a single Scotch and water!'

I proceeded to have 11 singles and two doubles that night and I've had a bloody good time ever since!

It was his magnificent way of telling us that nothing much had changed in cricket. We had the best of nights.

I'll value so many memories of knowing and working with Richie: the big things and the small.

He was 'Believable Benaud' — whatever he said got over the line. It didn't matter with whom he was communicating, from Kerry Packer to the fans.

And he was 'Backseat Benaud' — unless he had to, he never sat in the front in a car ... and *never* in row one on a plane.

RICHARD FISK

Richard Fisk's working life encompassed more than 40 years in sport, as an administrator, journalist, radio host and broadcaster. Among his varied roles he has been managing editor of the *New York Times'* European sports magazine, sporting director at Sydney radio stations 2GB and 2WS, and a senior executive with two National Rugby League clubs, Cronulla and the Sydney Roosters, and the Hunter Sports Group.

I HAVE seen or experienced many 'Richie moments', but two in particular have always stayed with me. At 2GB back in the early 1980s, when I was a rookie sports director and presenter, I had the good fortune of linking with Richie as 'our man' in England for the summer of cricket over there. Richie was the cricket correspondent on our Saturday morning sports show, which featured prominent rugby league characters such as Peter 'Zorba' Peters, Ray 'Rabbits' Warren and Greg 'Hollywood' Hartley.

I was hosting the show, which pretty much flew by the seat of its pants from week to week. Very early on we had a particular issue in cricket that required Richie's expertise, but it meant him staying up until well after midnight in England to make his contribution to the show. He did so in his usual calm, professional and good-humoured way. Being grateful for his input, I felt obliged to ring and thank him early the next morning.

'There is no need for thanks, Richard,' he told me. 'You have employed me to do a job over here and that's what I'll be doing to the best of my ability. Don't ever hesitate to call if you believe I can make a contribution towards us producing the best coverage we can.'

I remember, too, a special night two years later at the SCG when 2GB were having a crack at being the first commercial radio station to cover a one-day international series. Our commentary team comprised Mike Whitney, Kerry O'Keeffe, Len Pascoe, David Colley and me. At the end of our first, nervous night, there was a knock on the door of the 2GB booth and I opened it, to find Richie standing there. His work done with Channel Nine, he had made the effort of walking halfway around the ground to offer a few words.

'I just wanted to say I caught some of the coverage and it was fantastic,' he said. 'It was fresh, positive and different. Congratulations.'

With that, he was gone. I stood there, gobsmacked that he had not only taken such an interest in what we were doing, but had made the effort to deliver his views personally. It meant the world to me.

Always the professional, he was a man who chose his words carefully and, in my experience, always thought of the other person first. Several days later, he rang me with further encouragement, having organised for me to be his nominee as guest speaker at the Fiji Sports Awards later in the year.

'They are lovely people,' he said. 'I thought it would be a good way to help you broaden your experience.'

He was a wonderful man who taught me about the value of professionalism and humility, and about the ongoing obligation we all have to try to help young and less experienced people.

JOHN BRENNAN

John Brennan has been called the 'Godfather of Sydney radio' and 'the man who pioneered talkback radio in Australia'. The titles, from which the modest, gentlemanly 'Brenno' flinches, are not hyperbole. In a career spanning well over half a century, he was indeed a pathfinder and a star-maker — a unique figure in a rip 'n' tear industry. Brenno dearly loves his sport, especially rugby league (through his passion for the Balmain Tigers) and cricket.

WELL before I took over as programme director at Sydney radio's 2UE in the early 1980s, I was determined to fulfil a long-held hope — that if I ever ran a radio station Richie Benaud would be my cricket expert. When that plan became a reality and he joined up, it was a very special moment in my career and life.

We used Richie on the breakfast show with Alan Jones and in news bulletins. Later in the decade, after Kerry Packer bought 2UE in 1986, our new owner wanted me to cover cricket ball-by-ball. Kerry instructed me to organise broadcasting positions around Australia's major grounds and to go out and 'find some commentators'. A bonus existed — we could use his Channel Nine callers as 'colour men'.

I duly landed the commentators I wanted: Western Australia's ace caller, Dennis Cometti, and the colourful Henry 'Blowers' Blofeld from England. Epping Boys' High School graduate Andrew Moore was the third commentator; he would go on to be a top-class caller of cricket and rugby league and an accomplished general radio performer. The Great Benaud was the spearhead of the team ... and he loved it. We became good friends. The Christmas card from Richie and Daphne would be the first to arrive at our place each year.

When I shifted to 2GB in 2000 the station didn't have a cent to spare, and no extras could be hired outside the pool of our main stars. It was a difficult time. Finally, we reached the point where we *did* have a dollar to throw around, but Richie had signed an exclusive contract with Nine for the Australian summer and with that and his overseas commitments we couldn't use him. It was one of the great regrets of my years in radio.

Richie was an incomparable commentator and a magnificent man, loved and admired by all whose lives he touched. My life is richer and so blessed for having encountered him along the way.

DENNIS COMETTI

Dennis Cometti began his media career as a disc jockey in Perth. In 1973, he joined the ABC, where he covered a wide variety of sports, called WAFL football, and became known across the country as a cricket commentator. When the West Coast Eagles joined the VFL (now AFL) for the 1987 season, Dennis moved to the Seven Network and in the winters since has become a constant and highly respected figure on the AFL landscape, predominantly as a TV caller but also on radio and in newspapers. His reputation has been boosted, too, by his work in other sports, including Olympic Games swimming and as part of 2UE's coverage of international cricket in the late 1980s and '90s.

I'VE been a broadcaster since I was 18. And in all that time I think there's only one person I've worked with who intimidated me. It was Richie Benaud. Of course, it wasn't Richie's fault. It's just that I was a fan.

I always had been, ever since the West Indies toured Australia in 1960–61. Few sporting events are as vivid in my memory as that Test series. I remember it was a baking summer in Perth, the kind of summer that can grind down even a ten-year-old on school holidays. But somehow Richie Benaud and Frank Worrell managed to build something unforgettable.

The family radio on the fridge top barely got a breather.

Right away, Benaud became my hero. He was the captain, he could bowl, he could bat, and he did it all with a couple of shirt buttons undone and his collar up. There was a lot to like.

Fast forward to the summer of 1986–87. After broadcasting cricket for 13 years on ABC radio, I moved to the Seven Network. I wasn't at Seven to broadcast cricket; I was there to cover Australian rules football, or so I thought.

Things quickly changed when top-rating Sydney radio station 2UE decided it wanted to broadcast cricket. I was co-opted onto the coverage. This was how I first got the chance to meet and then broadcast alongside Richie.

Over nearly a decade, I found him to be both a generous broadcaster and a real gentleman. They say it doesn't pay to meet your heroes, but I've got to say in my experience, particularly in the case of Richie Benaud, it's best to disregard that advice.

As a broadcaster, he was insightful, he was understated and he was funny, often all in the same moment. He was respected and admired more than any other Australian broadcaster past or present. In the eyes of the Australian public, Richie was the voice of record.

More to the point, there was no sense debating things on air with him, because you couldn't win. I remember getting a reminder of that late one night in Adelaide.

We were broadcasting an eminently forgettable one-day international. Richie was sitting to my right, obscured beyond our producer and scorer, Andrew Moore.

For some reason, I felt compelled to suggest a couple of changes to the field and perhaps a bowling change as well.

Silence.

Unfortunately, there was a fast bowler bowling. I had all the time I needed. Too much time as it turned out! Calling on all my vast experience as vice-captain of green faction at Tuart Hill High School, I decided to go a little deeper into my tactics. More silence.

Andrew Moore is a big man, and suddenly I could feel him begin to vibrate.

I turned and saw that he had pulled back to reveal Richie, elegant as always, but appearing to be sound asleep. I quickly came to the conclusion this was my fault — I'd either bored him to sleep or, worse still, forced him into feigning sleep so he wouldn't have to tell me that he'd 'never heard such rot'.

As always, Richie Benaud managed to play things perfectly. Forgettable game, unforgettable memory!

JIM MAXWELL

Since joining the ABC in 1973, Jim Maxwell has covered more than 280 Tests in a career that has included numerous tours — among them those to the West Indies, South Africa and the Indian subcontinent, and to England for Ashes Tests. The distinctive Maxwell voice has been Australian cricket's 'sound of summer' on the radio for many years, just as Alan McGilvray's was before him. A straight shooter with expert knowledge, Jim has also covered many other sports, most notably both rugby codes, hockey (at three Olympic Games) and golf. He became president of the Primary Club of Australia in 2009.

IF cricket had ever anointed a pope it would have been Richie Benaud. He was the most influential, revered and respected person in the game for 50 years. As Australian captain, he never lost a series. As a commentator, he was precise, authoritative and deliciously understated — the master of the pause. Silence marked him as the best exponent of television's essential craft: let the picture tell the story, then utter, with appropriate gravitas, a memorably droll *bon mot*.

If you ran a poll today on who is the most popular cricket commentator in Australia, Richie would still rank No. 1. He is immortalised in beige, with that prominent lower lip and his acute analysis, and with Billy Birmingham's parody recalled by the fans' refrain: *two for two hundred and twenty-two.*

As a commentator, he concentrated on the game at hand, rarely dwelt on the past and was always respectful of the players — notwithstanding their foibles and failures. A wild-slog dismissal was 'clever bowling'; a rank delivery urged a reflective comment, such as, 'He might have lost his length there.'

He played in an era of austerity. No one earned any money then from playing in the Australian team. In his early years, there were no celebrations at the fall of a wicket. It was a game. Yet Richie was the first tactile captain, breaking the mould of restraint with enthusiastic enjoyment of the moment.

For a young lad at the SCG lucky enough to see so many great NSW and Australian players — the likes of Neil Harvey, Alan Davidson, Norman O'Neill, Bob Simpson, Brian Booth, Bill Lawry, Graham McKenzie and Wally Grout — Richie was one of many heroes. Positioned between the stellar careers of Bill O'Reilly and Shane Warne, he was the match-winning wrist-spinner of his time. The memory of listening on a crackling radio to his around-the-wicket performance at Manchester in 1961 reverberates now as much as does hearing his call of Shane Warne's ball of the century at the same ground in 1993.

He could surprise us, invariably with great effect. Richie was a long-time patron of the Australian Cricket Media Association, and one day in the 1980s he was asked to say a few words and present the annual 'emerging cricketer of the year' award to a young Steve Waugh. We were in Adelaide, in the old stand near the Chappell Bar, and Richie made a few observations about Steve and then added, 'But what I really like about him is that he's got a bit of shit in him.' And that was it.

I first met and interviewed Richie in 1975 for a programme on the 1960–61 Tied Test series. Looking back, it was a disappointment that he was never asked to work on the ABC-TV coverage in those years leading up to the start of World Series Cricket, which so transformed the presentation of the game on television.

My respect and admiration for him deepened through the last decade when he was Twelfth Man at the Primary Club. Every appearance he made at one of our functions was greeted rapturously by the audience, and he gave an ear to all comers who wanted a moment with him at the annual 'Marathon Cricket' matches at the SCG.

Richie Benaud was unique: a great all-rounder and leader whose devotion to the game will be remembered as nothing less than phenomenal.

MARK TAYLOR

Mark 'Tubby' Taylor succeeded Allan Border as Australian cricket captain in 1994. In the next four-and-a-half years, he led Australia to three Ashes triumphs, famous series victories in the West Indies, South Africa and Pakistan, and to the 1996 World Cup final. Arguably his two greatest achievements as a batsman came at either end of his playing career: 839 runs in his first full Test series, in England in 1989; and his epic 334 not out in the second Test at Peshawar in 1998, which equalled Sir Donald Bradman's then Australian record. A few months later, Mark appeared in his 104th and final Test, and was named Australian of the Year. Soon after, he joined the Nine commentary team.

IN the commentary box, Richie Benaud was not the sort of guy who'd tell you: 'This is how you do it,' or, 'This is when you speak and this is when you don't speak.' Richie's attitude was much more along the lines of: 'You've been employed to commentate on the game. Just go for it. Put forward your opinions. Speak when you think you've got something to say and you can add to the pictures.'

I started in the commentating business in 1999 and before too long Channel Nine was putting me in the box from time to time, sharing the hosting role with Richie. He was in the driver's seat as we ran through various things to be covered before the start of play. He would bounce things off me as I picked up some confidence and progressively I got the hang of it.

One morning at the MCG, in the 2002–03 season from memory, I sat with him during a rain delay. 'In you go, Richie and Mark,' was the direction that day. Richie took his time. The fact was he never rushed *anywhere*, but the way he moved this day was slow even for him. Finally, he arrived. By then, I was all wired up and 'plugged in' to the director. A voice came down the line: 'One minute to air, one minute to air.' And Richie was sitting there fiddling around with his earpiece. Eventually, he put it down, called the floor manager over and said, 'This earpiece is not working.'

With that, the floor manager ran from the room to get Richie's backup earpiece. Meanwhile, I'm hearing a new message: 'Thirty seconds to air, thirty seconds to air.' Finally, Richie gets the second earpiece. But immediately he declares, 'Ah, no, this isn't working either.' Next I hear: 'Ten seconds to air ...'

Alongside me, Richie casually pulls out his earpiece and says, 'It's all yours, Mark.'

Gulp!

It was down to me. I had to get us through the next five minutes of live television ...

There were butterflies that day, I can tell you. I needed to listen to the director in my ear, set the scene for our audience, direct questions to Richie ... provide something that would be worthwhile and make sense to the viewers.

To this day, I hold the deepest suspicions about the events of that morning. 'This earpiece is not working,' he claimed. I reckon it was Richie's way of saying: 'Here you go, Mark. You handle being in the No. 1 chair for a little while!'

I guess it was a vote of confidence, but I was thinking back then, *You bastard! You did that deliberately!*

I must have fumbled through okay; the fact being, I'm still around today.

There were many lessons to be learned from Richie, the prince of cricket commentators. Take, for example, the time at the WACA in Perth in 2001–02 when I was doing ball-by-ball commentary and Richie was sitting next to me. Shane Warne was batting and on 99. He had never scored a Test hundred. Australia's No. 11, Glenn McGrath, was at the other end. Warnie, no doubt, was a bit nervous about being stranded one short of his maiden ton. He blocked three straight deliveries from New Zealand's Daniel Vettori ... we all knew something big was going to happen ...

Vettori bowled a nice 'floater' and Warnie went after it ...

This was my call of the moment: 'He goes for it ... There's a man out there ... He's getting under it .... And he's got it! And Shane Warne ... tragically ... finishes on 99.'

That's how I left it. And I was thinking, *Well, that wasn't too bad. I'm quite happy with that.* I looked at Richie, whose job was to add some colour to my ball-by-ball. He said absolutely nothing. The silence was deafening. Then the director was in my ear, saying, 'Throw to the break, throw to the break.'

So I said, 'Australia all out 351. New Zealand's second innings will start after the break.'

The following morning, I was up the back of the box when Richie arrived. He walked up to me and said, 'Mark, can I have a little word?'

'Sure,' I said.

He steered me into a side room and there reached into his inside jacket pocket and pulled out a note. 'Do with this as you see fit,' he said.

It was like *Mission: Impossible*. I was almost waiting for the note to explode, as I opened it gingerly. It read:

> Tragedy. Kids dying in Ethiopia every day is a tragedy. The sinking of the Titanic was a tragedy. Shane Warne making 99 is not a tragedy.

Four weeks later, on the final day of the Boxing Day Test at the MCG, South Africa's Jacques Kallis was run out for 99. Up in the commentary box, I shouted again, 'What a tragedy!' Quickly, I glanced to where Richie was seated. He just gave me a little shake of the head.

Message received ... and understood.

It was in South Africa during the 2003 World Cup that I felt I really got to know Richie Benaud, even though by then we had worked together for more than three years. During an Australian summer, you often feel as if the work schedule is something like: go to the ground, commentate, quick dinner, back to the hotel to prepare for the next day, sleep, same again. If there is a gap between games, you head home, however briefly. You don't really get to know someone all *that* well with such a routine. But we were in South Africa for seven weeks, with sometimes days between games, so there was a lot of golf played. Richie loved his golf, because he could get away with just two or three other people for five hours or so without all the other distractions. I came to realise that he was really a shy man who didn't want to be the centre of attention. He enjoyed his own time and his own space.

I have to say that over there in South Africa he took my money regularly on various golf courses. He had a Honma two wood with which he just kept donging the ball down the middle, while I was spraying it everywhere. He kept saying to me, 'You should get one of these.' Early on, I was agreeing with him. By the time Ricky Ponting's team had won the World Cup, I was more inclined to say, 'Jam your Honma up your …!'

He was in his early 70s by then, playing off 12 or 14 — a steady golfer who enjoyed knocking it down the middle, say 180 to 200 metres, and chipping up. He was pretty competitive, but I think most of all, as I said, he enjoyed the peace and quiet of the golf course.

It was so special to have known Richie and to have worked with him. The experience of commentating with him was an invaluable masterclass. I am now fully aware that it is no easy thing to gaze down the barrel of the camera, with perhaps as many as two million people or more staring back at you, hanging on your every word and gesture. The early, pioneering days of TV cricket commentary must have been particularly nerve-racking. But he did it all supremely well.

Richie was on his own in the commentary business. To have been part of his team and to have worked with him was very special — a privilege and a pleasure.

TONY COZIER

Tony Cozier has been the West Indies' premier cricket writer and commentator stretching back to the 1960s.

IT was an opportunity not to be missed. It was September 2013 and Richie Benaud would be in Barbados for the first time since appropriately delivering the annual Sir Frank Worrell memorial lecture at the University of the West Indies, Barbados campus, 20 years earlier.

At 83, Richie was unlikely to come again; as it sadly turned out, it was his last chance to catch up with five of the West Indian survivors from the unforgettable 1960–61 series in Australia when he, as inventive home captain, and Worrell, his similarly minded West Indies counterpart, influenced their teams into an exuberant approach to the game that revived the fading image of Test cricket.

Immediately sparked by the unprecedented tie first-up in Brisbane, the series captured the public's imagination to such an extent that 100,000 people thronged the streets of Melbourne to hail their popular visitors at the tour's end. It was a phenomenon unheard of, before or since.

A lunch at one of Barbados' top restaurants, overlooking the spectacular Rockley beach on the island's south coast, seemed the ideal setting for Benaud to be joined by his 1960–61 challengers: Garry Sobers, Wes Hall, Seymour Nurse, Cammie Smith and Peter Lashley. Everton Weekes, 88 at the time, was also along; he had piled up runs while Benaud twirled his leg-spin in the final Test of the 1951–52 series down-under and the 1955 series in the Caribbean. Now they were Sir Garry, Sir Wes and Sir Everton.

I knew them all as friends, principally from years of covering the West Indies wherever they ventured, and Benaud from the eight seasons in Australia as part of the Channel Nine panel, learning the intricacies of television — as opposed to radio — commentary under his guidance. I first met Richie's wife and soulmate, Daphne, when she was secretary to the renowned cricket writer, EW Swanton.

I was in no doubt they would all be enthusiastic about the idea. Yet the exercise turned out to be not quite as straightforward as it appeared.

As keen as he was, Richie had one caveat. He was coming for an event unrelated to cricket (it was a special birthday celebration of a close friend of the Benauds, a Trinidadian long since resident in Sydney) and he didn't want any diversion from the occasion.

'One possible problem that springs to mind is if media outlets demand access with cameras, tape recorders and notebooks, something which, if it happens, would certainly detract from the idea,' he emailed when I put my lunch proposal to him. He was, after all, then as famous for his second career as television's most authoritative commentator as he was as captain and player.

I nervously assured him that wouldn't be the case, that I had it all under control. So the date was set, the restaurant booked, the local contingent confirmed and sponsorship agreed with the Cricket Legends of Barbados group. I got my son Craig busy designing a four-page menu, entitled 'Remembering the Great Times', carrying images of the seven players along with the iconic photograph of the final run-out of the Tied Test, the summarised scores of the matches and, of course, the menu: Opening Batsmen (starters); Middle Order (main course); Tail-Enders (sweets).

Then, suddenly, a setback.

Richie had fallen in the shower at his west coast villa and damaged his ribs. After examination at a nearby clinic, he was transferred to a private hospital on the outskirts of Bridgetown for a couple of days' observation.

Crestfallen, I cancelled the restaurant reservation and advised the others of the situation. Somehow, word got back to Richie. Daphne called to say that whatever I had done, I should undo it since Richie was adamant he wasn't going to let a little pain and some tight strapping around his upper body put him off. He would be there at the appointed time.

So the lunch arrangements were restored and, to their shared delight, the invitations to the local contingent reinstated. There was only one anxious moment when Richie arrived at the restaurant; as Wes Hall approached as if to greet him with a hug, he recoiled. 'No hugs today!' he exclaimed, pointing to his ribcage.

The group — including Daphne, Michele Kennedy-Green, the birthday girl from Sydney, and her sister, Patricia — took their seats at a round table at 1.10pm. We reluctantly broke up three hours later.

After glasses were raised in memory of those of the 1960–61 team who had passed on — Sir Frank, who died of leukaemia, aged 42, Sir Conrad Hunte, Gerry Alexander and Alf Valentine — the banter became increasingly animated, the stories more and more richly embellished, the laughter louder, Cammie Smith's as infectious as ever.

It was just what everyone had expected.

MARK NICHOLAS

Mark Nicholas, the former Hampshire captain, presents the cricket on Channel Nine in Australia and Channel 5 in Britain.

HE was father, uncle, brother and friend. He was our conscience and our guiding light. In an age of much madness, he made sense. He held firm when others doubted and let go when those around him needed to fly. His wise counsel was without compare, his kindness unconditional. There was something elemental about him, like the wind and the rain. And he was summer's sunshine. He was a constant in all our lives. But now he has gone. The memories, the sights and sound of him, will live with us forever.

We, that is the Channel Nine commentary team, last saw him in person at the Sydney Cricket Ground in November 2014. When he arrived on the outfield in front of the Members Pavilion where we had gathered, there was a general shuffling. Richie had been unseen and virtually unheard of for a year since the car crash that all but ended his career in television and the news that he was to appear at the Nine Network's launch of the 'Sizzling Summer of Cricket' was greeted with immense excitement.

The crash had damaged a couple of vertebrae and the suggestion of surgery to the spine had lingered around for most of the previous Australian summer. He made no fuss, of course, but admitted that he was far from ready to bowl 30 overs off the reel on a hot Sydney day. The surgery never happened. Apparently, a natural fusion was already taking place. Instead, the medics found some melanomas. Radiation and chemotherapy are not anyone's game. The treatment had taken its toll. I suggested that it had been a rough year. 'Roughish,' he replied, with the understatement that has hallmarked his life.

Anyway, Richie turned up bang on time for the photo shoot and though the joy in greeting him was uninhibited, we were all sad to see him so diminished. He carried himself with fortitude and typical grace but he was clearly weak. It seemed absurd that he had retired from the commentary box in England almost ten years earlier, but it is a fact. On that early September day at the Oval in 2005, the producer of Channel 4's cricket coverage, Gary Franses, had sent him across the ground to be alongside me and the others in our commentary team to say goodbye. Channel 4 had lost the rights to cricket in the UK.

The crowd rose to him with as much bonhomie as they had to the England team who, moments earlier, had won the Ashes after a summer of cricket that held the nation spellbound. Moved by their enthusiasm and warmth, Benaud shed a tear. At least, so said Tony Greig, who walked with him. Richie never denied it.

He was good to us all: always by our side, a constant source of wisdom and encouragement. No one has sold the game of cricket with greater skill; few played it with greater flair.

His minimalism was a lifestyle. The footprint was everywhere, though best illustrated in his television work both in front of the camera and behind the microphone. Witness: 'West Indies cruising to victory here — all Carl Hooper has to do is keep his head as Shane Warne switches to bowl round the wicket into the rough outside leg stump.' At which point, Hooper charges down the pitch and has a mighty heave at Warne. The ball spins and catches the leading edge of Hooper's bat. It is about to drop into Steve Waugh's hands as Benaud says, 'Oh Carl,' and nothing more.

When Channel 4 nicked the television rights off the BBC, Benaud was a must-get and entitled to first-class on British Airways. After Channel 4's first day on air, Giles Smith reviewed the coverage in the *Telegraph*. He opened with a sentence that went something like this: 'If Channel 4 put a programme to air about sex that revealed naked transvestites debating with one another the merits of their actions and then giving a display of their activities, it might just get away with it as long as Richie Benaud was there to say, "Morning, everyone."' With one of those superb catchphrases, Benaud had repaid the network's faith and introduced the game to its new, initially uncertain, audience.

At the end of the summer of 2002, we took him to lunch at The Ivy in London. The room was full of the great and the good — Frost and Parkinson, Mrs Beckham, Michael Winner, to name a few — but it went silent when he glided in. You should have seen the punters gawp. And the waiters, too. In general, Richie kept himself to himself, which is a powerful weapon. Because of it, public appearances became a parade.

I miss him. I'm sure we all do. To have him back amongst us that day in November brought such pleasure.

The day Richie died I googled the word 'dignity'. It says: 'The state or quality of being worthy of honour or respect.' There you go, that is Richie Benaud in a simple definition. From the first day of a glorious cricket career to his last as a universally admired and loved communicator of the most beautiful game, he was the very best.

Our privilege was to have sat at his table.

DAVID GYNGELL

David Gyngell became the chief executive officer of the Nine Entertainment Co. — which owns a string of businesses, including the Nine television network — in November 2010. A keen sports fan, David heads a network that for years has held broadcast rights to major top-rating sports, including cricket and rugby league. He has links that go all the way back to the introduction of television into Australia in 1956, being the son of the pioneering Bruce Gyngell, who was prominent in UK and Australian TV for 50 years.

RICHIE BENAUD was the gold plating around our logo at Channel Nine, akin to Steve Jobs at Apple. In any successful organisation there are always people of a certain persona, who provide an overarching element. That element is *class* — and it's an ageless quality that doesn't come and go with trends. I'm sure that to everyone who knew Richie even distantly, he epitomised class and respect. What he gave to Kerry Packer at the beginning of World

Series Cricket was this strong grounding in class, and it provided a calming effect in turbulent times. He was always surrounded by strong forthright figures in the commentary box, yet there was never any doubt who was the captain of our team.

Increasingly, from when I first met him when I was a teenager during WSC, to have the chance to spend some time with Richie was something of a religious moment. After all, as I came to realise, I was meeting the 'pope of cricket'! He was one of those blokes who, if you knew he was going to be there when you walked into a room, you always checked yourself. And you weren't doing it out of fear; it was out of respect. Richie had presence. He'd walk into a room to meet Kerry Packer and Kerry would stand up and pull out a chair for him. I never heard KP raise his voice to Richie. In my own life, there are only a couple of people whom I've held in such reverence and respect as I did Richie.

Of the Master Commentator, I think of the quiet moments and how he was the complete minimalist in approach. He could be intimidating from that point of view. Sometimes his silences — the things unsaid — were as powerful as things he did say.

Someone made the comment to me in the days after his death that Richie was 'bigger than Bradman'. It's an intriguing contention. Bradman's amazing statistics say what has to be said about him and people inevitably revert to them when talking about him. There is not so much mention of the man. Richie's statistics aren't anything like Bradman's, but as a human being and contributor to the game of cricket, he has no peer.

He never sought public attention. For a long time at Nine we tried to get him to do a *60 Minutes* story, or a *This Is Your Life* special to honour him at the Logies. He wouldn't accept any of it, just as the state funeral offered on his death was never going to be for him.

I learned many things about him along the way …

He never quibbled about money or asked for pay rises. He had no manager and arranged his own business. Agreements were reached on a simple handshake.

He became more statesmanlike as he got older, but there was always a dash of cheek and flair around when he 'let down'. You'd go to dinner with him on such a night and the waiter might ask, 'Red or white, Mr Benaud?'

And Richie would answer simply, 'Yes.'

He loved his trips to France and the never-ending summers, but Australia was where he was most happy. The last time I saw him was at his home at Coogee, and he told me how he was just finishing his first winter in Australia in 40 years.

And he loved the Australian Golf Club. It was so fitting that the farewell celebration, remembering his life, was held there overlooking the course, bringing together the people he and Daphne wanted to be there.

We'll never be able to replace Richie at Channel Nine. But we'll work hard to make sure that the qualities and the lessons and the colour and movement he brought to cricket commentary are still much in mind. One legacy (of many) he leaves is the link he had with younger generations via Billy Birmingham's work, with much of Billy's humour circling around Richie, and in the rise and rise of 'The Richies', with the numbers in that group totalling in the hundreds now and likely to be a colourful part of Sydney Tests for many seasons to come.

We'll all miss Richie Benaud. He was one of those rare people you brush against in life … and realise forevermore how fortunate you are that you did.

STEVE CRAWLEY

Steve Crawley, head of sport at Channel Nine, worked closely with Richie until the end. He marvelled at the seamless blend of man and commentator.

RICHIE BENAUD loved music, his favourite piece being Andrew Lloyd Webber's *Memory*. Not often but at times, in the quietness of a long day at the cricket, or in the evening, you'd hear him humming.

Memory
All alone in the moonlight

Richie in 2007, responding to his induction into the Australian Cricket Hall of Fame.

The 40th anniversary of the Tied Test was celebrated in Brisbane in late 2000. **Top:** Rohan Kanhai, Joe Solomon, Garry Sobers, Lindsay Kline, Ian Meckiff, Gerry Alexander, Richie, Wes Hall and compere Mike Coward on stage at the Brisbane Convention Centre. **Above:** Richie and Gerry Alexander, the West Indies vice-captain in 1960–61, on a lap of honour at the Gabba.

Above: Richie and Daphne help celebrate David Cox's 60th birthday at La Colombe d'Or restaurant, Saint-Paul-de-Vence, in 2004. The revellers are (from left): Kerrie Foskey, David and his wife Helen, Richie and Daphne, Rosemary Farr-Jones, Isobel and Clifford Hastings.

Right: Richie made his first England tour in 1953, the year of the Queen's coronation. Fifty-nine years later, the two met at the Royal Household Cricket Club ground at Windsor Castle.

The scene in the Nine commentary box at the SCG in January 2005, with Richie flanked by Bill Lawry and former Pakistan paceman Waqar Younis.

A section of the crowd at Trent Bridge pays tribute during the fourth Ashes Test of 2005, his 'farewell' series in England.

Above: Members of The Richies — (from left) Paul Stewart, Steven Blacker, Michael Hennessy and Andrew Colagiuri — on the beach at Bondi with their hero.

Below: The Richies at the SCG during the final Ashes Test of 2013–14.

Above: Richie at Grace Road, Leicester, still in his first decade as a sports journalist, covering the 1968 Ashes tour. To Richie's left are Daphne Benaud (in a headscarf, trying to avoid the driving rain) and another Australian journalist, Phil Wilkins. **Below:** A eulogy at the memorial service for Kerry Packer, Sydney Opera House, February 2006.

Channel Nine's commentators at the SCG in November 2010. **Above:** Tony Greig, Mark Taylor, Richie, Ian Chappell and Bill Lawry. **Below left:** Richie with Mark Nicholas. **Below right:** With Shane Warne.

Richie and Daphne (right)
on their wedding day,
London, 1967, and (below)
in their flat at Beaulieu,
France, 42 years later.

I can smile at the old days
I was beautiful then
I remember the time I knew what happiness was
Let the memory live again

He was a beautiful man, Richie, a gentle man and gentleman.

Even when Warnie bowled the ball of the century, Richie in commentary never yelled. All he said was: 'He's done it,' before adding after a pause, 'Gatting has absolutely no idea what has happened to it ... still doesn't know.'

Richie had rules. When it came to cricket commentary, they were written down:

- Your role is to be a well-informed friend — a friend who knows all the strategies, knows all the players, the officials ... for that matter, most of the fans in the stadium. And shares the viewers' deep love for and attachment to the sport.
- Don't ever talk over play. When the bowler begins his run, shut up. If you're in the middle of saying something — stop. Pick up again when you know the result of the ball.
- Don't fight the swell. Call the play quickly. Pause. Let the roar rise and drop. Then come back in.
- Never forget that silence can be the greatest weapon you have in your armoury.
- Television works pretty much like a sports team. At the risk of rolling out the clichés — there's no 'I' in team and there are two 'I's' in nitwit.
- The final word is to treat your viewers as family — respect them and they'll respect you.

In many ways, across a number of generations now, Richie's deep knowledge, insight and love of cricket have helped legions of people, particularly women, across the world better appreciate the game. Anyone could see the Chappell brothers, Tendulkar, Viv Richards and Malcolm Marshall, Botham and Gower, Sir Richard Hadlee, Lillee and Thommo, the Waughs and Warnie, Taylor, Gilchrist and Ponting ... anyone could see they were good. But Richie could tell you in a sentence why they were better than good. Just like that.

The calling stopped after his car crash at Coogee. October 23, 2013. On the way home from hitting practice balls at the Australian Golf Club, he mounted the nature strip in his beloved 1963 Sunbeam Alpine and slammed into a brick wall. Richie broke his sternum and damaged other parts that hurt and bled. We think he blacked out behind the wheel before crashing but we'll never know for sure.

Early in the rehab his doctors discovered the skin cancers that would lead to all the chemotherapy and then radiation treatment. In late March 2015, Richie, along with Daphne and the doctors, decided the treatment would stop. For a few days he slept. Then, on April 9, sitting at his bedside, Daphne smiled and said in her beautiful English accent, 'Rich, you don't have to keep up appearances anymore.' He died at 4.30 the following morning, aged 84.

Over the years much has been made of the fact Richie's mum, Rene, lived to 104 but as he'd tell you on the quiet, she had a fall when 102 and spent the next two years lying there wishing she were dead. Not Richie. Until the week before he died he never gave up hope. 'Going along slowly but nicely, thank you,' he'd say. 'Back walking. Steady as she goes.'

We worked together on a number of pieces for Nine's summer of cricket in 2014–15. I'd write the words, he'd read them and then we'd get the broadcast team together and cover it with pictures, always with the understanding he could change any word at any time. And he only ever changed the scripts once.

We were doing a sad piece about the death of young cricketer Phillip Hughes, when Richie changed the line 'God bless you, son' to 'Rest in peace, son'. He looked up afterwards and whispered, 'I don't do God.'

Such an interesting man; he could tell you so many fascinating yarns without ever sounding boastful or big-headed or up himself. Not once did he accept an individual award because he always felt part of a team. He spoke of Don Bradman and Robert Menzies not like they were knights of the realm, which they were, but as mates, plain and simple. Richie and Daphne were close to Don and Jessie Bradman.

'Don and Richie had a great rapport,' Daphne would say. 'I could listen to them for hours — and did. Don's quiet wit never failed to entertain.'

Sir Robert taught Richie the power of the pause ... Menzies cleverly using the tactic to add theatre to prime ministerial speeches. Richie? Lip ribbon microphone in hand, Richie would adopt the art of the pause to command circumstances and audiences much more important than Canberra.

Still, most kids today wouldn't know he even played. A right-handed all-rounder, he bowled leg-spin, taking 945 first-class wickets and scoring almost 12,000 runs. So proud yet typically humbled to have been the first player in history to achieve the magical Test double of 2,000 runs and 200 wickets.

His Test debut came in 1952 and he was captain of Australia from 1958 until 1963. He played with Miller, Davidson, Harvey and Lindwall, Morris and Lawry. Bill Lawry. Richie loved Bill Lawry, even though he was a Victorian. It took a West Australian, DK Lillee, to break his bowling record, the most wickets by an Australian. So he could play, don't worry.

But he was a better commentator. The best ever.

Richie Benaud. A beautiful man.

– 10 –
POSTSCRIPT

The final contributions are from Richie's sons
Greg (born in 1955) and Jeff (born in 1958). Jeff has written
the book's postscript. Greg remembers a father who became
an inspiration ...

GREGORY RICHARD BENAUD

HE WAS A GENTLE, loving father to me and my brother. He firmly but gently applied discipline to us when we were children. He was successful at his job as a journalist and after that as a commentator.

In his day, he was the world's foremost cricketer and the world's best leg-spin bowler — captain of the Australian XI and the NSW XI, and the first player from any country to take 200 wickets and score 2,000 runs in Test cricket ...

The words above were part of a 'best wishes' that I wrote to say on a *Richie Benaud ... This Is Your Life* TV show in 1975. Due to circumstances, I was unable to deliver my message at the time.

I'm fortunate now to be able to convey some of the respect and love I have for Dad. To say thank you for the kindness and love shown to me by Dad and by Daph, both now and over many decades.

When I last spoke to Dad, he said, 'We've been privileged to know each other the way we have.'

I've often thought the privilege has been all mine.

Dad, may you continue to inspire us, and also young cricketers and everyday Australians.

THE RICH TAPESTRY
OF LIFE

By Jeff Benaud

'IT'S just part of the rich tapestry of life, son.'
That is a phrase I will always associate with Dad. Said with a slow, dry, slightly sardonic delivery.

It was a phrase I did not hear very often. That's because it usually referred to some person or event that wasn't at the absolute apex of his list of favourites.

It wasn't a complaint, really — because my father very rarely complained about anything. It was just an observation about another of the many challenges that life throws at all of us. Some large, some small.

The rich tapestry of life.

It's not a bad way to describe Dad's life.

There were certainly some very varied threads that formed the tapestry of his life. The thread of his Australian bush upbringing with a pioneer family. A Gallic shrug of the shoulders in adversity. The thread of a raw core of talent. But also understanding that talent alone is not enough. The thread of the unique professional in his work: he knew when to speak ... and when to let the game speak for itself.

There are some other threads in his tapestry of life. There was the thread of being a good and gentle person that went to the very core of his being.

He was a strong person, very determined and not easily dissuaded from his objective. But it was strength that came without any threat of violence. His strength was strength of character. And what a rare and invincible Excalibur that gentle strength of character always proved to be against some mighty opposition.

Hard work was another thread. Not mindless slog for no purpose, but a determination to do what was required to meet the

311

deadline, to be professional, not to let people down, to maintain standards and improve them, and to add something positive wherever he could. Dad wanted to win — but there was no honour in winning if it was achieved outside the rules and without good sportsmanship.

Dad could take some considerable time to make a decision, weighing up all the pros and cons and balancing all the options. He could not be pressured or rushed into anything — only good sense and fair play had a chance of success. He could not be forced into the mould — only reasoned into it. But once the decision was made, it was almost always final.

Another thread was a sensitive radar for hypocrisy.

At times my father was labelled a 'rebel', especially around the time of World Series Cricket. But the term 'rebel' was a misnomer. A rebel sounds like someone who is against anything and everything, including the traditional establishment. That wasn't Dad.

What he was against was *injustice*. The injustice of a fair day's work without a fair day's pay. It was the injustice that motivated him to do whatever he could to right such a situation. World Series Cricket allowed him to do it in an ideal way. No one was happier than Dad when that injustice was righted and the cricket world was reunited.

And there was another thread in Dad's life — the single golden thread around which his life was woven.

That thread was his genuine, gentle, enduring and consistent love for Daphne. Having Daphne as a partner in business, in laughter and in life was the defining thread. Daph made him happy. She gave him the chance to be all that he could be. Of all those many times he was asked to name his 'greatest team in history', I know the one team he always wanted to be in was his team with Daphne. They were the best team going.

My father has now lived his wonderful life. His time with us has passed, but his legacy lives on.

His legacy lives on in the game he loved and made better and stronger. And his legacy lives on in all of us who knew him, as a husband, son, brother, friend and colleague, or simply as the voice that reminded us it was summer. We remember him as a valued part of our life — a part of our life that is worth remembering with affection.

And when I remember him it is my very first memory that I treasure most ...

I'm a three-year-old being tossed high into the air.
I'm soaring higher, higher,
Up to touch the bright, clear, clean sun.
I'm flying up, up, like I'll never come down.
Laughing with a pure innocent joy.
Soaring.
Then falling, plummeting, sure to smash hard on the ground.
But strong hands and arms catch me and I can see Dad's laughing face,
his jet black hair, tanned skin, flashing white teeth.
'I've got you, son.'
Then launched sunwards again. Squealing with delight, arms
outstretched like a bird. Then down to the safety of Dad.
Again and again. Never missing. Always there. Never letting us down.
Ever.

FOR THE RECORD
RICHIE BENAUD

Right-hand batsman; right-arm leg-spin bowler

Born: October 6, 1930, at Penrith, NSW

Died: April 10, 2015, at Woollahra, NSW

Major teams: Australia (1952–1964);
New South Wales (1948–1964)

Captain: Australia (1958–1963);
New South Wales (1956; 1958–1963)

Test Cricket (debut: fifth Test v West Indies, Sydney, 1951–52)

Tests	Inn	NO	100	50	Runs	Ave	Ct	Balls	Runs	Wkts	5w	10w	Avge
63	97	7	3	9	2201	24.46	65	19108	6704	248	16	1	27.03

First-Class Cricket (debut: New South Wales v Queensland, Sydney, 1948–49)

Mat	Inn	NO	100	50	Runs	Ave	Ct	Balls	Runs	Wkts	5w	10w	Avge
259	365	44	23	61	11719	36.51	254	60481	23370	945	56	9	24.73

Test Batting and Fielding, by series

Season	Opponent	Tests	Inns	NO	100s	50s	HS	Runs	Avge	Ct
1951–52	West Indies	1	2	0	0	0	19	22	11.00	0
1952–53	South Africa	4	7	1	0	0	45	124	20.67	4
1953	England	3	5	0	0	0	7	15	3.00	5
1954–55	England	5	9	0	0	0	34	148	16.44	3
1954–55	West Indies	5	6	0	1	1	121	246	41.00	8
1956	England	5	9	1	0	1	97	200	25.00	3
1956–57	Pakistan	1	2	0	0	1	56	60	30.00	0
1956–57	India	3	4	0	0	0	24	53	13.25	0
1957–58	South Africa	5	7	1	2	0	122	329	54.83	5
1958–59	England	5	5	0	0	1	64	132	26.40	8
1959–60	Pakistan	3	4	1	0	0	29	84	28.00	2
1959–60	India	5	8	2	0	0	25	91	15.17	5
1960–61	West Indies	5	9	0	0	2	77	194	21.56	3
1961	England	4	6	1	0	0	36*	45	9.00	4
1962–63	England	5	7	0	0	2	57	227	32.43	9
1963–64	South Africa	4	7	0	0	1	90	231	33.00	6
Total		63	97	7	3	9	122	2201	24.46	65

NOTES

1. * indicates not out
2. Richie's three Test centuries were: 121, batting eight, in the fifth Test v West Indies at Sabina Park, Kingston, June 1955; 122, batting seven, in the first Test v South Africa at the Wanderers, Johannesburg, December 1957; 100, batting four, in the fourth Test v South Africa at the Wanderers, Johannesburg, February 1958.
3. Richie twice took three catches in one Test innings: in England's first innings of the fifth Test, Melbourne Cricket Ground, February 1959; in England's second innings of the fifth Test, The Oval, August 1961. He took four catches in a Test once: two in each innings of the first Test v West Indies, Sabina Park, Kingston, March 1955.

Test Bowling, by series

Season	Opponent	Balls	Mdns	Runs	Wkts	5w	10w	Best	Avge
1951–52	West Indies	35	0	14	1	0	0	1–14	14.00
1952–53	South Africa	846	23	306	10	0	0	4–118	30.60
1953	England	408	19	174	2	0	0	1–51	87.00
1954–55	England	935	23	377	10	0	0	4–120	37.70
1954–55	West Indies	1109	47	485	18	0	0	4–15	26.94
1956	England	924	48	330	8	0	0	3–89	41.25
1956–57	Pakistan	102	5	36	1	0	0	1–36	36.00
1956–57	India	1019	52	388	23	3	1	7–72	16.87
1957–58	South Africa	1937	56	658	30	4	0	5–49	21.93
1958–59	England	1866	65	584	31	2	0	5–83	18.84
1959–60	Pakistan	1344	94	380	18	1	0	5–93	21.11
1959–60	India	1934	146	568	29	2	0	5–43	19.59
1960–61	West Indies	2145	56	779	23	1	0	5–96	33.87
1961	England	1287	76	488	15	1	0	6–70	32.53
1962–63	England	1864	58	688	17	1	0	6–115	40.47
1963–64	South Africa	1353	37	449	12	1	0	5–68	37.42
Total		19108	805	6704	248	16	1	7–72	27.03

NOTES

1. 'Best' indicates best innings figures. Richie's best match figures in a Test were 11–105 v India at Eden Gardens, Calcutta, November 1956.
2. Richie's 16 five-fors in Test cricket were: 7–72, first Test v India, Madras, 1956–57; 6–52, third Test v India, Calcutta, 1956–57; 5–53, third Test v India, Calcutta, 1956–57; 5–49, second Test v South Africa, Cape Town, 1957–58; 5–114, third Test v South Africa, Durban, 1957–58; 5–84, fourth Test v South Africa, Johannesburg, 1957–58; 5–82, fifth Test v South Africa, Port Elizabeth, 1957–58; 5–83, third Test v England, Sydney, 1958–59; 5–91, fourth Test v England, Adelaide, 1958–59; 5–93, third Test v Pakistan, Karachi, 1959–60; 5–76, first Test v India, Delhi, 1959–60; 5–43, fourth Test v India, Madras, 1959–60; 5–96, fourth Test v West Indies, Adelaide, 1960–61; 6–70, fourth Test v England, Manchester, 1961; 6–115, first Test v England, Brisbane, 1962–63; 5–68, first Test v South Africa, Brisbane, 1963–64.
3. Richie's economy rate in Test cricket was 2.10 runs per over (calculated on all overs being of six balls). Of all wrist-spinners with 75 or more Test wickets, only Bill O'Reilly (1.95 runs per over) has a superior economy rate.

Test captaincy, by series

Series	Opponent	Venue	Won	Tied	Drawn	Lost	Results	Toss
1958–59	England	Home	4	–	1	–	WWDWW	1/5
1959–60	Pakistan	Away	2	–	1	–	WWD	1/3
1959–60	India	Away	2	–	2	1	WLDWD	1/5
1960–61	West Indies	Home	2	1	1	1	TWLDW	2/5
1961	England	Away	1	–	2	1	DLWD	2/4
1962–63	England	Home	1	–	3	1	DLWDD	3/5
1963–64	South Africa	Home	–	–	1	–	D	1/1

NOTES

1. 'Results' indicates the results of each Test in a series. 'Toss' indicates how many tosses Richie won in a series. Thus, against England in 1958–59, he won one of five tosses.
2. Richie's overall Test captaincy record is 12 wins, one tie, 11 draws and four losses. He won 11 of 28 tosses.
3. Richie missed the second Ashes Test of 1961 because of a shoulder injury. Vice-captain Neil Harvey took over, lost the toss and led Australia to victory.

4. Richie led Australia in the first Test of the 1963–64 series against South Africa. He broke a finger in a grade game and had to miss the second Test. As he was retiring from first-class cricket at the end of the season, he proposed that Bob Simpson remain as captain. Australia won the second Test, drew the third, lost the fourth and drew the fifth.

5. Australia's results in Test series from Richie's debut in 1951–52 to his appointment as captain were as follows:

Season	Opponent	Venue	Series result	Test results	Captain
1951–52	West Indies	Home	Won 4–1	WWLWW	AL Hassett
1952–53	South Africa	Home	Drawn 2–2	WLWDL	AL Hassett
1953	England	Away	Lost 0–1	DDDDL	AL Hassett
1954–55	England	Home	Lost 1–3	WLLLD	IW Johnson
1955	West Indies	Away	Won 3–0	WDWDW	IW Johnson
1956	England	Away	Lost 2–1	DWLLD	IW Johnson
1956–57	Pakistan	Away	Lost 0–1	L	IW Johnson
1956–57	India	Away	Won 2–0	WDW	IW Johnson
1957–58	South Africa	Away	Won 3–0	DWDWW	ID Craig

6. Richie debuted in the fifth Test of 1951–52, and played in the final four Tests of 1952–53 and the first, second and fourth Tests of 1953. He did not miss another Test until the second Ashes Test of 1961. Arthur Morris captained Australia in the third Test in 1951–52 and the second Test of 1954–55. Ray Lindwall was captain for the second Test v India in 1956–57.

First-Class and Grade Cricket

1. As well as representing NSW and Australia, Richie played for the following first-class teams: the Australians during tours of England (1953, 1956, 1961), the West Indies (1955), New Zealand (1956-57), South Africa (1957-58) and India (1959-60); Australian XI and Combined XI teams against various touring sides in Australia; the International Cavaliers in Rhodesia (1960) and India, South Africa and Rhodesia (1962-63); an International XI in New Zealand (1961-62); EW Swanton's XI in India (1964); and a Commonwealth XI in Pakistan in 1968. He also played in three testimonial games that were given first-class status — for AR Morris' XI v AL Hassett's XI (Lindsay Hassett testimonial at the MCG in 1953-54); IW Johnson's XI v RR Lindwall's XI (Arthur Mailey-Johnny Taylor testimonial at the SCG in 1955-56); RN Harvey's XI v RR Lindwall's XI (Stan McCabe-Bill O'Reilly testimonial at the SCG in 1956-57) — and led R Benaud's XI against RR Lindwall's XI at the Gabba in 1959-50 in a game staged to celebrate Queensland's centenary.

2. Richie's highest first-class score was 187 for Australians v Natal at City Oval, Pietermaritzburg, January 1958.

3. His best bowling in a first-class innings was 7-18 for NSW v MCC, Sydney Cricket Ground, 1962-63. His best bowling in a first-class match was 13-134 (7-46 & 6-88) v Natal at Kingsmead, Durban, November 1957.

4. Richie played for Cumberland (now known as Parramatta) in the Sydney grade competition. He played first grade from 1946-47 to 1967-68, scoring 5,692 runs at 40.95, and taking 362 wickets at 18.55 and 76 catches. He scored 12 centuries and took five wickets in an innings on 17 occasions in first-grade matches for the club.

ACKNOWLEDGMENTS

In the manner of sport at its best, this book was in the truest sense the result of a wholehearted 'team effort'.

Very special thanks are with the Benaud family. Richie's wife Daphne and his brother John were wonderfully supportive and towers of strength throughout, playing the necessary 'sheet anchor' role as the book evolved. We are grateful for the support of Richie's sons, Greg and Jeff, whose personal reflections provide a wonderful postscript.

Our thanks also go to the people at Channel Nine, not least for granting us permission to use excerpts from the tribute to Richie that was broadcast so soon after his death, and for helping us locate Brendan Read, whose cover photograph is superb. We appreciate the continued support of Pan Macmillan Australia and the Opus Group, and the efforts of those involved in the physical making of the book: Graeme Jones, Luke Causby, Robert Stapelfeldt, Elizabeth Cowell, Sarah Shrubb and Steve Keipert.

And, crucially, we must thank the wonderful cross-section of cricket people and the many contributors from outside the game who so generously shared their time and personal memories and reflections of the late Richie Benaud. The co-operation of friends, teammates, opponents, old school mates, workmates and others who had encountered Richie along the way was wonderfully selfless, precise and professional. We suspect that Richie, meticulous in both work and play throughout his life, would have approved, though being the private man he was — ever modest about his own considerable achievements and never a seeker of attention — the suspicion is he would have flinched at the sheer volume of words and photos that flowed onto the desk of publisher Geoff Armstrong.

Our hope is that, in the quality of the contributions and the breadth of its coverage, this book does justice to a great and popular Australian.

Norman Tasker and Ian Heads

NOTES ON SOURCES

Contributions

David Hill's story, which begins on page 155, originally appeared in *The Australian*, April 11, 2015. In the footnote on page 210, John Cutler is quoted from *Making the Cut*, by David Dowsey (Peleus Press, Sydney, 2013), a history of the Sydney tailoring firm, JH Cutler. Jack Bannister's contribution, which begins on page 252, originally appeared in *The Guardian*, April 11, 2015. The excerpts on pages 261-264 were taken from the Channel Nine special, *Richie: A Marvellous Life*, April 12, 2015. Mike Atherton's story (page 276) originally appeared in *The Times* (London), April 11, 2015. Billy Birmingham's tribute (page 279) originally appeared at *foxsports.com.au*, on April 10, 2015. Tony Cozier's contribution (page 295) and Mark Nicholas' story both originally appeared at *espncricinfo.com*, on April 10, 2015.

The extract on page 62 from the Parramatta High School magazine, *The Phoenix*, appears by permission of the school. The editors are grateful for the support of school principal Domonique Splatt and historian Tony Lennon.

The support of Clayton Murzello — who arranged for Nari Contractor to contribute to the book and organised the photo from the GK Menon collection of Richie from 1959–60 — is much appreciated.

The lines from *Memory* (page 302) are reprinted by permission of Faber & Faber Ltd. The song's lyrics are by Trevor Nunn, music by Andrew Lloyd Webber.

The stanza from John Betjeman's *Seaside Golf* on page 334 was chosen by Daphne Benaud as an apt way to close the memorial for Richie that was held at the Australian Golf Club in Sydney on April 15, 2015. It comes from *Collected Poems*, by John Betjeman, first published in 1955, and is reproduced by permission of John Murray Press, an imprint of Hodder and Stoughton Limited.

Prelude

The quotes and comments in the prelude come from the following sources:

Page 3: Alan McGilvray, *Captains of the Game* (ABC Books, Sydney, 1992)

Page 5: AG Moyes, *Benaud* (Angus & Robertson, Sydney, 1992)

Page 7: Lou Benaud, *Cumberland Argus*, February 18, 1953

Page 8: Ray Robinson, *Green Sprigs* (Collins, London, 1954)

Page 9: Sir Neville Cardus, *The Playfair Cardus* (Dickens, London, 1963)

Page 10: Keith Miller, *The Sydney Morning Herald*, December 2, 1975

Page 10: Wally Grout, *My Country's Keeper* (Pelham Books, London, 1965)

Page 11: Alan McGilvray, *Captains of the Game* (ABC Books, Sydney, 1992)

Page 11: Wally Grout, *My Country's Keeper* (Pelham Books, London, 1965)

Page 12: CLR James, *The Cricketer* (UK), May 1967

Page 12: Jack Fingleton, *The Greatest Test of All* (Collins, London, 1961)

Page 13: Jack Fingleton, *Australian Cricket* magazine, February 1970

Page 14: Frank Worrell, *The Observer*, August 6, 1961

Page 14: Sir Neville Cardus, *World Sports* magazine, September 1961

Page 14: Bill O'Reilly, *Sun-Herald*, January 14, 1962

Page 15: Lou Rowan, *Umpire's Story* (Jack Pollard Pty Ltd, Sydney, 1973)

Page 16: Bill Jenkings, *As Crime Goes By* (Ironbark Press, Sydney, 1992)

Page 17: Jim Laker, *A Spell From Laker* (Hamlyn, London, 1979)

Page 17: Alan McGilvray, *Captains of the Game* (ABC Books, Sydney, 1992)

Title Page Quotes

Page 19: Norm O'Neill, *Ins and Outs* (Pelham Books, London, 1964)

Page 43: Bill O'Reilly, *Sunday-Herald*, October 30, 1949

Page 67: Ian Wooldridge, official programme for the 1988 Bicentennial Test and One-Day International

Page 123: Christopher Martin-Jenkins, *The Top 100 Cricketers of All Time* (Corinthian Books, London, 2009)

Page 153: Richie Benaud, *The Cricket Revolution*, by Eric Beecher (Newspress Pty Ltd, Melbourne, 1978)

Page 175: Frank Tyson, *Century-Makers* (Hutchinson, Melbourne, 1980)

Page 205: James Packer, *The Sydney Morning Herald*, April 11, 2015

Page 237: Alan McGilvray, *Captains of the Game* (ABC Books, Sydney, 1992)

Page 267: Sir Michael Parkinson, *Richie: A Marvellous Life*, broadcast by Channel Nine, April 12, 2015

PHOTO CREDITS

The editors are very grateful for the work of photographers of many generations — professionals and enthusiastic amateurs alike — who found themselves somewhere around the life of Richie Benaud and took the photos that feature in these pages. A number of the photographs come from private collections, with original creators unknown. Sincere thanks go to the Benaud family and others who dug deep into files and cupboards to help ensure that the book could be special in both its words and images.

Where possible, sources are recognised:

Brendan Read: cover image (www.brendanread.com)

Jugiong Public School centenary book: section 1, page 3 (bottom)
Parramatta High School: section 1, page 4 (top and bottom right)
GK Menon collection: section 1, page 6 (bottom)
SCG Museum collection: section 1, page 7 (top)
Shirley Plowright: section 1, page 7 (bottom)
Getty Images/Hulton Archive: section 1, page 8
News Ltd/Newspix: section 1, page 6 (top); section 2, page 2 (top right); section 2, page 6 (bottom); section 2, page 7
Jim Fenwick/Newspix: section 2, page 3 (top)
National Archives of Australia: section 2, page 3 (bottom)
Getty Images/Hulton Archive/V. Wright: section 2, page 4 (top)
Getty Images/Hulton Archive/Dennis Oulds: section 2, page 4 (bottom)
Getty Images/Hulton Archive/Central Press: section 2, page 5 (top)
RL Stewart/Fairfax Photos: section 2, page 6 (top)
H Martin/Fairfax Photos: section 2, page 8 (top)
Parramatta District Cricket Club: section 2, page 8 (bottom); section 3, page 5 (bottom)
Ray Saunders/Newspix: section 3, page 2 (top left)
John Woodcock: section 3, page 2 (top right)
National Library of Australia: section 3, page 2 (bottom)

Notes on specific photos

1. The portrait of Richie that appears on page 19 was painted in 1961 by Maureen Roberts, the wife of Ron Roberts, the English freelance cricket reporter. Beyond his often superb writing, Ron Roberts also organised and managed several overseas cricket tours, including trips by the International Cavaliers. He died in 1965, aged 38.

2. The men in the Stan McCabe-Bill O'Reilly testimonial match group photo (first photo section, page 7) are: (back, from left) Johnny Martin, John Freeman, Barry Shepherd, Ken Mackay, Ray Strauss, Richie Benaud, Sid Carroll, Billy Watson, Les Favell; (middle) J. Daly (umpire), Lindsay Kline, Graeme Hole, Ron Gaunt, Norm O'Neill, Jack Treanor, Peter Burge, Len Maddocks, J. Bowden (umpire); (front) Alan Davidson, Wally Grout, Ian Meckiff, Ray Lindwall, Stan McCabe, Bill O'Reilly, Neil Harvey, Colin McDonald, Bob Simpson. The match, RR Lindwall's XI v RN Harvey's XI, was played at the SCG, January 5–9, 1957.

3. On page 67, the Australian XII for the fourth Ashes Test of 1962–63, at the Adelaide Oval, is: (back, from left) Norm O'Neill, Brian Booth, Graham McKenzie, Ian McLachlan (12th man), Bill Lawry, Barry Shepherd, Wally Grout; (front) Alan Davidson, Bob Simpson, Richie Benaud (captain), Neil Harvey, Ken Mackay.

Brian Booth: section 3, page 5 (top)
Mark Ray: section 3, page 8 (top)
Getty Images Sport/Simon Fergusson: section 4, page 1
Getty Images Sport/Nick Wilson: section 4, page 2 (top)
David Cox: section 4, page 3 (top)
Bob Barker/Newspix: section 4, page 4 (top)
Philip Brown: section 4, page 4 (bottom); section 4, page 5 (bottom)
Sam Ruttyn/Newspix: section 4, page 5 (top)
Lindsay Moller/Newspix: section 4, page 6 (bottom)
Brendan Read: section 4, page 7 (all)
Getty Images/Hulton Archive/Ronald Dumont: section 4, page 8 (top)
Rodney Cavalier: section 4, page 8 (bottom)

The photographs that appear on the 'title pages' for each section of this book are:

Page 19: A portrait by Maureen Roberts (Benaud family)
Page 43: Accountancy clerk (Benaud family)
Page 67: Australian XII, fourth Test, 1962–63 (Brian Booth)
Page 123: At the news desk (Fairfax Photos)
Page 153: First night match at the SCG, WSC Australians v WSC West Indians, November 28, 1978 (Peter Leyden/Newspix)

INDEX

INDEX

Egar, Col 15, 106
Eisenhower, Dwight 108
Ekland, Britt 139
Endean, Russell 127
England v South Africa (in
    England) 144
Erby, Jon 45-8
Erskine, James 214-16
Ewens, Wilf 58-61

Favell, Les 97, 134-5, 245, 269
Ferrett, Graham 219
Fingleton, Jack 12-13, 38, 127
Fisk, Richard 285-6
Flindt, Rex 66
Flintoff, Andrew 143
Flockton, Ray 25
Fordham, John 207-10
Fordham, Nick 207
Franses, Gary 276, 299
Frith, David 24-7
Frost, Sir David 236, 299

Garnsey, George 54
Gatting, Mike 198
Gauld, Cathy 223-4
Gilchrist, Adam 79, 188, 303
Gilligan, Arthur 127
Gleeson, John 48, 180-2, 185
Goddard, Trevor 127
Goodman, Tom 6, 7, 126
Goodwin, Harold 51-3, 178
Gough, Darren 142
Gould, Ernie 46, 87
Gould, Phil 261-2
Gould, Shane 187
Gover, Alf 187
Gower, David 261, 262, 303
Grace, WG 157
Granger, Stewart 188
Graveney, Tom 99
Gray, Grace 149-52
Gray, Katherine 152
Gray, Robert 148-52, 170-1,
    271-4

Greig, Tony 22, 130, 158-9, 191,
    200-1, 209, 226, 228, 264, 299
Griffith, Billy 188
Griffith, Charlie 65, 119
Griffiths, Richard 146
Grimmett, Clarrie 8, 12, 37, 202
Grout, Wally 10-11, 30, 70, 92, 107,
    118, 291
Gupte, Subhash 114
Gyngell, Bruce 300
Gyngell, David 261, 300-2

Hadlee, Sir Richard 303
Hadley, Ray 261, 263
Haigh, Gideon 35-6
Hall, Wes 5, 30, 45, 70, 92, 100, 114,
    193, 296-7
Hanson, Pauline 34
Hardy, Ken 4
Harmison, Steve 279
Hartley, Greg 285
Harvey, Neil 10-11, 13-15, 26, 31-
    2, 40, 71, 75-80, 89, 105, 107-
    8, 132, 190, 195, 291, 305
Hassett, Lindsay 6, 37, 79-80, 284-5
Havers, Nigel 236
Hawke, Bob 260
Hayes, Colin 110
Healy, Ian 209, 283-5
Heine, Peter 127
Henley, Len 127
Hennessy, Michael 228-9
Hill, David 23, 155-66
Hill, Jack 7
Hill, Julian 163
Hill, Lachie 163
Hillier, Kevin 280
Holding, Michael 261, 263
Hole, Graeme 25, 86
Holland, Bob 179
Hooper, Carl 299
Howard, John 33-5
Howarth, Peter 47
Hughes, Phillip 252, 261, 304
Hunt, James 141

Hunte, Sir Conrad 30, 297
Hutchinson, Kim 229-31
Hutchinson, Neil 229-31
Hutchinson, Norm 229-31
Hutchinson, Ron 111
Hutton, Ben 213
Hutton, Charmaine 213-14
Hutton, Sir Leonard 26-7, 50, 103, 213
Hutton, Ollie 213
Hutton, Richard 213

Illingworth, Ray 129
Imran Khan 141
International Management Group (IMG) 138, 215, 255-6
Inverarity, John 125
Invincibles 7, 71-2, 75, 80, 203
Irwin, Hale 225-6

Jackson, Archie 6
James, CLR 12
James, Ron 5, 8, 56, 58, 60
Jarman, Barry 110-13
Jeffery, Michael 40
Jenkings, Bill 16
Jenner, Terry 37
Jobs, Steve 300
John, Sir Elton 144, 236
Johnson, Brian 220-1
Johnson, Ian 7, 9, 31, 82, 128, 134
Johnston, Brian 17, 247
Johnston, Bill 80-1, 107
Johnston, Pauline 247
Jones, Alan 29-33, 287
Jones, Geraint 279
Jones, Ross 171
Jones, Vicki 235-8

Kallis, Jacques 294
Kasprowicz, Michael 279
Katich, Simon 175, 199-200
Kennedy-Green, Michele 297
Kentridge, Sir Sydney 145
Kernahan, Jim 171

Kershaw, John 86
Kissell, Ron 184
Kline, Lindsay 30, 107-8, 113, 115, 173
Knight, Annette 188
Knight, Barry 186-9

Laidlaw, Renton 238-41
Laker, Jim 9, 17, 108, 128
Langer, Justin 31
Langley, Gil 10
Lashley, Peter 296
Lawry, Bill 21-4, 76, 79, 118, 121-2, 158, 186, 188, 191, 200-1, 252, 278, 291, 305
Lewis, Tony 257-60
Lill, John 112
Lillee, Dennis 79, 129-30, 217, 261, 263, 303, 305
Lindwall, Ray 10, 12-13, 24, 26, 31, 39, 71, 77, 79-80, 85, 116, 203, 275, 305
Lloyd, Clive 168-9
Lloyd, David 271
Lloyd Webber, Andrew 302-3
Loader, Peter 11
Lock, Tony 9, 128
Longhurst, Henry 16, 161, 241
Loxton, Sam 73, 75, 76
Luxton, Ron 220-2

Macartney, Charlie 1, 18
Mackay, Ken 25, 127
Madden, John 163
Maddocks, Len 76-7
Mailey, Arthur 54
Mandela, Nelson 145
Mangan, Stephen 146
Marks, Alec 86
Marks, Neil 105-9
Marsh, Rod 217, 283
Marshall, Malcolm 168, 303
Martin, Johnny 127
Martin-Jenkins, Christopher 123
Maskell, Dan 16, 161, 241

SEASIDE GOLF

How straight it flew, how long it flew,
It clear'd the rutty track
And soaring, disappeared from view
Beyond the bunker's back —
A glorious, sailing, bounding drive
That made me glad I was alive.

— John Betjeman